M000287474

GREAT CHANGE

GREAT CHANGE

THE WAY TO GET BIG STRATEGY DONE

ADAM BENNETT

WILEY

First published in 2023 by John Wiley & Sons Australia, Ltd
Level 4, 600 Bourke St, Melbourne, Victoria 3000, Australia

Typeset in Warnock Pro 11pt/14pt

© Adam John Bennett 2023

The moral rights of the author have been asserted

ISBN: 978-1-394-20372-7

A catalogue record for this book is available from the National Library of Australia

All rights reserved. Except as permitted under the *Australian Copyright Act 1968* (for example, a fair dealing for the purposes of study, research, criticism or review), no part of this book may be reproduced, stored in a retrieval system, communicated or transmitted in any form or by any means without prior written permission. All inquiries should be made to the publisher at the address above.

Cover design by Wiley
Cover and background image: © Andrii/Adobe Stock Photos

Disclaimer
The material in this publication is of the nature of general comment only, and does not represent professional advice. It is not intended to provide specific guidance for particular circumstances and it should not be relied on as the basis for any decision to take action or not take action on any matter which it covers. Readers should obtain professional advice where appropriate, before making any such decision. To the maximum extent permitted by law, the author and publisher disclaim all responsibility and liability to any person, arising directly or indirectly from any person taking or not taking action based on the information in this publication.

SKY9AE13623-F48E-48E9-A10D-5526E21FCCB7_081723

To my best friend, Belinda. Thank you. For everything.

Contents

Acknowledgements

I'd like to offer my most sincere thanks to all of the people who have helped me on my journey so far.

In corporate life, I'm a great believer that there are those who extend ladders and are committed to helping those around them develop and succeed; and those who close hatches and are determined that no-one else will follow their ascension path through the organisation. I've been incredibly lucky to have had many people extend ladders to me and genuinely help me develop and learn.

Thank you to Grace Chopard (former VP, Global Strategy & Transformation, IBM) for taking a chance on me as a trainee management consultant and getting me started at Price Waterhouse Urwick. Thank you also to Martin Green (former Partner, KPMG) for recommending me for my first meaningful project management role, and to Lawrence Owen, Sarah Cole and Carlos de Carvalho for your support over many years, and for giving me constant challenges that stretched me out of my comfort zone. You each provided valuable lessons and examples that provided me with an early solid foundation.

Thanks also to Gavin Slater (former Group Executive, NAB) for letting me get on with things and giving me lots of rope (and sometimes Red Bull) to try the ideas and approaches I outline in this book in a real-world environment. Thanks also for your trust, aircover and support.

A special thanks to Cameron Clyne (former Group CEO, NAB) for his support and wise counsel throughout my consulting and banking careers, and for his continual example of inspirational and authentic leadership.

Thank you also to Andrew Dutton (Chairman, NSW Land Registry Services) and the board for placing their trust in me as the first CEO of the newly privatised company, and for the shared ambition to truly transform the organisation.

Thank you to Paul Starling (8th Dan, IKGA Oceania Vice President) for providing a pathway in traditional Karate-Do that ignited a lifelong passion in the philosophies and lessons associated with Japanese martial arts. Thanks also to Ray Beattie OAM and Trevor Lawler for the lessons and hard knocks along the way.

Thank you to Horden Wiltshire, CEO, former submariner and long-term Karate-Do sparring partner, for your friendship and the deep discussions over many years that have contributed ideas to this book.

For me, writing a book was a little uncertain: would anyone be interested in what I'd have to say? I'd therefore like to acknowledge the support, encouragement and constructive feedback provided by John O'Donnell, Tyrone O'Neill, Matt Englund, Mark Devitt, Melinda Smith, Nicole Mathias-Browne, Steve Barrow, Barbara McKee and Stephen White.

I'd like to thank the team at Wiley. Thank you to Lucy Raymond and Leigh McLennon for their initial enthusiasm for my book, and for guiding me on the publishing journey, and to Chris Shorten and Sandra Balonyi for their patience in working with me to fine-tune the manuscript that is now the book you're reading.

To my children, Jack and Renae, hopefully this book gives you some additional insights into what your dad was doing these many years ... and Renae, contrary to your eight-year-old-self's observation, I'd like to think I did more than just 'chat with people all day'.

Lastly, I'd like to thank my wife, Belinda Kerr, for her ongoing encouragement, chapter reviews and provocative challenges, and most critically, her down-to-earth bullshit meter, which has made such a positive contribution to this book.

Thank you all.

About the author

Adam Bennett is an experienced transformation leader with direct experience in leading and advising transformation programs across a diverse set of blue-chip companies and industries in Australia, and the Asia–Pacific.

His career spans three decades as a CEO, CIO, digital executive and management consultant. He's observed what works and what doesn't with a dry humour and is a keen observer of the many characters, good and bad, that inhabit corporate life. He is the Principal of Great Change Consulting, a specialist transformation advisory practice that helps CEOs and executives successfully implement their transformation programs.

Adam has a Bachelor of Business from the University of Technology, Sydney, where he is an Adjunct Professor (industry) and regular guest speaker on transformation. He's also a graduate of the Advanced Management Program at Harvard Business School. He has a long-term addiction to martial arts, holding a 3rd Dan black belt awarded by the International Karate-Do Gojukai Association, headquartered in Tokyo, Japan.

Introduction

Our world continues to change at an incredibly fast pace, and we've not reached 'peak change' just yet. How we frame this change — whether as a threat or an opportunity — is important. While the accelerated pace of change may be new, the challenges associated with transformation are not. In this book I'll unpack how to navigate these challenges, and how to leverage the lessons and examples provided by those who have come before us.

We've not yet reached peak change

The impact of technological change enabling new and innovative business models is threatening and disrupting established businesses and organisations around the world. This disruption will accelerate, so all leaders must be interested in managing change and successfully transforming their companies and organisations.

This is a book on how to do it. It defines and outlines a 'way' of transformation that can help leaders at all levels to adopt the right mindset and understand the very real pitfalls and challenges that make transformation difficult. It also examines how to pull the right corporate and operational levers to effect change and help a corporate transformation be successful.

It's worth noting that there are many techniques and approaches to transforming organisations, and many of their proponents approach transformation with fanatical zeal as though they're the first to deliver material change within an organisation. They may think that the challenges associated with the design and execution of large-scale transformation are different from those in the past because the objectives (build a platform business) or techniques (create automated processing interfaces) are somehow new or different from anything that's gone before. Or worse, in an environment in which no-one can be perceived to be disadvantaged, that they must pretend everyone working happily (or otherwise) within their company's status quo has the right to the same or a better role in the newly transformed organisation or company.

This makes no sense.

| Leading transformation is not new

Leaders have been grappling with change since time immemorial. While there are new technologies (remember when 'cloud' used to just be something in the sky) and some new techniques, such as Agile, most of the transformation challenges we face today have been solved before, and many of the approaches used are just as relevant now as they once were. It's just that in many cases we never learned them, or we've forgotten them, or we've invented new words for old ideas.

There's a WAY of transformation — and by 'way', I mean a combination of science, proven practices, methodologies and historical examples — that can be used to help give a leader the best possible chance of successfully transforming their company.

Let's also agree that transformation and managing change is difficult.

Transformation is not impossible, but it's hard. It's empirically difficult and challenging. Many successful businesses over the past several decades — despite being full of clever, earnest and motivated people — have been unable to successfully change. I've observed the difficulty of transformation while consulting to and working in multiple blue-chip companies around the world over the past three decades.

I've set out to write a book that encapsulates what I've learned so far in a career involved directly, and almost exclusively, in the development of corporate and/or divisional strategy, and the implementation and execution of transformational change. Throughout this period, I've definitely tried to — in the words of Mickey Connolly, founder and CEO of Conversant — 'reserve the right to get smarter.'

Being involved in the conception of corporate strategy and leading transformation is hugely exciting, satisfying and rewarding. Using tools to quickly get to grips with the essence of an industry and company — to really understand what the company needs to create value and make money, and to understand the strategic opportunities and threats it faces — is incredibly mentally stimulating.

Meeting and understanding a set of motivated people earnestly grappling with the challenges of industry change, trying their best to make sense of things, and worried for the future of their company and their own careers, has also been humbling and sobering.

To then craft reality-based strategies and initiatives to help a company adapt and thrive in the face of a changing landscape — and to actually lead their transformation efforts, to design and then pull different 'levers' to effect organisational change and take people on the journey — has been at once a privilege and massively energising.

| What this book is about

As it says on the cover, this book is about Great Change. Great in that it is material, significant and worthwhile; and great in that it is also successful, fun and engaging. For the sake of clarity (and brevity), let me ensure that we're all on the same page right from the get-go by providing four definitions:

1. *WAY*: I'll explain more on this concept later, but for now, this book is predominantly about the 'how' (i.e. the execution, or the 'means') of transformation, not the 'what' or 'why' of transformation (i.e. the strategy, or the 'ends'). It's a blueprint and its objective, above all else, is to be useful to those who might use it.

2. *Big*: although much of what I've learned is applicable to all kinds of change, this book is not about re-engineering your accounts payable department. It's about leveraging all the tools and levers necessary to ensure that a significant transformation is successful. And by significant, I mean a business division or, ideally, an entire corporate enterprise or government organisation.

3. *Strategy*: while this book will inevitably help you develop cogent strategies, it broadly assumes that you know what you are looking to achieve, and that you've got a long-term objective for your organisation.

4. *Done:* the transformation must be achievable and measurable, and something that you or anyone else can point to once implemented, and call 'done'. Done doesn't mean 'going to', 'nearly' or 'success is close — all we need is another $50 million' and all the other garbage claims that many leaders of failed transformations make to feel better or to justify wastage of time and treasure. Done means done. The change or transformation must be objectively complete and deliver its original scope and benefits.

Let me also state right up front that I've observed that too many business books are dry and highbrow, so this book is a somewhat irreverent take on a serious topic. It tries not to take itself too seriously.

Who this book is for

This book is for anyone faced with understanding what's happening in the world, developing a strategy and ultimately changing their organisation. You might work for a private sector company, big or small, a government department, or some other kind of organisation. You might be the newly appointed chief executive officer, or you might be leading a large division or business unit, and you're out of your comfort zone of managing the business-as-usual operations and pushing your boat out into the uncharted waters of transformation. You might even have just been appointed as the leader of a transformation and you're seeking more tools and techniques to give your project a better chance of success.

Or you might be none of these things. You might be that young, emerging leader watching many disruptive forces play out and wondering how you'll affect the organisation that you work for. Or how you affect your career and how you might get involved in the management and leadership of transformation.

In all these cases, this book offers practical and pragmatic lessons for igniting, leading and implementing transformation, regardless of whether your team is measured in the hundreds or the thousands.

| Three inspirations for this book

This book pulls together lessons from three areas I've practised closely and observed for more than 30 years:

- the study of world history
- the close practical study of traditional Japanese Gōjū-ryū Karate-Do
- business transformation (as a long-term management consultant and hands-on executive).

Here's why I've woven these themes into the blueprint:

- *World history*: I've been actively reading books about history since I was about 12 years old, and after all these years, I'm one of those people who simply cannot walk past a brass plaque on a wall that explains some obscure fact from the past. Historical figures such as George Marshall, Barbara Jordan and Matthew Ridgway can still speak to us about how to tackle our very real contemporary challenges. Their leadership, psychology, and geo-political and strategic lessons have helped me throughout my career in leading transformation. Importantly, many of the concepts for thinking, developing and getting big strategy done were first developed and then honed by military leaders throughout history, so there's a strong relevance. However, let me state right up front that I'm not one of those armchair strategists who equates business with warfare. I've never been in the military, and I've never been in a war. As an avid reader of history, I know that business and organisation change is a lot easier. The stakes are not as high and, typically, every business leader goes home to their comfortable apartment, house or even mansion at the end of the day. When it comes to reading and applying military history, let's acknowledge the service of our citizens who've actually been in the military and put themselves in harm's way. Those who have had to make incredibly critical decisions. We must never kid ourselves that we are in some kind of narrow macho corporate battlefield, nor that our business jobs are as difficult. However, equally, let's also agree that we who've made our careers in business can still be incredibly competitive. We take our accountabilities and the commitments we make extremely seriously, and we are very focused on beating the competition, whoever that may be.

- *Gōjū-ryū Karate-Do*: Karate-Do translates as 'the way of the empty hand'. I started studying Gōjū-ryū, one of the most traditional karate schools, in 1985. The word *Gōjū* translates as 'hard/soft' and I've found it's a great metaphor for navigating life. Gōjū recognises extremes while also encompassing contrast and acknowledging that each has its place. The underlying philosophy is that you remain courteous and humble at all times. You stay flexible and understand that you shouldn't rely on only one style of thinking or moving. Some situations require a hard response, some a soft response. Paradoxically, a hard situation may require a soft response, or vice versa. Martial arts training has given me a somewhat unusual (and relatively safe) way to develop my ways of thinking and has itself served as an entrée into interesting psychological mindsets and Eastern philosophies that are relevant for leading transformation.

- *Business transformation*: I was extremely lucky to join Price Waterhouse Urwick as a junior management consultant in 1994, which allowed me to consult to a diverse set of companies across a range of industries around the world. While I often worked on the development of corporate strategy, my passion and area of focus was on the implementation and transformation of the client's operations and company. I was never interested in the development of a strategy for its own sake, or in writing a strategy report that then stood on the client's shelf gathering dust. After 13 years as a hands-on consultant, leading the delivery of projects and client engagements, I then worked as an executive in the National Australia Bank. Over the next dozen years, I worked in a variety of roles including as chief information officer and leading digital teams. This was followed by being the first post-privatisation chief executive officer for NSW Land Registry Services as it transitioned from a former government department to its current incarnation as a highly profitable digital infrastructure business. All of these experiences have been formative and provided a huge set of lessons that I've now brought together in a cohesive whole. It's been quite the ride so far, and I've loved (nearly — let's be honest) every minute of it.

Okay, now I've got all of that off my chest, let me explain how I've laid out this book. My goal is to share some of the observations and lessons learned along the way and to be constructively provocative to challenge and complement some of the perspectives you'll already have.

How you can use this book

To be successful, any 'way' of transformation must acknowledge and address the difficulties associated with change. It must help an organisation make sense of the world, develop its response and most importantly (and the main subject of this book) help drive transformation and results.

Once you understand why an objective is difficult, it's easier to design actions to overcome these difficulties and achieve your goal.

This book has five key chapters intended to help you understand why change is difficult and to navigate your way forward to achieve real and meaningful — or in other words 'great' — change.

Each chapter lays out ideas, illustrative stories and examples, and finishes with a summary of the key points raised.

Let me briefly introduce the five chapters of the book.

1. The WAY things get done

The WAY can be defined as the very essence of how things get done in every human endeavour. In all organisations, there's a 'way' of doing things, and these methods, approaches and cultures combine in a manner that defines the very core of the organisation. Whether a branch of the military, a company, a school, a university, or, as I'll explain later, a martial art, all organisations evolve a distinct 'way' that permeates right to the very core of how its people perceive the world, think, operate, change (or not) and manage the many interactions they have internally and externally with the outside world. If you've ever been part of an organisation — and that's all of us — then you know intuitively the 'way' that your organisation works, what it stands for and why it exists.

2. Understanding transformation

When I use the term 'transformation' I'm talking about three elements, all of which are needed for success:

- the identification of disruptive forces
- the crafting of strategy
- the successful implementation of change.

Transformation is inherently difficult because all organisations have an existing way of being that creates its own inertia, and the status quo never has to argue its case. Introducing change collides and grinds against this status quo and the well-entrenched way of being that so deeply defines the organisation seeking to change. The transformation is also likely to be resisted or sabotaged by the culture and interactions of the personalities and corporate characters that inhabit every organisation.

3. The mindset for great change

Leading and managing a transformation effort is different from managing the business-as-usual operations of an organisation, so you may need to think a bit differently. Different doesn't mean better or worse. This chapter describes some of the timeless and positive ways of thinking that can help you unlock opportunities and an organisation's potential, and personally lead a transformation effort.

4. The mechanics of great change

Just as there's a WAY of being, there's also a WAY of changing. Management consulting firms, companies and academics have long studied how to change organisations. As a result, there are different proven and time-honoured techniques and methods — or mechanics — that can help you accelerate your transformation and set it up for success. The mechanics detailed in this book are a pragmatic, commercial and practical guide for leaders of all levels that will help you take action and deliver transformation outcomes. Given the inherent complexity and difficulty of transformation, there are no silver bullets to guarantee your success. However, following a clear framework will definitely help you to give it a red-hot go.

5. Creating your 90-day blueprint

There's very little time to make a good first impression. It's something I quickly realised as a junior management consultant when I had to maximise planning time before starting a consulting engagement, and quickly build momentum at the client site to start adding value. Time is money and the meter is always running. Executive life is no different, so this chapter covers how to quickly build momentum in your new role and a 'how to' for building your own transformation blueprint. The world is moving fast, and expectations of you in your new role will be high, so there's no time to waste. Get at it. This chapter therefore provides you with ideas and approaches that you can put into immediate practice to build momentum.

A caveat: these mindsets and mechanics are not intended to be locked in stone. At the very heart of the approach is continual improvement. Use or discard some or all of these at your own discretion. You may also have techniques that you already use that are better. Great. This book is intended to promote your thinking, so you can develop and refine your own templates and transformation style.

It's always about the people

Transformation is an endeavour ultimately dependent on the scale of ambition of its leaders, and the power and patience of its resisters. Above all, it's the competition of ideas, views, biases, hopes and aspirations of an organisation's leaders and employees, with no guarantee that any particular idea or view will win. Whether an organisation successfully senses the disruptive forces that might put it at existential risk, is able to craft a compelling strategy, and then, most critically, can implement the changes required is not pre-ordained. Success will always depend upon the people involved.

To be successful, a transformation leader must assess the people around them to balance the degree to which they will promote or prevent change. Understanding people and their very human motivations, and then being willing to take action — whether that means promotion or demotion — based on that understanding, is one of the most important skills a transformation leader can develop.

It's always the people — and the very rich set of attributes, good and bad, that people exhibit in their everyday interactions — that makes corporate life so interesting. And when these people are thrust into the Petri dish of transformational change, where their very deepest assumptions are challenged, their greatest fears come true, their personal ambitions are laid bare and they face the greatest opportunity for personal development, then everything becomes absolutely fascinating.

Along the way I'll therefore share some observations of the corporate characters I've come across. I've been incredibly fortunate to have had some great role models, bosses, mentors and colleagues, and awesome people working beside me in my own executive teams. All of these people have invested in me, been patient, inspiring and tough in equal measure, and I carry something from all of them in how I approach transformation.

Equally, and let me rip the band-aid off quickly, there have also been some narcissists and psychopaths. In this book, I'll share elements of both the positive and negative personalities. Though, if I'm honest, it's far more interesting and (hopefully for you) entertaining to joke about the narcissists and psychopaths and to describe the crazier and less self-aware characters that inhabit corporate Australia and the business world more generally.

It's also worth noting that unless you understand these corporate characters and how some of them can, and no doubt will, obstruct your transformation efforts, it's impossible to design and execute a logical and thorough change program that can overcome their resistance and enable a successful transformation. In the case of corporate psychopaths, narcissists and authoritarian disbelievers, forewarned is truly forearmed.

Finally, I've made a metric shit-ton of errors and mistakes over the past 30 years. I've taken a balanced approach to these errors and professional regrets, there being things I should've done and didn't, and things I did do and shouldn't have. Let me confess that some of the lessons and recommendations in the coming pages are definitely things of which I should've taken note. Sometimes it's not until you make a mistake and feel its impact and implications that you realise that there was a better way of doing things. Hopefully you can avoid some of the mistakes I've made. Let no-one think I got everything right!

So, without further ado, let me introduce the first corporate character: the 'self-righteous', that special breed of executive who simply can't believe they have anything to learn. The one who could not possibly show any of the traits that I'm going to describe, and is, therefore, by definition, without an existing fault (or future potential). If this sounds like you, stop now, send me an email, and I'll refund your money because this book is definitely not for you. Otherwise, read on.

CHAPTER 1

The WAY things get done

Game of Thrones is an American fantasy drama series created by HBO based on the stories in *A Song of Ice and Fire* by George R R Martin. Since it debuted in 2011, each of its 73 episodes has been watched by more than 44.2 million people, according to Fiction Horizon (fictionhorizon.com). It's a huge epic, shot on location across Europe and North America, involving a massively talented cast, amazing production values and a political web of intrigue across the storylines. Its combination of drama, sex and romance, and action scenes involving sword fights, pitched battles and dragons, saw it win 59 Primetime Emmy Awards, the most by a drama series.

The sword fights are amazing and play a central role in the storyline to punctuate the drama with violence. From the choreography to the way that it's portrayed, the producers have done a great job of capturing the techniques and strategies associated with the long-lost art of sword fighting. Of course, no-one really knows what it was like for two European knights to go at it with their swords because this knowledge has dimmed and disappeared over the past 500 to 600 years. Although there are some medieval swords gathering dust in some cathedrals or museums, the actual way of applying the physical sword techniques, the ways of thinking and the approach to strategy and combat are long gone. These ways, which were so critically important to the social, political and military fabric of Europe for so many centuries, haven't made it across time to be available to us now, and so the producers of *Game of Thrones* have had to make it all up.

Imagine if this was not the case.

Imagine that, within a taxi ride from Heathrow Airport, in the green fields outside London, you could still learn such things. For example, the traditional techniques, strategies and philosophies of wielding a European long sword, mace and halberd, and for jousting on horseback against an opponent in full plate armour, taught just as they were back in the day.

This is exactly what you can do in Japan.

Within Chiba Prefecture, near Tokyo's Narita International Airport, there's a special place. It's the Tenshin Shōden Katori Shintō-ryū, a classical sword school founded in 1447. At the school, you can learn how to use a samurai sword to fight a man wearing medieval armour and wielding a sword, halberd, spear, or long and short swords. The school's aims have remained the same since they were laid down by its founder, Iizasa Chōisai Ienao, more than 575 years ago: to produce swordsmen versed in every aspect of the art of war, from weapons skills to tactical, logistical and medical knowledge.

At the time of writing, the headmaster of the school is Iizasa Shūri-no-Suke Yasusada, the 20th generation in line from the founder. The teachings of the ryū were designated an intangible cultural asset of Japan in 1960. The curriculum incorporates a comprehensive set of actual combat techniques, organised into different 'kata', or groups, of pre-arranged techniques for the *katana* (samurai sword), *naginata* (halberd), *rokushakubo* (six-foot staff), *yari* (spear), *shuriken* (blade throwing), *kumi-uchi* (unarmed grappling and striking), strategies, philosophies and teaching methods. The interactions of the headmaster, teachers (*sensei*) and senior students — passed down verbally, in written teaching scrolls and via certain protocols over the centuries — form a distinct culture.

The curriculum, the physical location or *dojo* (literally, the way/place), the history, ethos and culture, combined across all of its forms and elements, comprises a martial 'way' (known as *budo* in Japan) that contains all of the physical and mental components necessary for success in sword combat.

In Japan, the concept of the way (pronounced as 'dough' in Japanese and written as 道 in kanji) can be loosely translated as the 'path' or 'road'. The concept of the way is deeply ingrained in Japanese culture and philosophy, and has its roots in the *Tao Te Ching*, written by Lao Zi, a Chinese philosopher, around the 4th century BCE. At its heart is a conceptual idea that there's a way of doing things. There's a way of being a farmer, priest, soldier or merchant, and each of these pursuits has definite characteristics underpinning what they do and how they do it.

Hence, in Japan, the now international Olympic wrestling sport of *judo* translates to 'the way of softness'. The striking and kicking art of Karate-Do translates to the empty (*kara*) hand (*te*) way (*do*). In my personal experience, Gōjū-ryū, a traditional school of Karate-Do, has its own 'way', which is a combination of closed and open hand striking techniques, throwing and joint locking, predominantly low-level kicking techniques, and short and stable stances. Its philosophies and strategies combine these technical aspects with distancing and timing strategies that best suit close quarter self-defence. In any case, each style has its own way that's distinctive. Watching an exponent of one of these martial arts, you can tell which art it is by the techniques they use and how they use them.

Many physical and spiritual pursuits in Japanese culture recognise this connection to a distinct way of doing things. For example, there's a way of preparing tea (*cha-no-yu*, the tea ceremony), a way of arranging flowers (*ikebana*) and a way of ink painting (*sumi-e*). The way permeates and defines how people in a range of activities understand, think about and perform their jobs, hobbies and sports. Critically, the way is not to be confused with what's often defined in our modern corporate context as culture. Throughout this book I use the term 'way' in a far broader sense than culture.

| Elements of the WAY

The concept of a way is, therefore, an all-encompassing method for collecting the techniques, philosophies and modes of thinking required to undertake, and succeed in, a certain task or goal.

In traditional Japanese martial arts, these philosophies, strategies and techniques were formulated into 'kata', comprising long sequences of defensive and attacking moves. These individual kata, starting with sets of beginner techniques and progressing up to sets including more sophisticated techniques, can be likened to the chapters of a book, and form the curriculum of the martial arts school. Their pattern and practice are jealously guarded to ensure that they remain unchanged.

In a modern business, these philosophies, strategies and techniques would be expressed as policies, procedures, business processes and cultural expectations. Combined, they define 'how we do things around here' for an organisation.

In essence, then, a 'way' can be distilled down to its two consistent elements: mindset and mechanics.

Mindset means how people think and perceive the world. It encompasses the ways of looking at what's occurring in its context, whether that be a 15th-century sword fight, a 21st-century sports competition or a multinational business. Something happens as stimulus, you perceive it happening and then your mindset — or ways of thinking — will determine how you respond. Stimulus, perception, thinking, then response (hopefully in that order).

Putting aside sword fighting, let's think about the business world. When something happens, such as the emergence of a new competitor, the launch of a new regulation or problems with a loyal customer, your prevailing mindset will determine how you respond. The culture of your company, its approach to customer service and competition, and its procedures and training will all influence how you perceive what's happening and how you'll intellectually and emotionally respond.

These personal and professional experiences, beliefs and the culture of your company will all influence you very deeply. Perhaps more deeply than you think. All of these experiences will have laid down what are sometimes referred to as 'sacred beliefs' that are very powerful, difficult to challenge and fundamentally drive your behaviours. In essence, according to Changing Minds (www.changingminds.org), sacred beliefs are 'those that people hold to be unquestionably true'.

Mechanics means how people actually respond, based on events and their mindset. The mechanics relate to the actions you take and the techniques you apply to respond to the stimulus. Depending on your mindset, you might take the following responses:

- *The emergence of a new competitor:*
    a) you immediately commission a study to find out what's happening, or
    b) you immediately cut your prices, or
    c) you wait to see what happens.

- *The launch of a new regulation*:

    a) you start researching what your company needs to do, or

    b) you assess whether the regulation is actually in effect, or

    c) you seek an immediate clarification meeting with your regulator.

- *Problems with a loyal customer*:

    a) you tell them to suck it up, or

    b) you immediately call them to find out what's happening, or

    c) you remain silent and see what happens.

The range of potential responses — the mechanics — is dependent on your mindset.

While we do not use the term 'do' or 'way' in Western societies, we certainly would recognise the distinct methods of playing our familiar sports (everyone can tell the difference between batting techniques in cricket and baseball), learning musical instruments or cooking certain international cuisines. Just because we don't name it as such doesn't mean we don't actually study and use certain approaches.

Think about something that you do regularly and well: it could be a sport, a hobby, managing a meeting, closing a sale or coaching a colleague. If you do these well, I suspect that you've learned, practised and honed your skills over many years, and that you typically approach different circumstances and people with a somewhat standard set of principles because you've applied them over and over, and you know that they're likely to work. And again, I suspect that if you were asked to teach this special personal skill to someone else, you would be able to talk at length, and with passion, about what you do, how you do it, what typically leads to success, and the mistakes and pitfalls to avoid.

If you were to reflect on what makes you successful in your sport, hobby or business context, I can almost guarantee that it would probably be based on the mental methods that you use to make sense of what's happening (i.e. your mindset) and then the manner in which you respond (i.e. the actions, or mechanics, that you apply). Without knowing the terminology of what the Japanese call a 'do', what you've inadvertently done over these many years is develop your own 'way' of doing things.

The corporate WAY

Companies and other large organisations are no different. They develop their own way of being and doing things. We are sometimes tempted to think about this as culture, being the beliefs, behaviours, symbols and style of the people within these companies. This definition is too narrow. A 'way' is far more and all encompassing.

Just like the Tenshin Shōden Katori Shintō-ryū, with its weapons, techniques, strategies, philosophies and teaching methods — in essence, its way — passed down from generation to generation unchanged through time, so the modern company also has its own way.

This will encompass its products, patents and proprietary ways of design and manufacture (think Apple), the business processes it follows, its enabling technologies (think Amazon), the methods it uses to recruit staff and familiarise them with the company, how it inculcates the culture into new recruits through scorecard setting, and performance appraisals and rewards (think Goldman Sachs). It will also extend to the corporate stories told, perhaps about the original founders (think Bill Gates and Paul Allen at Microsoft), or in written statements (think Johnson & Johnson's customer credo), or reinvention over the course of generational technological change (think IBM). The people within each of these organisations may never acknowledge the existence of a way, but regardless, that's exactly what they're working within, and contributing to, each day they go to work. It's the collection and organisation of all the elements within the company that constitutes a way, and it's what makes a company like Apple the remarkable success it is.

All these elements form the way that the company works. They are the reason that new recruits (regardless of their level in the hierarchy) take a while to settle in and get their footing: because they're learning how everything works, who and what's important, who are the most profitable or influential customers, what the key processes and systems are, what's celebrated and sanctioned, what's tightly or loosely believed, and the cadence of meetings, processes and decision making. It's also why not all new starters fit in, regardless of the rigour of the process that recruited them, the depth of psychological testing they endured, or the number of interviews they sat through, smiled, and repeated their schtick in.

These elements define how the company works and its essence, or way of being. They have typically built up over a long time for long-established companies, or reflect the strongly held sacred beliefs of the founders of younger companies. In both cases, the power of longevity and traditionally held beliefs, or the power of the founder's personality and biases, make these elements deeply ingrained, and materially powerful in driving how people think and respond to various stimuli. Above all, the accrued power of time or connection to the current senior boss makes them very hard to change.

| Adaptation or extinction

Wars are no longer fought with swords, halberds and staffs. The world has moved on, and the armed forces of all countries are now equipped with the most modern weapons available. The bladed weapons of medieval Japan have been replaced by guns and tanks and aircraft.

The Tenshin Shōden Katori Shintō-ryū has therefore itself evolved from the cutting edge (pun intended) of military science, martial thought and physical sword technique, to become, in the face of changing circumstances 575 years later, an intangible cultural asset. The very traits that made it relevant and effective in the 15th century now consign it to be like a living museum. Its strategies, philosophies and techniques are no less valuable. It's just that now, instead of being valued for their efficacy in self-defence when confronted by someone with a three-foot razor blade, they're valued for their fierce beauty, discipline and cultural connection to historical Japan.

Companies too need to confront the harsh reality that their own way of doing things, while relevant today, will inevitably be pressured by changing circumstances, new competitors and more innovative methods. Without focus, attention and maintenance (or even reinvention), the existing way of doing things will eventually become tired, irrelevant or, worst of all, it will become a *Harvard Business Review* case study that warns prospective executives of what not to do. The equivalent of a 'corporate' museum piece.

This can be hard to take, especially by those who founded the company, or designed and implemented the ways of doing things that may now be under threat. Challenging the business practices that someone has implemented can be like telling them that their baby is ugly. It creates a visceral defensive response. Such a response makes it even more likely that the company won't change and address the very forces that are threatening it.

Every human organisation has an established way of doing things: every sports team, private company, publicly listed corporation, high-tech startup, government agency, martial art and religious organisation. There's not a single organisation of like-minded human beings organised to achieve a collective goal that doesn't establish and develop its own way of doing things. It permeates all of human endeavours and fundamentally defines how we, as people, get stuff done.

And that represents the threat and the opportunity. The established way of doing things in your organisation, and whether it's capable of itself changing in the face of changing circumstances, will be the most important element in whether the organisation continues to successfully navigate a changing world.

As Charles Darwin is reputed to have stated, 'It's not the strongest of the species that survives, nor the most intelligent, it's the one most adaptable to change.'

Key points from chapter 1

- All organisations develop a way of being, and all people in these organisations develop a way of performing their roles. Both of these forces are very strong and naturally resist change.

- When disruptive forces emerge in an organisation's environment and then collide with the existing, deeply held ways of being that characterise the company and the people within it, things become interesting. This collision is real and it plays out in how the company and its leaders perceive the threats and opportunities created by the disruption (mindset) and how its people then respond to this disruption via the tactics and techniques they pursue (mechanics).

- Just as there are many different martial arts, and many different corporate 'ways', there are also undoubtedly many different 'ways' of leading and managing transformation.

- The various consulting firms have all invested significantly in the creation of different methodologies, approaches and philosophies based on their experiences, all designed to ensure the success of their transformation offerings to clients. Many large companies have drawn on these firms and their alumni to develop their own 'in-house' methods for transformation and change.

- When the new way of transformation collides with the existing way the company is being run and operated, things truly get fascinating. It's then that you have existing mindsets challenged, wars of ideas and influence and new ways of doing things introduced that throw all of the traditional mechanics up in the air, to fall back down in hopefully more effective and efficient patterns.

- Let's face facts: 575 years from now, no-one will be hanging out in a small hall on the quiet green outskirts of a major city practising the strategies, philosophies and techniques we use each day in our companies. Insensitive to a changing world, unchanged and static, our companies will go broke and simply cease to exist. Unlike the Tenshin Shōden Katori Shintō-ryū, I guarantee that none of them will become intangible cultural treasures.

CHAPTER 2
Understanding transformation

Before proceeding too far into a book on transformation we'd best be on the same page with regards its definition, what is typically driving it, and why it's hard.

If you're a leader, or you aspire to be one, then you *must* care about transformation.

You should understand the elements of transformation and what's involved because there's not a single industry that's not undergoing significant change. Strong forces such as technology and innovation, industry forces, societal forces and even internally generated forces unique to each company, are continually placing pressure on the business models of many organisations. There's no sign of this abating, so we've not reached peak change in society or business yet, and it's inevitable that you'll be faced with transformation.

If you're seeking to embrace transformation, you should also acknowledge that transformation is difficult. Leaders have long grappled with transformation in different societal, military and business contexts. Leading transformation has not become inherently easier.

Acknowledging that transformation is difficult, it's important to understand *why* it's difficult. Transformation is difficult because the status quo never has to argue its own case. There are many deeply ingrained and hard-wired ways of being within every organisation that actively resists change, and many organisations are also filled with executive personalities who actively resist change.

A successful transformation program must be designed and executed to directly acknowledge and address the inherent difficulties associated with change, and ready for the resistant personalities that it will inevitably uncover. If you don't know what creates these difficulties, then it's hard to design a transformation program that addresses and overcomes them.

So what exactly is transformation?

The Merriam Webster dictionary definition of transformation is 'Transformation (noun) — a complete or major change in someone's or something's appearance, form, etc.'

If we're going to be focused on transformation throughout this book, it's a good idea that we all get on the same page and work with the same understanding of the term. Putting aside the dictionary definition, transformation in a business or corporate sense can best be described as:

- understanding and making sense of what's happening and changing in the world (i.e. *disruption*)

- developing a planned and purposeful response to this change (i.e. a *strategy*)

- taking action to make changes to the various components of the business to address the identified disruptions (i.e. *execution*).

The net result of this three-step process is transformation, whereby the new or current organisation is significantly and measurably different from its previous form. Its financial health and trajectory, as evidenced by its balance sheet, profit and loss and free cash flows, must also be objectively better. It's no use claiming success in a transformation initiative that has delighted customers, simplified the organisation and energised the employees, but has left the company financially weak or depleted. Or in other words, claim that the operation was a success but unfortunately the patient died!

Transformation is then, by definition, significant or material. As stated in the introduction, transformation is not re-engineering the accounts payable department.

Equally, transformation is not something that should be measured in weeks or months. A transformation program measured in weeks or months is most likely lacking in ambition and scale, even if undertaken in a small organisation. True transformation takes time, but it shouldn't take too long. The longer a transformation program goes without delivering its objectives or measurable benefits, the less support and resources it will attract as it proceeds.

Transformation in the context of this book covers:

- whole of business (of any size)

- whole of operating division or business unit (i.e. a product line business; or sales, manufacturing etc.)

- whole of business function (i.e. finance, human resources, technology, and the like).

An easy rule of thumb should be that the organisation unit that's subject to the transformation should be at least several hundred people and can then obviously range up to thousands or tens of thousands of people for large organisations.

With more people involved comes new challenges. An exponential increase in the number of personal relationships and interactions increases complexity and complication. There are more opinions, contexts, excuses, aspirations and ambitions, all of which must be considered.

This doesn't mean you have to tailor a plan to address every individual's needs and concerns. It just means that you'll have to take the time to understand the typical views and ambitions — for or against the transformation — and develop plans to get large groups of people behind the transformation and its goals. And strangely, it seems that in modern organisations, if you put 10 people in a room, you typically get 11 opinions.

We've not yet reached peak change and disruption

We live in an incredible time of disruption, change and opportunity. Jack Welch, the former, and now increasingly somewhat controversial, CEO of General Electric, observed that 'If the rate of change on the outside exceeds the rate of change on the inside, then the end is near.' The management of change and transformation has been a clear feature of the last decade, and every year business and social commentators seem to claim that everything is moving and changing so fast. We are yet to see the news headline, 'Change finally slowing down'.

Well, we've not reached peak change yet, and the combined effect of pressure from several different trends and forces means that this disruption is likely to keep accelerating. In his book *Principles for dealing with the changing world order,* Ray Dalio, the legendary founder and co-chief investment officer for Bridgewater Associates, states that 'it seems obvious that the rate of invention and improvement in most areas will accelerate at an even faster pace, rapidly raising productivity and living standards'.

The biggest impact of these accelerating and colliding forces is that they put your organisation's existing business model, and the corporate 'way' by which you already do things, under constant pressure. This means that the period over which your business model and its established way of doing things continues to be appropriately calibrated to the external environment is becoming shorter. Which means you have to work harder just to keep up, let alone get ahead.

Quite simply, being open to transformation, being alert to disruption, developing appropriate strategic responses and then implementing these responses is becoming more and more important. In some respects, the cultivation of appropriate transformation skills and approaches is becoming ever more necessary and will eventually represent a business-as-usual skillset for all people leading companies, and certainly many of the rest of the wider employee group.

The large-scale shifts likely to impact your organisation include geo-political forces such as the rising ambitions of China, impacts from the Russian invasion of Ukraine, industry forces unique to your company, growing regulation and societal trends such as consumer activism, skills shortages due to COVID-19, and economic factors such as high inflation and volatile interest rates.

This chapter is not intended as a deep summary of each shift your business is likely to face, but there are three shifts worth considering for the potential impact they may have on you and your company:

1. the climate crisis
2. population growth
3. technology and innovation.

Climate crisis

The Earth is warming and the human-induced concentration of greenhouse gases in our atmosphere is increasing, and these two things are related.

In his book *How to avoid a climate disaster*, Bill Gates describes this process as greenhouse gases trapping heat, raising the Earth's surface temperature. He explains that

> the more gases there are, the more the temperature rises. And once greenhouse gases are in the atmosphere, they stay there for a very long time; something like one-fifth of the carbon dioxide emitted today will still be there in 10 000 years.

In the book, Gates references five questions, all of which will affect customers, businesses and suppliers involved in providing goods and services. These questions are significant and the answers we develop to address them over time will fundamentally impact how we live our lives as individuals, how our communities work, and the absolute and relative wealth our countries can create and retain. Gates' macro questions address:

- *how we plug in* — or, in other words, the generation and distribution of electricity from renewable sources such as solar, hydro and tidal, and the share that remains based on traditional fossil fuels

- *how we make things* — including the design, manufacture and assembly of capital assets such as infrastructure, buildings and roads, through to consumer items that we use in our everyday lives

- *how we grow things* — recognising that the manner in which we grow a range of grains, fruit and vegetable crops, together with raising livestock such as cattle, chickens, pigs and sheep for human consumption

- *how we get around* — meaning the transport modes we use each day, such as cars, trains, ships and aircraft, the materials that make up these products, together with the manner in which they are manufactured

- *how we keep cool and stay warm* — covering the quantum and type of fuel sources required to heat and cool our homes and places of work.

This is quite a comprehensive list, and it gives rise to opportunities and threats for businesses. It's difficult to imagine a single company that will not be directly or indirectly affected by at least one of these questions being asked and subsequently answered. Every industry will be affected: for some the impact is right now, while for others, it's only a matter of time.

The need to respond to these impacts, to develop responsive strategies and to implement transformation will be an existential challenge for many companies. The leadership of these companies will be faced with a somewhat stark choice: do they acknowledge the threat or disruption and do something about it, or do they kick it into the long grass for the next generation of leaders to deal with?

Population growth

The world's population continues to increase, although it will increase at different rates in different geographies.

The late Hans Rosling, a Swedish physician, academic and public speaker, had a simple PIN code for the world's population: 1-1-1-4. This represents the Americas, Europe and Africa having 1 billion people each, and Asia having 4 billion people, resulting in an average current world population of 7 billion.

Rosling's 2018 book, *Factfulness: 10 reasons we're wrong about the world — and why things are better than you think*, elaborates:

> Like all PIN codes, this one will change. By the end of this century, the UN expects there to have been almost no change in the Americas and Europe, but 3 billion more people in Africa and 1 billion more in Asia. By 2100 the PIN code of the world will be 1-1-4-5. More than 80% of the world's population will live in Africa and Asia.

People are living longer across the globe, and based on the generational arithmetic calculated by Rosling, it's inevitable that the world's population will get to about 11 billion.

What does this mean for society? How many Nobel prize winners could arise from these extra 4 billion people? How many innovations, inventions and transformations might they initiate or influence? What kind of political pressures might they bring to bear? Economic and political stability are not guaranteed. As Voltaire memorably said, 'History is filled with the sound of silken slippers going downstairs and wooden shoes coming up'. Or in other words, those wealthy and comfortable populations can be very surprised when they're awoken by those who've come to challenge the wealth and comfort they might take for granted.

What does this mean for business? What does it mean for commodities, for building materials, food, clothing, consumer goods, connections to the internet, travel consumption, health spending ... The economic power and demands of 4 billion extra people is likely to be enormous.

What does it mean for your business, your customers or the businesses that supply your company?

When the imagination and invention, the societal expectations and the resultant consumption and needs of these people are taken into account, what does it mean for the growing climate crisis or nationalism? Could this particular force be fuel for other forces? Time will tell, and the opportunities and threats that emanate from just this one force are impossible to predict with certainty.

What we can say with absolute certainty, however, is that this increase in population will inevitably create disruptions and opportunities that businesses will have to understand and respond to.

Technology and innovation

Technology change will continue to accelerate and impact the customer offerings, processes and business models of organisations in all industries. Cloud computing, technology services on demand, the metaverse, the internet of things, blockchain and quantum computing will all continue to play out. I suspect the biggest change, however, will come from the continued and rapidly accelerating impact of artificial intelligence.

In very simple terms, as defined by Encyclopedia Britannica, 'artificial intelligence (AI) is the ability of a computer or a robot controlled by a computer to do tasks that are usually done by humans'. AI algorithms and computers, also harnessing the massive computing potential of the cloud, will revolutionise jobs across every organisation and industry. So far, AI applications have typically been used to perform low-level processing tasks, but as it becomes more sophisticated and powerful it will start to replace or augment more cerebral tasks.

Significant change is coming, and it's coming quickly. Ray Dalio explains this well in *Principles for dealing with the changing world order*:

> *The ability of both computers and humans will improve at an increasing pace. Perhaps most importantly, advances in the wider use of quantum computing with AI will lead to unimaginable advances in rates of learning and improvement and changes in global wealth and power. These changes will occur in varying degrees in the next five to 20 years but will add up to the greatest shift in wealth and power that the world has ever seen.*

IBM's Watson supercomputer has been able to digest thousands of images and characteristics of individual melanomas, digest the free text of the latest research findings, and teach itself to improve the diagnosis of melanoma in humans. What's most interesting about this is not what Watson can do, but that this was its capability in 2017. It's even better now.

Full self-driving (FSD) is emerging as one of the next automotive battlegrounds as traditional car companies, together with new companies such as Tesla, and also technology companies such as Apple and Google, are competing to develop the best AI algorithms to take passengers safely from point A to point B. Once (if) cracked, this kind of FSD AI will have massive business and societal implications. American entrepreneur and Venture for America founder Andrew Yang writes 'there are over 3.5 million truck drivers in the US, and another 7.2 million workers who serve the needs of truck drivers at truck stops, diners, motels and other businesses' in his book, *The war on normal people*. This means that more than 10 million individual workers could be negatively affected by the introduction of FSD AI into just one industry.

Some commentators might imagine the ease at which truck drivers and taxi drivers can retrain into new jobs (notwithstanding the challenges and personal disruption associated with this), but does that also hold true when senior lawyers in law firms are dislodged by algorithms that can determine the facts of a case, trawl the legislation and precedent law in seconds, and craft an argument overnight before the human lawyers even get their morning coffee? Not to mention the medical diagnostics staff already affected by Watson.

ChatGPT exploded into our societal and business context in November 2022 as a powerful tool for searching, developing and augmenting written text. ChatGPT took just two months to achieve 100 million users, the fastest adoption rate ever. While there have been some early and highly publicised mistakes in its responses, it's important to remember that ChatGPT and AI generally are the dumbest they will ever be. According to British online newspaper *The Independent*, 'machines can learn unsupervised at the speed of light'. They will only get smarter. And the rate they get smarter is either exhilarating or daunting depending on your point of view.

The one thing we know for certain is that the rate of improvement and availability of these AI technologies will not slow down any time soon. When combined with other developments in cloud storage, cyber, data collection and analytics, the potential changes become exponential. In such circumstances, what will be the response of the current crop of senior executive leaders? Will they grab hold of and wrestle with these forces and their potential impacts — both positive and negative — or will they lean back and hope that they can just make it through the rest of their career without having to change their organisation?

Company-centric forces

As all of the general technology, industry and societal forces play out, every organisation (yours included) is also inevitably facing its own unique forces that generate the need for transformation. These forces are those things that have been bubbling along quietly, sometimes noticed by the more strategic or astute leaders, who realise that significant investment and effort is going to be required to solve them, or sometimes they're not noticed or acknowledged at all. They're those big things that, if they're spoken about, might be discussed in hushed, frustrated or resigned tones, or worse, are buried on page 79 deep within the operational risk register. These are the forces that are about your organisation, and only your organisation.

By definition, these forces are a function of your organisation's industry, age, culture, historical business performance and, if listed, the shareholder return expectations placed on it by the market. They're a direct reflection and result of your company's way of doing things.

Most critically, these internal forces typically arise and affect the ability of your organisation to invest in transformation right at the time that many of the other industry, technological and societal forces are simultaneously landing on your plate.

Example themes that generate the need for transformation include:

- product obsolescence
- technical debt
- skills demographics
- growing headcount and the emergence of 'bullshit' jobs
- regulatory pressure
- investment slate pressure.

It's worth exploring each of these themes to understand how they affect transformation.

Product obsolescence

It's Friday, 19 October 2001 and let's imagine that you're the divisional head for the Sony Walkman. You're sitting in your office in Tokyo — a decent office, I assume, given the success your core product has enjoyed since it evolved from its earliest days, through its subsequent waterproof incarnation with the cool yellow case, and into the Discman that enabled millions of people to listen to their favourite CDs on the run. You're ready for the weekend, not realising that by Tuesday, your cherished and highly successful product will be obsolete.

Because on Tuesday, 23 October 2001, Apple — who you maybe didn't even register as one of your competitors — will launch the first iPod. A solid-state device that can download hundreds of songs and has a cool interface that allows the user to select and shuffle songs and curate their own playlists. And, amazingly, they download the songs over the internet. 'Holy shit!' (or a Japanese equivalent) you say. 'Why didn't we think of that?' Especially because you've already got all the ingredients in-house: the screens, the battery, the computing smarts, the precision manufacturing capability and even a music division that's signed some of the best and biggest global artists.

Without an ongoing investment, it's quite easy for your company's main product offering to fall behind those of your major competitors. This problem is industry agnostic, and all companies can (will) at some stage fall prey to it. It's literally economic Darwinism, where natural selection thins the herd of competitors, and only the most adaptable survive.

Quite simply, product obsolescence becomes apparent when your competitors introduce features that improve and differentiate their product from yours — or worse, a new competitor introduces a product that blows yours out of the water.

Numerous articles have been written about why Sony couldn't make the iPod: some offer suggestions that it was because of what American academic and business consultant Professor Clayton Christensen called the 'innovator's dilemma'. This is when large companies that listen to their customers are ultimately undercut by offerings from other disruptive competitors. Some suggest that the Sony organisation structure and silo-based incentives prevented cross-divisional collaboration. Whatever the cause, its product was made obsolete very quickly, and all organisations remain at risk of their main product falling behind competitors with regards to features, reliability, price point and value proposition.

Technical debt

Technical debt can be defined as the fact that your legacy technology or physical assets are constantly wearing out and therefore need replacement.

First, let's acknowledge that technical debt is bad because its existence points to the fact that you have technology systems that are old. While they continue to run, they might also be written in old languages that are hard to upgrade and improve, they may have specialist key-person risk associated with their maintenance, they may create cyber risks and patching difficulty, and they may limit your optionality with regard to the transformation of your business model and/or business processes.

The currency of an application compares what you have with the latest version released by the technology vendor. It's exactly like your own smartphone, and the repercussions are similar. Systems should be regularly upgraded to the latest version to ensure that you can access all of the latest features and improvements, and critically, so that you're covered and protected from the latest cyber threats. The challenge for many businesses is that it's boring and unexciting to invest in the maintenance and/or replacement of old systems, when you can invest in the implementation of shiny new toys that grab everyone's attention and make the sponsor look strategic, dynamic and hard driving.

There's no easy way to address technical debt, which arises across applications and infrastructure alike. The big challenge to businesses is that technical debt is largely invisible. If you take manufacturing, it's obvious when you go to a factory if the plant is tired and the machines are run-down and old. Not so for technology: it's hidden deep inside the data centre or the networks, desktop or applications, quietly getting worse unless new projects are undertaken to fix, upgrade or remove it.

The state of your assets, whether physical or technological, is a function of the preventive and corrective maintenance, and the straight-out replacement, you've done over the years to keep them in optimal condition. Do you remember that time a couple of years ago when times were tough, and your company cut the maintenance budget for your plant and equipment to prop up short-term profitability? The market consensus earnings per share had to be hit, and you had to get the money from somewhere. Or the time when they cut the graduate program during the recession and unfortunately created a skills gap that could never seem to be closed? It was then made worse when the training budget was cut the following year. These are the kinds of short-term-focused decisions that create technical debt.

The current state and usefulness of your physical, technological and human capital assets will therefore be a function of the time at which you first implemented these various assets (yes, that first mover advantage can eventually become a liability) and the degree of investment you've made since.

In very simple terms, if unaddressed, your legacy assets will inevitably become:

- less efficient as better ways of doing things emerge that your old assets simply cannot keep up with

- a brake on transformation as they cannot cope with the opportunities that start to present themselves

- inherently riskier because the people, processes and procedures to operate them come under pressure as people resign, knowledge is lost and general apathy permeates their operation (after all, which young and ambitious software developer wants to learn that old computer code, or which graduate engineer wants to work on maintenance of that old steam-powered machine in your factory).

Skills demographics

'I'm happy to report to shareholders that the people in our business simply don't matter. None of them. All of them are replaceable!' said no Chief Executive Officer, ever (notwithstanding that some board directors might quietly think 'especially you!' if they ever heard this statement).

Instead, companies pride themselves on the degree to which they invest in the skills of their people, and in improving the correlation between these skills and the quality and profitability of their outputs. All organisations claim some kind of competitive advantage from the recruitment, training and retention of a skilled workforce. Over time, they become adept at clearly identifying the skills and expertise they require, and then buying or building this expertise.

So, what happens when an industry disruption changes this equation?

Let's consider the automotive industry. For more than 100 years, this industry has built strong linkages to technical colleges and universities around the world for the development of skilled mechanics and engineers. These skilled workers have then joined the large automakers; been further trained in the design, improvement and manufacture of internal combustion engines; and contributed to the high output and low energy consumption engines that power the modern world. The automakers are filled with specialists who work directly on the creation of the core products of their company.

Although this model has worked for decades, it's now under threat. With the global move to electric vehicles, the automotive companies will be faced with a stark choice: keep making internal combustion engine powered cars, or switch to electric. Part of their consideration set will be what to do with their existing highly skilled workforces. It's unreasonable to expect every individual mechanic and engineer to transition their skills — in many cases acquired over decades of their career — into the design and manufacture of a completely new technology.

How do these automotive companies manage the fact that the skills of their oldest, most experienced and highly paid workers may well become irrelevant to the products they now need to design and manufacture?

The automotive industry is not unique. Many traditional white-collar workers — think banking, professional services, healthcare — will be required to augment their existing skills with artificial intelligence and work in new ways that simply do not reflect how the work has traditionally been done. The degree of change will be significant.

The advent of new technologies, industry shifts and changing customer preferences will therefore inevitably put pressure on the existing skills demographics of organisations. Human resources departments will have to respond in very strategic and thoughtful ways, and potentially compete for new recruits in a different manner, and from different sources, than they have traditionally.

Success in this changing world will go to those companies who can indeed teach their old dogs new tricks.

Growing headcount and the emergence of 'bullshit' jobs

Over the past 30 years, I've observed in many different industries the remarkable dynamic that, in large companies, it's typically easier to justify the recruitment of new people than it is to remove people. Left alone, the work that everyone is responsible for seems to expand, leading some executives to request more and more resources. As a result, many companies, especially large ones, are at risk of having too many people with the wrong skills doing the wrong things.

The degree to which your company falls prey to this dynamic is driven by its culture, financial expectations, and profit and performance motives of the executive leadership and governance group. Different companies in the same industry can have a very different appetite and ambition for high performance and profitability. This ambition will determine the degree to which the company maintains excess capacity, the relative productivity of the workforce, and most importantly, the number of 'bullshit jobs' that they maintain.

David Graeber's definition of a bullshit job (taken from his book *Bullshit jobs*) is 'a form of employment that is so completely pointless, unnecessary, or pernicious that even the employee cannot justify its existence'.

According to Graeber, there are several broad categories of bullshit jobs, three of which are:

- 'flunky' jobs: those that exist only or primarily to make someone else look or feel important, such as doormen and receptionists

- 'duct tapers': employees whose jobs exist only because of a glitch or fault in the organisation; who are there to solve a problem that ought not to exist, such as those who staff a help desk because the underlying process and technology they support has been so poorly designed that it simply doesn't work

- 'taskmasters': employees who oversee and supervise the work of others who either don't need supervision, or only need supervision because they're doing a bullshit job. Sometimes, the taskmaster will invent new bullshit jobs to give themselves something to supervise.

Let's consider some of Graeber's categories.

An example of a 'flunky' role in a large organisation is the 'executive manager' role, which seems to have evolved as a crutch for many senior executives, and whose job it is to read everything their boss should be reading, and then discuss progress and actions with the executive managers of all of the other senior executives. They typically attend these meetings with a 50-page PowerPoint presentation that they've put together using other people's reports, to which they've added their own stylish clipart and company logos. These meetings typically achieve nothing.

An example of a 'duct-taper' role is when a customer applies to do something online — for example, open an account in a bank — and then has to input a code or information that's only available if they're already online. Or worse, information that must be verified by calling a contact centre. Despite the inevitable cheery disposition and helpfulness of the duct-taper, if the underlying business process and enabling technologies were better designed, their job would not be required.

Then there's the 'taskmaster'. The first type of taskmaster is typically hard wired into companies through poor organisation design, whereby the spans and layers of the structure are out of proportion to the work being completed. An example is a structure where a middle manager (level A) has, say, three direct reports (level B), each of whom has three direct reports (level C), so the team is 13 people across three layers. There's an immediate opportunity to remove the three managers at level B and have the level A manager supervise nine level C people. Not exactly rocket science to fix, but common in large companies.

The next type of taskmaster is usually found in cultures that promote the easy and uncritical recruitment of new people into an organisation, without challenging whether every role represents a business case for the shareholder (in that they create more value than they consume). Once recruited, the system will find work for those people even when the original work they were recruited for has run its course. This is very common in large organisations that use daily rate contractors to do project and technology work. These contractors are expensive (because of the daily rate), offer a different employment model (because they're not counted as permanent, full-time equivalent employees) and typically bring new skills that the company needs. This all seems logical and would make absolute sense if the contractor was let go at the end of their assignment. However, often contractors come in for a discrete piece of work and do a good job, while simultaneously ingratiating themselves with the management to obtain more work. This occurs so much so, that 10 years later, they're on their 17th assignment, doing generalist work that a lower level employee could do — or work that's not really even required — and no-one can quite recall who originally hired them or what they're supposed to be doing.

The broad cost of all of these bullshit jobs adds up. Over time, companies can amass a weight of roles that simply don't need to exist. Roles that no-one would notice if the person in each role actually stopped performing the requirements of the bullshit job. In addition to the financial cost, bullshit jobs also create friction that slows things down as information and decisions slowly navigate the structural 'fat' throughout the organisation.

These jobs also negatively influence the culture because the people actually performing the real work of the organisation know about these bullshit jobs and the uselessness of them. The frontline workers see the culture of entitlement and largesse and the people sitting in head office sipping lattes at will. They know that it's at odds with the 'you can't claim overtime' or 'you can't take your drink break' or 'you have to work harder' demands they get each day from the managers inhabiting these bullshit jobs.

And when pressured to change, how many people in the bullshit jobs are ever going to put their shoulder to the transformation? As they say in the classics, turkeys never vote for Christmas dinner.

If you want to transform, then get rid of the bullshit jobs and reinvest the savings in your frontline roles, or something worthwhile such as product research and development, capital investment or paying bigger dividends.

Regulatory pressure

Every industry has some kind of regulation. Some industries, including financial services, health, pharmaceutical, aviation and mining, are very, very highly regulated. Industry regulators typically introduce more regulation for industry participants to respond to. After all, regulators do not kick back over their summer break thinking up rules to remove.

Regulatory pressure is an industry force that all industry participants must respond to. However, the specific issues that regulators call out, and the manner in which the company responds, will inevitably be based on:

- the perceived clarity of the regulation
- the relationship between the regulator and the company (driven by the personalities and quality of relationship between the responsible stakeholders)
- the degree to which compliance can be satisfied with existing technologies, processes and approaches, or whether it requires significant extra investment

- the level of competing investment options that crowd out the regulatory investment (see 'Investment slate pressure')

- the cultural propensity of executives to comply, which may well be based on the level of short-term incentive compensation they have at risk

- the culture of transparency between the board and executive, and the degree to which the risk appetite requires full (absolute maximum letter of the regulation) or part (bare minimum to get a pass mark) implementation of compliance to regulations.

This is not an exhaustive list. It's a pragmatic list of how different companies may respond. Depending upon how each company responds, circumstances can arise where different companies in the same industry, with the same rules, can end up with very different regulatory outcomes.

A company can easily become the outlier if it responds to the regulator poorly, if it takes too long to remediate problems, or if its personnel antagonise the regulator. It may then have to invest significantly to close compliance gaps that other participants have addressed along the way, and this can happen at the very time when management attention and customer demands require focus and investment that's now not available because it's being monopolised by the regulatory compliance remediation work that should have been done earlier.

Investment slate pressure

Not many companies have an infinite ability to invest more capital, because even if you have very deep pockets there's a limit to how many skilled resources you can deploy, and on the business's capacity to absorb significant change simultaneously. In the end, there are some business problems that can't be solved simply by throwing more resources at them: sometimes you just can't get another mechanic around the engine of the car.

In these cases, the company's investment slate — or capital expenditure budget — will itself become a limiting factor on what can be done. Not just the quantum of funds available, but also the relative priority of all of the many competing initiatives that are jockeying for a finite amount of funding. Sometimes, the eventual need to address regulatory requirements that have been deferred or to address technical debt and replace core infrastructure that's been sweated too long, will crowd out other perhaps more strategic or profitable investments that would otherwise have propelled the company forward or made its products more competitive.

When this happens, the current executive team may experience frustration at the inability to invest in more exciting strategic and customer-focused initiatives and will exert pressure to rush or complete the regulatory projects on the cheap, thus making things worse. A corporate investment slate full of the wrong things at the wrong time can be deadly.

Why *you* must care about transformation

It's easy to take some comfort that if all of the forces just mentioned are affecting you, then they'll probably have an effect on your competitors. Given the same set of pressures and forces are affecting your organisation and each of your competitors, then — all things being equal — success, or at least a more secure future, will probably go to whichever organisation is most alert to the disruptive force and responds in the most effective and efficient way. This is why *you* must care about transformation. Your professional relevance, and the relevance of your organisation to your customer, will depend on the capacity that you have to identify disruption and what you do in response.

We haven't reached peak change, so the level of disruption and pressure will keep growing. Someone is going to have to step up to identify these disruptive forces, craft clear and cogent strategies to address them, and execute and implement real change — some of which will inevitably be painful — that transforms the organisation and ensures it continues to be successful. Will it be you?

Transformation has always been difficult

As a former management consultant, one of my favourite quotes is the following:

> *And one should bear in mind that there is nothing more difficult to execute, nor more dubious of success, nor more dangerous to administer than to introduce a new system of doing things: for he who introduces it has all those who profit from the old system as his enemies, and he has only lukewarm allies in all those who might profit from the new system.*

Before you read on, when do you think it was written?

The answer is 1532: it was written by Niccolò Machiavelli nearly 500 years ago.

According to an article by Nohria and Beer in *Harvard Business Review*, 'the brutal fact is that about 70% of all change initiatives fail'. It's important to remember that transformation has always been difficult. The empirical historical record is very clear on this and the following quick review of societal, military and corporate difficulties will confirm this.

Societal difficulties

It's 1854 in London, and people are dying in large numbers. Cholera is back. In the 1840s and 1850s it was the scourge of the UK with regular outbreaks killing tens of thousands of people. A two-year outbreak in England and Wales claimed more than 50 000 lives.

So far, since this latest outbreak started during 1853–54, there have been another 10 000 deaths in London alone.

The government health authorities are worried, but clear on the cause of the outbreak. Everyone knows that this scourge is caused by the 'miasma': the unhealthy and unpleasant vapours, or 'bad air' that permeates London and the big cities and towns across the UK.

The authorities and their entire organisational resources are geared towards solving the problems associated with bad air.

Unfortunately, despite their efforts, people continue to die.

What if all these efforts, resources and people are focused on the wrong thing? On solving the wrong problem? But that's impossible: it's the 'miasma', there can be no doubt.

Or is there?

Dr John Snow has been doing his own study. He's developed some maps and models documenting the concentrated spread of cholera across London. He has a theory, and he's spent four long years lobbying the government authorities. Month after month he presents his case to resistant and closed ears: cholera is a disease caused by contaminated water supplies and not carried through polluted air or vapours.

Let's pause the narrative here as we imagine the distinguished specialists working for the health authorities. The 'learned' men rolling their eyes and guffawing after Dr Snow left the room. Or them joking about who would even meet with him to hear his latest quackery, which challenged what they knew to be true: that it's the 'miasma'. Perhaps they laughed out loud in his presence, as they discredited his training, perspectives, views and character.

Eventually, though, he wears them down and they agree to what today we would call a 'pilot'. The handle on a simple water pump on Broad Street in London's SoHo district is removed. The local people, who have been dying in droves, have to get their water from somewhere else. Miraculously, they stop dying.

Dr Snow has proved his theory: cholera is a water-borne disease. The health authorities have been wrong all along, and they have been trying to solve the wrong problem.

While we celebrate the achievement of Dr John Snow — and others, such as Joseph Bazalgette, the talented engineer who led one of the 19th century's greatest engineering achievements: the creation of

London's sewer system — it's easy to overlook the characteristics and nature of organisations that were difficult to change and transform. The public health officials — with all the government resources within their control, combined with their apparent motivation to protect the public from disease and poor health outcomes — nonetheless took some convincing.

In the language of transformation, they failed to countenance 'disruption', or the potential impact of forces (positive and negative) that could affect their organisation and its aims or the dogma that they stubbornly adhered to. Therefore they failed to develop a strategy to move forward. It took four years of argument and evidence from Dr Snow to eventually shift them. Or, as Steven Johnson postulates in his book *Extra life: a short history of living longer,*

> *a rogue medical detective, challenging the authorities in the midst of unbelievable terror, [and] whose sleuthing and empirical method [ended] up transforming our understanding of disease and saving untold millions in the decades that follow[ed].*

Military difficulties

Let's consider the experience of several Western armed forces, especially between the two world wars. Each of the long-established organisations of the British Army and Royal Navy resisted change. Both organisations, with long histories of successfully defending Britain's interests around the world, and existing in a period of international tensions and disruptions, failed to innovate and transform. Given the high stakes of inaction, it's intellectually safe to assume that the army and the navy were full of some of the best and brightest minds of their age, and that both would use whatever technology was available to give themselves a strategic or tactical advantage. That they would adopt the new technology, adapt their organisations and strategic approaches to it, and train and develop their people to maximise its use. Not so.

First, let's consider the actions of the army of Great Britain between the world wars. After being on the winning side of the allies in World War I and having been exposed to the success of innovative and new styles of planning and executing offensive operations in the last 100 days of the war, Britain resisted permanent changes to its army. Despite the introduction of new combined arms warfare first utilised at the Battle of Hamel (more on this later), Britain ignored these developments in the planning, equipping and operations of its army. Britain thought that World War II would repeat the tactics of World War I (although ironically not the last 100 days of World War I, which had by then become a war of combined arms and manoeuvre) so they quickly got to France, dug some deep trenches and waited for the Germans to attack.

History is clear on what happened next. The Germans unleashed Blitzkrieg (or 'Lightning War'), which combined fighter planes, dive bombers, tanks, artillery and infantry into a mobile, cohesive and lethal force that completely overwhelmed the combined French and British armies. In World War I, the Germans had failed to take Paris after more than five years of focused attacks. In 1940, with their new tactics, it took them just over six weeks.

On Britain's failure to embrace armoured warfare in time to influence the fighting in 1940, Basil Liddell Hart, a leading British military intellectual, said (as cited in Norman Dixon's book *On the psychology of military incompetence*), 'If a soldier advocates any new idea of real importance, he builds up such a wall of obstruction — compounded of resentment, suspicion and inertia — that the idea only succeeds at the sacrifice of himself; as the wall finally yields to the pressure of the new idea, it falls and crushes him.' Liddell Hart considered the British army's problem of institutional rigidity and stuffiness so great that he equated it with an illness.

The British Army proved itself a case study in failing at all three parts of the transformation equation: detecting the disruption (of new ways of waging war), developing a plan or strategy to address it (incorporating doctrine and tactics to combine their different forces), making changes (to introduce new weapons, training, communication methods, and the like).

The Royal Navy was equally poor at transforming. In his book *The blunted sword*, David Divine wrote about the resistance of the British Admiralty to embracing change.

Despite being the custodians of the very sea power that guaranteed the security of the British home islands and their extensive empire, Divine, as quoted by Norman Dixon, writes,

> *of the twenty major technological developments which lie between the first marine engine and the Polaris submarine, the Admiralty has discouraged, delayed, obstructed or positively rejected seventeen. The essential and necessary incorporation of these developments in the structure of modernisation has been achieved by individual and sometimes undisciplined officers, by political and industrial pressures, or—and most frequently—by their successful adoption in rival navies.*

What about other armed forces, in other countries? Just to round things out, at this time, in the United States, the US military establishment was grappling with its own challenges. Brigadier General Billy Mitchell, who is considered the founding father of the US Air Force, certainly had his work cut out for him. Convinced of the emerging importance of air power, and the potential for aircraft to defeat and sink the capital ships of the world's navies, he incessantly lobbied for the conduct of some tests to prove his point.

Reluctantly, in 1921, the US Navy agreed to a series of tests (on German ships captured in World War I) that were supposed to reflect real-world conditions. Except that the agreed-upon rules of engagement limited the size and number of bombs that could be dropped on each ship, the time they could be dropped and how many could be dropped in a certain period. They were not allowed to use aerial torpedoes. The rules also specified that each successive attack had to pause after its predecessor while tests were made on the progress of damage.

The air attacks were ultimately successful. However, the navy cried foul because the original rules of engagement were not satisfied to the letter. No matter that several ships were lying on the bottom of the ocean.

Having proved his point, you'd think Billy Mitchell would be fêted. Um, no. He was seen as too controversial, and too abrasive. Within four years of the successful tests, he'd been demoted to colonel and transferred to rural Texas to command ground forces. Clearly frustrated, Mitchell later spoke out against the 'establishment' and its reluctance to invest in developing US air power. This was the opportunity the army, and especially the navy, needed. In October 1925, Mitchell was charged with insubordination on the direct orders of President Calvin Coolidge. He was found guilty by a board of 13 senior officers drawn from the ranks of the most senior officer corps and suspended from the army without pay. He resigned from the army in 1926. As Liddell Hart had suggested, the establishment that Mitchell had challenged did indeed fall on him and crush him.

As a result, it would be several years before the United States developed its air power, and the commencement of World War II would find it severely lacking.

Between the wars, individual elements of the armed forces of both the United States and the UK failed across all three elements of a successful transformation:

- They failed to identify the disruptive forces of change happening outside their organisations. Somehow, they managed to miss the disruption caused by the rise of militarism in Europe and Japan, the rearming of Nazi Germany and Imperial Japan, and the military incursions by each of these countries into the Sudetenland, and China respectively. But most importantly, they failed to engage with how Germany and Japan were rearming and the weapons, technologies and tactics they were developing.

- Because they remained ambivalent about these newly emerging technologies, they failed to develop a coherent strategy for their use and incorporation into their own existing offensive or defensive doctrines.

- Having no strategy for adoption, there was obviously no implementation into their established organisations. The status quo within each organisation was preserved.

Corporate difficulties

Failure to transform is not the sole preserve of military establishments. Many corporates across many industries have fallen by the wayside and failed because of an inability to identify disruptive forces, craft appropriate strategies and implement the changes.

In his brilliant book *The innovator's dilemma*, Harvard professor Clayton M Christensen outlines many examples of companies (and whole industries) that failed to transform.

His first example is the hard disc drive industry. This industry was at the forefront of technological breakthroughs and innovation at the start of the computer age. Christensen writes, 'When the best firms succeeded, they did so because they listened responsively to their customers and invested aggressively in the technology, products and manufacturing capabilities that satisfied their customers' next generation needs.' However, all of these same participants missed the transition to 3¼ inch disc storage, then networked storage and ultimately cloud storage. Few, if any, of them are still in existence.

Steel making is the another industry Christensen talks about. The incumbent operators of large-scale blast furnaces failed to identify the threats of new technologies such as minimills, which took just 15 years or so, starting in 1960, to totally dominate the North American markets for rods, bars and structural beams.

Christensen goes on to discuss retail and the rise of the big box retailing model, laser jet and ink jet printers, and personal computers. In all his examples, Christensen is at pains to point out that each of the companies in these changing industries wasn't filled with idiots (my word) that didn't know what they were doing. These industries were comprised of sophisticated companies, run by competent and motivated managers who either failed to adequately sense what was truly happening in their industry or, having seen disruption, somehow didn't craft appropriate strategies to address what they saw. Or, they managed to see what was happening, crafted good strategy, but then failed to successfully execute. We may never know the exact causation, but we do know the impact: they failed to transform, and therefore, they failed.

Let's consider some high-profile corporate failures.

Unfortunately for their shareholders, management and employees, Kodak became the pin-up example of corporate failure of the past couple of decades. Its inability to see the looming disruption of digital photography on the rivers of gold delivered by their film and photographic paper printing business is legendary. And I guess when you see one of your core products — in Kodak's case, a camera — included as a feature in someone else's product (mobile phone), you know you have real problems. What's most ironic about the Kodak story is that the first digital still camera was developed by Eastman Kodak engineer Steven Sasson in 1975. Sasson made a prototype using a movie-camera lens, some Motorola parts, batteries and electronic sensors.

What about Blockbuster video? Many years ago, the lengthy perusal of movies, row after row, in the local Blockbuster sometimes seemed to take longer than the actual watching of the selected movie. Who hasn't seen the title box of a long-coveted movie across the aisle, and rushed over only to find it empty because someone else has already rented it? At its height in 2007–09, Blockbuster boasted more than 7500 physical stores around the world, a by-mail business and a growing digital business. Blockbuster's biggest failure may well have been not accepting an offer to buy Netflix for $50 million in 2000.

Kodak and Blockbuster were full of clever, committed people. And yet they failed to transform. Neither was able to identify the reality of the disruptions coming, despite being in close contact with that very disruption in the form of ignoring the commercial possibilities of the digital camera in Kodak's case, and, for Blockbuster, not seeing the value in buying Netflix.

So, let's agree: transformation is difficult.

While clearly not impossible, it's empirically difficult to continually look outwards at a changing environment and identify the forces that could disrupt your organisation. And even if you should successfully identify these forces, it can be difficult to develop cogent strategies to address what you see. Should you manage to successfully identify disruption *and* develop a great strategy it can still be difficult to implement and execute the transformation program that actually changes your organisation.

Having established that transformation is difficult, and before introducing some methods and approaches for increasing your chance of leading a successful transformation, let's first propose a hypothesis for why transformation is difficult. By doing so, we can ensure that the methods and approaches cut to the heart — or the *kokoro*, as discussed in chapter 3 — of making transformation successful.

Three reasons transformation is so hard

To design a successful transformation program and tailor it to the circumstances of your organisation and your professional context, you should not only acknowledge that transformation is hard, you should also understand why it's hard. It's only by understanding the causes of these difficulties that you can design the strategies and actions to overcome them.

There are three reasons why transformation is difficult:

- the status quo never has to argue its own case
- many corporate factors actively resist change
- many corporate personalities actively resist change.

The status quo never has to argue its own case

I remember learning about Sir Isaac Newton and his three laws of motion in my year 7 science class. As a quick recap, Newton proposed three laws that describe the relationship between the motion of an object and the forces that act upon it. These laws, first published in 1687, can be paraphrased as follows:

- *law 1*: a body continues in its state of rest, or in uniform motion in a straight line, unless a force acts on it
- *law 2*: a force acts on a body and moves it in such a manner that the time rate of change of momentum is the same as the force

- *law 3*: two bodies exerting forces on each other are equal in magnitude and opposite in direction.

I wasn't that good at physics in year 7, or anytime really, so these technical descriptions are not exactly clear to me. Thus, I decided to reference Physics4kids.com for a simpler explanation. Their explanation is that Newton's first law of physics basically says that an object at rest stays at rest, or an object in motion stays in motion, unless something happens. If you're going in a specific direction, unless something happens to you, you will always go in that direction. Forever.

What we can interpret from this is that something stays in its current state unless something is done to change it. It won't — or can't — typically change of itself. In other words, the status quo, or current state, will tend to remain the status quo.

Let's have a crack at turning the first Newtonian law into a statement about organisations and transformation projects:

- *Law 1*: a ~~body~~ *company or organisation* continues in its state of rest, or in uniform motion in a straight line, unless a ~~force~~ *transformation project* acts on it.

In a company, the current state that delivers the business-as-usual outcomes associated with the normal manufacture of a product, the generation of revenue, the supporting business functions, and so on, will all tend to remain quite static unless someone or something implements an action to change them.

In most corporate cases, especially for those in mature industries, it takes a lot of work over many years to actually create the status quo. Year after year, extra layers are added — a little like the growth rings of a tree — as the minutiae of small, incremental day-to-day decisions and actions play out, all of them adding weight and mass. People come and go, as one retires and another is promoted, each adding to the flavour of what's important and what's not, their personalities and personal biases signalling what's focused on and those things that can go through to the keeper. Over time, the processes and enabling systems also undergo small customisations and upgrades, typically under the radar screen of management.

These business-as-usual processes, systems and structures continue to deliver, day after day, year after year, unless change is actively and formally implemented. Someone has to actually do something to make it change.

And when that someone eventually turns up and proposes a change, their proposal will be evaluated. Some will rejoice and support it, others will dig in and obstruct it. Their proposal will be poked and prodded, tested for its pros and cons, and compared against other options. It may even be compared with the status quo: the 'do nothing' option. All the while, as the evaluation plays out, the 'status quo' will be busy plodding on, doing what it's always done, unaware of all the new and recent activity and the discussion about whether it needs to change or not.

Status quo bias in the minds of people is a real thing. The website Behaviouraleconomics.com explains this well:

> *Status quo bias is evident when people prefer things to stay the same by doing nothing (or by sticking with a decision made previously). This may happen even when only small transition costs are involved, and the importance of the decision is great.*

Never forget that, even when a decision is actually made — or when the decision is deferred, or more information is requested — the status quo proceeds onwards, undistracted by all the new noise. The status quo is like some kind of Arnold Schwarzenegger Terminator-type force that will just keep going and never stop unless someone actively stops it. For now (and quite literally, forever), the 'do nothing' option is the one with actual momentum. Things don't change when a decision is made — they change when defined and determined *action* is taken.

At Harvard Business School, the lecturers continually alluded to 'CEO-itis', a peculiar disease that caused those afflicted to think that just because they said something should happen or change, it *would* actually happen or change. Things change *only* when formal actions are taken to redesign and implement new processes and enabling technologies, and to hire, fire or redeploy people. Without action, the status quo remains.

While this is perhaps self-evident, it's at the core of why transformation is difficult: the status quo never has to argue its case.

Many corporate factors actively resist change

The status quo, or current state of a corporation, has its own unique inertia that makes change difficult. There are also several factors hardwired within most organisations that actively resist change, including:

- difficulty in identifying sometimes weak signals
- competing investment priorities and the power of last year's budget
- corporate relativism
- unwritten assumptions
- sunk cost bias
- cultural signals
- talented people on the move.

Let's examine each of these factors to understand them and just how they actively resist change.

Difficulty in identifying sometimes weak signals

Potential disruptions to a corporation do not typically show themselves to the executive team with an advertisement in the *Australian Financial Review*. Disruptive forces might start off as a largely unnoticed quirky news story, or only make true sense when viewed with the benefit of hindsight. Sometimes — rarely — the disruption actually turns up in your boardroom and presents itself to the executive group. An example, as we've already seen, is when CEO Reed Hastings offered to sell his Netflix streaming idea to Blockbuster for $50 million in early 2000 and Blockbuster laughed him out of the boardroom. The rest, as they say, is history.

Many corporations also lack the resources, or do not see the need to allocate a budget, for a continuous scan of the external environment to identify potential disruptions. It would be hard to sell a job description during budget time titled 'External environment watcher'. Instead, people might assume that the strategy function of large corporations will always be on the lookout for disruptions, and then be perfectly placed to identify the threat and craft the action required. This is rarely the case.

Unfortunately, the pull of business-as-usual operations, involvement in the setting of budgets, administration of the investment slate for capital decisions, and identification of potential acquisitions or divestments and their subsequent implementation, all serve to occupy the time of the strategy team. This leaves little time to actually scan the world and the rapidly changing environment.

And even if the disruption signals are picked up, as noted in the book *The execution premium* by authors David Norton and Robert Kaplan, '[many] companies generally fail at implementing a strategy or managing operations because they lack an overarching management system to integrate and align these two vital processes.' Sometimes the strategic evangelist who actually sees the change coming cannot communicate the threat effectively, or people just don't want to know (see the section below titled 'Many corporate personalities actively resist change').

Ironically, disruptive warning signs become even harder to see the more successful the organisation becomes. This is because if the organisation is successful, it can seem as though the good times will last forever, and the potential warning signs identified by the constructively paranoid executive can be dismissed by the 'if it ain't broke, don't fix it' mindset of the less strategic or reflective executives who believe their own bullshit.

In any case, the signals are missed, nothing happens and the organisation continues through the water oblivious to the looming icebergs.

Competing investment priorities and the power of last year's budget

The capital budgeting process and the setting of the investment slate is always one of the most entertaining times in companies as the different executive personalities spar and jockey for the lion's share of available funds. The investment slate is a tangible indicator of the corporate strategy translated to action. It's where the rubber hits the road.

Unfortunately, despite the enthusiasm of most executives for grabbing significant chunks of the budget, the investment slate up for grabs in any typical year is generally quite low because the decisions and projects of last year — the inflight projects — have already taken their share first. This means that the last remnant of the investment slate is less like a large African prey animal being cautiously eyed off by lions, and more like some hot chips at the beach, being fought over by hungry seagulls.

All kinds of projects might be inflight, including regulatory remediations, or the maintenance and replacement of infrastructure to 'keep the lights on'. They may also include big projects from last year, aimed squarely at last year's problems, which may or may not still be relevant, and once they're inflight, it becomes very hard to stop them for a range of reasons discussed below.

In any case, last year's capital budgeting decisions hang over the current process, consuming significant resources and reducing the amount available for anything new.

Corporate relativism[1]

It's human nature to compare ourselves to those around us and to those in a similar circumstance. From our first days at school, we were compared and ranked with one another in the classroom based on our answers to exam questions and our submission of assignments.

---

[1] Thank you to Brian Hartzer (former CEO, Westpac), who used this term over a coffee when we were discussing the difficulties associated with leading corporate change.

In sports, we were graded against others and allocated into appropriate teams based on our skills and talents within that sport. As employees we are also graded against our scorecard and/or role expectations to establish a performance rating relative to our peers.

Companies are no different. Especially public companies. Investors and analysts continually benchmark similar companies against their peers to establish absolute and relative performance. This allows convenient and easy analysis and works well when comparing the performance of large retailers (think Woolworths and Coles), miners (BHP and Rio Tinto), banks (ANZ, CBA, NAB and Westpac) and a host of other industries.

Over time, the executive and management teams, especially those with deep industry experience, can easily start to focus heavily on what the rest of their industry is doing as their main point of reference. They become experts in what their competitors are doing or not doing and follow their every move. Overdone, this external but limited and narrow focus can quickly become corporate relativism.

Corporate relativism can be defined as the trap whereby executives evaluate the opportunities, threats and disruption relevant to their company through a contextual lens instead of an absolute lens. This context is then unconsciously and gradually narrowed to include only their own company's operations relative to those of their nearest competitors. It leads to questions such as 'What are our closest competitors doing?' instead of questions such as 'In a rapidly changing world, what should we be doing?' and therefore puts the organisation at risk of being blindsided.

In *The innovator's dilemma*, Clayton Christensen references technological change in the mechanical excavator industry. Long story short, according to Christensen, not a single cable actuated mechanical shovel manufacturer from the late 19th and early 20th centuries made the transition to hydraulics. None of them. Christensen makes the point that 'each cable shovel manufacturer was one of at least twenty manufacturers doing everything they could to steal each other's customers'. And yet in this wide and highly competitive field, not one successfully made the transition from one technology to the next. None of them were able to transform themselves.

It's a safe bet to imagine that these mechanical excavator manufacturers were filled with bright people who followed the developments of their competitors extremely closely and sought to emulate them in a series of improvements over time. Unfortunately, by focusing too narrowly on one another, and by asking themselves only what their competitors were likely to do, they each missed the key question of what they should be doing in the face of a disruptive technology such as hydraulics.

Corporate relativism can be a serious brake or limiter on the degree of transformation a company is prepared to make because it will unconsciously limit the ambition, risk and scope of any potential change so as to remain within the industry pack. Doing what everyone else is doing can certainly seem sensible, safe and logical. However, it misses the point. Transformation is about sensing the disruption, crafting a strategy and then implementing and taking action to propel your organisation ahead of the pack.

If a change project doesn't differentiate your company from the industry pack it's not called 'transformation', it's called 'keeping up'.

Unwritten assumptions[2]

Companies can develop powerful unwritten assumptions that quietly but firmly guide the imagination and decision making of executives. They reflect the combined wisdom, custom and logic that's been built up over time, and act as a set of guard rails that limit how people think about disruption, transformation and the possible changes and actions that can be taken.

After more than 30 years in management consulting and direct executive experience, the two most powerful unwritten assumptions I've observed are:

- don't lose any revenue
- don't lose any customers.

---

[2] Thanks again to Brian Hartzer, who used this term also: it was a very valuable and illuminating coffee discussion!

These assumptions seem very logical. After all, why would you want to lose revenue or lose customers?

Well, there are some reasons why you might want to do both as soon as you can, and the first is based on the work of Vilfredo Pareto, an Italian engineer, economist and philosopher.

According to his principle, for many outcomes roughly 80 per cent of the consequences come from 20 per cent of the causes. This holds true for many business situations, and in many industries it's absolutely true of revenue generation. For these companies, 80 per cent of the revenues come from 20 per cent of the customers, suggesting that there's a tail of customers who add a diminishing share of revenue until, sometimes, there's a small group of customers who actually generate negative revenue. For this customer subset, their business and patterns of engagement may consume greater resources, through significant customer service interactions or the use of expensive channels, than their custom actually delivers to the business.

Any rational analysis would say to stop serving any customer for whom the service economics don't add up. If the revenue they generate is less than the cost of the service, then it's an easy decision, right?

While logical, it's often not so easy for a number of reasons. First is that the analysis required to provide the insight is not always done. Determining the relative cost, volume and profit characteristics of a given customer and product set requires considerable ongoing analysis. When this analysis is done, it can also fly in the face of established wisdom and generate considerable resistance from those who will be affected by any change.

Back in the day, I was part of a consulting engagement working to identify enterprise cost reduction opportunities for a global company that made electronic sound and vision products. We were told that the sale of the largest big-screen TVs into the most popular retailers was driving big revenues and profits for the company. We were sceptical and performed an activity-based costing exercise. Counter-intuitively, the analysis found that the company was losing money on every big-screen TV sold after the logistics, holding costs and such things as retailer rebates were taken into account. Several of the client's executives found our analysis very confronting.

What makes these situations difficult to solve is the unwritten assumptions associated with them. It's just not considered possible to either significantly increase the price of big-screen TVs or eliminate customer rebates. Or even worse, stop selling that latest TV model to that channel. What will the customer think? What would we tell head office? How would we show that in the budget? Executives would claim that they'll miss their scorecard revenue goals.

In such cases, the rational answer for the company is to rid the system of unprofitable customers and to actually reduce revenue to make more money. However, because of the unwritten assumptions — and the resultant budgetary, cultural and public relations challenges associated with them — it's easier to preserve the unprofitable relationships than it is to rock the boat.

Over time, these unwritten assumptions limit the degrees of freedom that any transformation program can traverse because there may be pockets of existing customers, and their associated revenues, that cannot be lost or challenged regardless of how unprofitable they may be.

Sunk cost bias

Sunk cost bias is based on the fact that we as humans can find it psychologically difficult to stop something that we've invested significant time, effort, resources and emotion into. We've all probably heard the admonition to 'not throw good money after bad' but that's exactly what happens due to sunk cost bias. Executives can easily think that the embarrassment, loss of face or financial write-offs associated with a project that's gone bad are simply too much to bear, and so they push on. And on. And on. Sunk cost bias is real, and is easily recognised by irrational feelings such as:

- 'But we've come so far; we must keep going.'
- 'We are so close. Just another million dollars and we'll be done.'

- 'If we stop the project then we're all stuffed,. What will we tell the board?'
- 'It doesn't matter that the project is taking too long, it's over budget and the benefits case has evaporated. We simply must finish.'

We all know that not every project will run perfectly or be a winner, but for some reason, when faced with a full investment slate and last year's budget carried forward, we can find it excruciatingly difficult to stop a project and write off the money already spent.

Corporate leaders are not alone in falling for the sunk cost bias. Let me reinforce what I mean.

It's May 1996, and an expedition led by Rob Hall and Scott Fischer is summiting Mount Everest. The expedition is in full swing after months of training, detailed preparations and meticulous planning, and the climbers are getting ready to leave their Camp IV base for their final push to the summit. The dangers at this altitude are very real because Camp IV is an incredible 7925 metres above sea level, placing it squarely in the 'Death Zone', where the air is so thin it cannot sustain life for an extended period.

After all the time, and financial and physical exertions, to get to Base Camp IV, with climbers now already tired and cold, with lungs burning, drawing on their body's last fat reserves, the final push to the summit is simply a shocker. Climbers must take note of the weather, wait for their window of opportunity and then quickly start their ascent while it's still dark. Once at the top, they mustn't delay, and must keep reserves of energy and daylight for their trip back down.

Annie Duke describes the climbers' quandary in her book *Quit: the power of knowing when to walk away*:

> *Climbers on the descent can suffer from [the same] combination of fatigue, oxygen deprivation, frostbite, changing weather, becoming lost or disoriented, falling into a crevasse, and darkness if they persist too long in their summit attempt. A misstep can cause you to fall 8000 feet to your death into Tibet, or 10000 feet to your death into Nepal.*

The climbing rules are therefore very simple, explains Duke: 'Climbers need to turn around if they realise that they [will] not reach the summit until mid-afternoon or later.'

Everyone on the expedition is aware of the rule — known as the 'two o'clock rule' — because Hall and Fischer, the two experienced expedition leaders, continually reinforce the need to turn around if you haven't reached the summit by 2 pm. But human nature being what it is, a scenario has been created where it's almost impossible to make the right decision. From a paid guide's perspective, the customer is paying to get them to the top, not near the top. You can imagine the scene: the customer panting in tortured breaths, 'But the summit's so close, it's just there', or 'But what will I tell my family and friends?'

No-one celebrates the rational person who *almost* summits Everest. And this desire — in the mind of someone already strongly motivated enough to put in months of training, who pays heaps of cash and who might also be suffering from hypoxia and may not be making completely rational decisions — means that it's very difficult to stop them proceeding to the very top of the world.

And this is precisely what happens on this day. Despite the warnings, despite the repeated commitment to the two o'clock rule, only four individuals on the expedition adhere to the turnaround time philosophy. Everyone else keeps climbing up. Up and up, just a couple more feet... pause... a couple more steps, chests heaving, minds focused. The summit so close you can feel it. Six people make it to the top by 2 pm. The schedule, with its checks, balances and warnings, has fallen away. Nothing matters except to summit.

Duke explains that although no-one yet realises it, due to the elation of summiting, Hall and Fischer have

> *ignored their own rules designed specifically to combat the sunk cost bias and put themselves and their clients in grave danger. Long story short: Hall, Fischer and three members of their expedition died as a storm enveloped the mountain during their descent. Others barely escaped with their lives after many hours wandering in the dark while braving sub-zero temperatures.*

So, back to comfortable corporate life: although difficult, painful and potentially embarrassing to the company, it's usually better to call it and stop a project when you know that it's not going to deliver what it promised. Even if it does deliver, what it delivers is now irrelevant. Don't throw good money after bad and stop riding the dead horse. There's no need to always keep pushing every single thing forward.

Avoid sunk cost bias.

Cultural signals

All organisations have a way of earning prestige, recognition and promotion. These cultural norms are among the most powerful forces within nature because they motivate corporate animals to go above and beyond in the pursuit of what they perceive to be the critical determinants of their professional and personal success. In other words, those that want to get ahead do exactly what they think will help them do so.

Think about your own organisation. Whatever its industry, there's a set of people in your organisation who deliver the core product or service of your business, and vie for the spoils of prestige, recognition and promotion at the highest level. For example:

- if you're a banker, you've had to lend money, and the more the better
- if you're a technologist, you've had to cut code
- if you're an automotive engineer, you've had to design an engine or major car component
- if you're a firefighter, you've had to hold a firehose
- if you're a doctor, you've had to make people better.

And so on.

Unfortunately, for many organisations this recognition and prestige comes from doing things in the established and traditional ways, without any hint of change.

As an easy example, let's imagine the rock star automotive engineer working for a prestige car brand who is the foremost engine design expert. They know everything there is to know about designing the most high-performance petrol driven internal combustion engines (ICE). They've worked their way up the corporate food chain, they're an acknowledged expert, and all the junior engineers revere them and want to replicate their experience. The executives indulge them, and pay them well, because it's obvious how important they are to the company. They induct the graduates and share the corporate stories. They design and deliver the training for young engineers and the entire system celebrates them.

Except that now, cars are becoming electric.

But what about the ICE engineers? They don't want to give up their prestige and the importance of their specialist knowledge, and potentially become irrelevant. They're tempted to deny the disruption and resist the potential transformation, hoping they can hang on just a little bit longer. And the corporate culture reinforces this, because so many executives themselves grew up in the system, or themselves identify as the gun ICE engineer, and they simply cannot countenance a company — or even a world — where the ICE engineer is not revered.

Having bone deep experts in the company — regardless of industry — can make transformation very difficult. And these resistors of change can easily be perceived as the defenders of the existing way of doing things because they stake out and claim the high ground as the traditionalists who value the company and its ways more than the change agents who want to transform it.

Talented people on the move

Talent management has always been at the core of successful organisations. Great organisations have always identified, developed and moved their talent through different roles and challenges to develop their skills and broaden out their experience. This is nothing new.

What perhaps is new is the speed and velocity at which people are being moved. Many companies are moving their most talented people through different roles every two years. This might seem reasonable until you consider that for someone on a talent placement program:

- their first six months in the new role are about getting up to speed with the role and the new part of the business

- the next 12 months is typically spent hoping that nothing stuffs up in their business-as-usual world to threaten their status on the talent program

- the last six months in the role are spent finding their new dream role and then lobbying everyone hard to actually get it.

None of this is conducive to transformation. Identifying disruptive forces takes time, as does developing a cogent strategy to address the forces you've identified. Implementing and executing the changes to address the disruption takes even longer.

Even if people have a desire to initiate and lead change, if they're moved too often, there's a disincentive to actually address the real disruptions because it takes too long. If you want to stay on the talent program, it might be a safer bet to find something smaller, more digestible and short term, so that you can be seen to have done the work and the short-term benefits accrue to you while you're in the role. After all, it's better that you get the recognition rather than your successor, right? (I'll introduce the 'Dale dug a hole' executive in chapter 4.)

So you can see that the organisation's existing way of doing things, its approach to scanning and understanding the market in which it operates, and the way it responds by allocating scarce investment budget to address what it finds, can make transformation very difficult, or at least unlikely. Even more powerful resistance is encountered from the sunk cost bias and the natural human desire to see things through, regardless of any change in circumstances. The most powerful resistance comes from those whose prestige, recognition and promotion prospects are heavily rooted in the existing ways of doing things, and the strong cultural signals that they receive every day that reinforce the status quo.

Large-scale transformation can be resisted (or at least stymied) by the very talented people who should be most expected to drive it, simply because they're never in the role long enough to initiate or lead it, or because they don't want to do things that don't deliver an immediate benefit that's directly attributable to them.

There's no two ways about it: transformation can be very difficult. The entire corporate 'way' that has been built up within the company over many years is working against the transformation. The weight of established business processes, the way the technology is wired, the culture, stories and history, the KPIs and measures, the way budgets and forecasts are developed, and the corporate roles that are celebrated, all combine into a sometimes immovable weight that's difficult to shift and that works to maintain the current state.

As well as these hard-wired corporate factors that prevent transformation, there are also certain personalities that kill transformation projects stone cold dead.

Many corporate personalities actively resist change

American anthropologist Margaret Mead observed that we should 'never doubt that a small group of thoughtful, committed citizens can change the world; indeed, it's the only thing that ever has'. This quote equally relates to companies, and with a tweak or two, perfectly describes corporate reality, which is:

> *Never doubt that a small group of thoughtful, committed* ~~*citizens*~~ **executive leaders** *can change the* ~~*world*~~ **company**; *indeed, it's the only thing that ever has.*

It's the people (executives and employees) who change and transform companies. It's not outside forces, or management consultants, or new machines — it's always those people most passionate about their company and its success.

While the status quo never has to argue its case, and there can be very real corporate factors that resist change, these difficulties can all be overcome if you have the right people, with the right temperament and skills, committed to the transformation.

Or not. It's a sad and often unspoken fact of corporate life that many people are just not up for it. Some people just do not want to get involved in transformation. They hope for the continuation of their quiet life running the business-as-usual part of their company that they know so well.

As a management consultant working with clients and an executive working with colleagues and direct reports, I've seen many corporate personalities resist change. In chapter 4, where I talk about building the team and getting the right people, I'll share some of the many entertaining—but sadly uninspiring and value destroying—corporate characters that inhabit Australian companies large and small, all of whom can derail, obstruct or kill transformation efforts. For now, though, let's outline some of the reasons why senior executives resist change.

Executives who resist change and transformation do so because they fall into one or more categories:

- *Losers*: These executives can see the writing on the wall and suffer from loss aversion, which is the concept that the psychological pain people feel when they lose money, or something else of value, is twice as strong as the pleasure of gaining the same thing. Loss aversion can explain sunk cost bias, and possibly also status quo bias. Executives may look ahead to the impact of transformation and know that they'll genuinely lose power, responsibility or prestige. It might mean that their role is diminished or eliminated, that they'll have to move roles, that they'll leave the company or that it may have some other negative impact on them. In other words, that the results of the transformation will not be good for them. These people are clever enough to see what's coming, and as a result they want no part of it. As Machiavelli declared, people live peacefully as long as their old way of life is maintained and there is no change in customs.

- *Defenders*: These executives are generally defensive. They have a toxic reaction when someone points out how something could be changed. They like things exactly as they are, and they have 'paved the goat track' rather than taken a chance on exploring new and better paths.

- *Wimps*: These executives are weak, fearful and unadventurous. They don't trust the uncertainty and ambiguity of the potential change because they simply cannot bear to put themselves at professional risk. The expectation of embracing the uncertainty and ambiguity of transformation makes them run a mile, and it's therefore easier to either hide under their desk and hope that it passes, or aggressively shit-can it at every opportunity.

- *Rationalists*: These executives are likely to resist. American writer Upton Sinclair nailed this dynamic well when he declared that 'it is difficult to get a man to understand something when his salary depends upon his not understanding it'. Sometimes corporate incentives create perverse outcomes whereby one set of executives are busy working towards an outcome that has been overtaken or made redundant by a later strategy or program. In such cases, the executives will continue to pursue what's on their scorecards, and what they think is the corporate expectation of them. Scorecard robots. The good news, though, is that if you change their incentives, most of them will change tack and get behind the transformation.

- *Autocrats*: These authoritarian executives think they have all of the answers. It doesn't matter what the disruptive forces are, they simply don't recognise them. It's all fake news. They simply cannot agree with the announced strategy or direction of the transformation effort underway. They think they know best and they'll actively resist anything that's not in accordance with their own established worldview.

- *Incompetents*: These executives lack the skills. They may not have been involved in leading change and project management, and may be daunted by the approach, language, jargon and pace of the transformation project. If they feel insecure, it just might be easier to not turn up to the meeting, rather than be caught out as being ignorant of how to run transformation projects.

- *Disinterested*: These executives are disengaged, go through the motions in their roles and simply don't give a shit. Regardless of their motivations for being disengaged (they might have been overlooked for a role, or in a role too long or generally tired after what seems like 100 years with the same company), they're unlikely to put their shoulder against the wheel of anything, let alone the dangerous and risky transformation project that's rolling into town. As a result, it's all too hard, and it's easier to just go through the motions, or to quietly 'white-ant' the effort.

As an aside, imagine how much easier transformation would be if all of these corporate personalities would put up their hands, self-identify as obstacles and then quietly head for the exits. Or better yet if, instead of coloured hats like Edward de Bono's six thinking hats, we could have a coloured badge system. Can you imagine: 'Would all of the disinterested please pick up a green badge? Red is for the autocrats, and oh, for you incompetents, Bill is over there waiting to help you put on your orange badge. Once you've got your badges on, please go and stand over there in your group.' Instead, these people will identify themselves as the transformation progresses, and you will then be faced with deciding what you do about them.

Above all, one of the most common and powerful reasons I've seen for executives resisting a transformation effort is because they simply cannot get their heads around the need to change. These executives are … drum roll please … the:

- *Traditionalists:* These executives simply cannot imagine that their industry or company could work any differently from how it always has. Their mental models simply cannot keep pace with the high rate of change, and so they continue to look at every new problem through their traditional lens. To them, what has worked in the past will work in the future. They're the ultimate example of the adage that if your only tool is a hammer, every problem starts to look like a nail.

In fairness to the traditionalists, let's acknowledge a simple truth of business: it's hard to rethink how an established industry should change and evolve to address a changing world and changing customer expectations when you're a deep expert in that industry. I get it.

You already know of plenty of businesses, such as Kodak and Blockbuster, that were filled with intelligent people who, for a number of reasons, just couldn't get their act together to address the momentous changes that surrounded them and their industry.

From what I've seen, the already difficult task of changing an organisation becomes even harder if you've worked in that same industry for many years. Now, I've not commissioned any independent research, but I suspect that there's a strong correlation between the number of years you've been in an industry, and your ability to rethink it. Said another way, your ability to rethink the industry you're an expert in diminishes with every extra year that you remain in that industry. And the longer you've been in an industry, the greater the chance you'll self-identify as an 'expert' and the less likely it is you're going to challenge your own thought processes and biases.

If you're an executive with many years of experience in an industry, my last statement might sting a little, so let me offer a challenge and some examples.

The challenge: reflect on your own career, and that of some of your longstanding colleagues who claim 20 years of experience. Is that 20 years of real, lived and varied experience, or is it one year of experience 20 times? They're two very different things. And if pushed, I'd say that many people in senior company roles in many industries have grown up in the company absorbing how their organisation and the industry does things. They've predominantly managed business-as-usual (BAU) operations, and they've had limited experience in managing and leading transformation projects. Why? Because the management of BAU is always less risky than the leadership of transformation and, therefore, more attractive to the risk averse.

Let me be clear that I'm not talking about every role in business or society. There are many roles for which the years of acquisition of knowledge are critical — for example, brain surgery. I'm pretty sure that the best person to challenge how to do brain surgery better *is* actually a brain surgeon. However, what I am saying is that that same brain surgeon is probably not the best person to challenge how to run the whole hospital system better.

Equally, its ridiculous to assume that deep industry knowledge doesn't have a place in running companies. It does. Let me say that again, lest anyone think I'm advocating for the wholesale removal of deep industry specialists from every industry: *industry deep knowledge is critical. However,* it has to be balanced with openness to new and innovative ways of doing things.

Let me explain. As I've told my kids (until they're sick of hearing me), talent plus hard work will *always* beat talent on its own. Likewise, deep industry expertise plus a transformation mindset will always beat deep industry expertise on its own.

I'll give you an example using the banking sector (which I have some experience in) to make a couple of points.

Australian banking's love affair with the status quo

Let me state right up front that I'm not unduly picking on the banking industry, and certainly not commenting on its ability to generate profits from its BAU operations. Many large companies in many industries clearly find transformation difficult and I don't think banking is necessarily better or worse than any other well-established global industry that also grapples with the need to change. However, let me put my cards straight on the table: I worked for one of these banks for nearly 13 years in a variety of roles — and I consulted with clients in a variety of industrial, retail, pharmaceutical and service industries — so I've observed the challenges big companies face first hand.

The banking industry in Australia is dominated by the big four incumbent banks: CBA, Westpac, NAB and ANZ... and arguably now five with the emergence of Macquarie Bank's retail offering. These banks are very profitable in an absolute sense when compared to other large Australian corporates, and massively profitable in a relative sense (return on equity or return on assets) when compared to most overseas banks.

Each of these banks typically makes most of its money by offering four key services:

- *institutional banking*: lending to large corporates at the top-end of town
- *business banking*: lending to small-to-medium enterprises

- *personal banking*: lending to consumers for mortgages, personal loans and credit cards

- *payments and other services*: facilitating small (think credit card terminals) and large value payments (think real-time gross settlements and the international Swift system), and other assorted things such as foreign exchange rate desks and trade finance, and taking a clip on each transaction.

All of the big four banks have abandoned their wealth management divisions. (It's ironic to consider that at some point in the past, a group of bank executives did very well from the bonuses associated with successfully buying these wealth businesses and then another generation of bankers made their bonuses by finally getting rid of them. Go figure.)

When you think about the strategic landscape of the financial services industry, there are numerous threats and seismic shifts coming. It obviously won't happen overnight, and the Australian banking system will continue to be profitable well into the future, but change is coming. It's inevitable. The halcyon days of Australian bank profits may well be unsustainable into the future. It would take too long to list all of these threats, but let's create a quick list:

- *Institutional banking threat:* Many large corporations have extremely strong balance sheets, so when they do need to borrow, they can drive extremely strong competition and tight margins into the institutional divisions of the big four banks. The amount of lending is usually huge, but the actual margin and profit is rarely so. This is likely to continue.

- *Business banking threat:* Very credible competitors — such as the newly listed Judo Bank — are emerging as real threats to the big banks. Technology companies such as Xero (accounting software) are also amassing huge amounts of data on the operations of the small business customers who make up their customer base. Over time, companies like these may either use or sell this data to facilitate credit provision from a range of different companies that could be specialist financial services or industrial or technology companies that have excess cash, or that white label the balance sheets of major banks as a form of utility.

- *Personal banking threat #1:* The COVID-19 pandemic has helped people continue to make the leap to online banking and a migration away from using branches. Again, very credible competitors such as Athena are offering digital home loans funded by Australian superannuation funds. Many Australian banks will be struggling to respond to the challenges of unravelling all of their channel complexity together with the facilities, people, processes, policies, technologies and strong cultural and remuneration practises that entrench it. For many banks, their branch networks are now a cost base looking for an objective.

- *Personal banking threat #2:* As if the first personal banking challenges were not enough, all of the big banks are at risk of having their businesses hollowed out as they become utility-like balance sheets. All of the banks have become addicted to the mortgage origination flows provided by the broker and wealth management sector, which in some banks provide up to 50 per cent and more of the flow. These loans are so much more expensive to acquire and originate than their proprietary loan books because of the significant commissions paid to the brokers, and the incentive that this provides brokers to flip their customers (and they are the broker's customer) every couple of years. It's a fascinating case study on how a short-term lack of strategic perspective and customer service thinking has created a long-term monster that will significantly reduce the profitability of the mortgage loan books of the banks.

- *Payments threat:* The prospects of this little-understood — even within the big banks — river of gold that the big four have mostly monopolised for the past several decades is coming to an end as Apple (Apple Pay), Afterpay (buy now pay later) and a range of other innovative payment companies pick at the margins associated with the facilitation of payments between individuals and businesses. The banks will continue to make money from payments, but they'll inevitably make less revenue and less margin.

Within each of the big four banks is a team of people tasked with assessing and countering these threats. Typically, these teams will be led by a senior executive who 'grew up' in banking (e.g. a 'business banking' specialist, a 'retail banking' specialist or a 'payments' specialist) and is now tasked with re-engineering and overturning the orthodoxy of the very industry they grew up in. I'm not saying that they cannot do this. I'm just saying that it's difficult. And it becomes more difficult the longer the executive has been in banking.

Again, if you're in banking — and specifically Australian banking — you might yourself call bullshit on my thesis and be very optimistic about the ability of some of the big four to evolve. Maybe. It's too early to tell. But we can perhaps all agree that some of the biggest recent innovations in banking (e.g. Apple Pay, buy now pay later) were not invented by the big banks.

And this is because the big four banks typically think like ... the big four banks.

Let me bring this to life a little by sharing how, as recently as a few years ago — albeit before the challenges of COVID-19 forced their hand — at least one of the big four thought about their branch network.

Despite all of the evidence indicating that the number of branch transactions was falling, the branches continued to be cherished. Every now and then, as members of the executive team, we'd prepare for a series of branch visits by setting aside a day, breaking into pairs and going out on the road.

The visits were organised with military precision. We'd be told the exact time to attend, and for how long, while a couple of days out the branch staff would get the branch ready for our visit. This would inevitably mean that they would tidy it from top to bottom, and literally paint the rocks in advance of the senior folks from head office visiting. In many cases, someone would bake a cake. Sometimes, as a special treat, we'd hit the sentimental jackpot, and an executive would have the chance to visit the branch where they first worked as a graduate or trainee when they joined the bank last century.

While we'd have a lovely time talking with the staff, and learning how busy it all was, the statistics — which we'd generally studiously avoid — didn't bear this out. The transactions per branch just stubbornly kept falling. I suspect that there were tumbleweeds blowing through some of the branches, so seldomly were they visited by customers. There was also an assumption that the customers loved coming into the branch to do their banking because, well, they came into the branch. The only survey — which we'd do as we spoke to customers waiting in line at the branch — was of the customers actually in the branch. We never got the opportunity to meet the thousands of bank customers living in each catchment area who used digital channels because they never set foot in the branch — and never had any intention of ever returning again.

And yet the whole system remained geared around the branch: the original branch that opened someone's original account then benefited from every successive product that customer opened regardless of the channel they used to open it or the channel they actually used to access it. Whoever was in charge of the retail network would get the sales credit of every channel. It was madness.

When I look back, the visits reinforced in the minds of the branch staff that they were the most important channel, and they in turn made the visiting executives feel good about things. Inevitably, executives would return with a list of things to fix from frayed carpet to broken printers, which they then made a special effort to 'jump the queue' to get fixed, and thus be able to show that they got things done, even if the money had to be allocated from the digital channels. Crazy town.

Meanwhile, the thousands of staff who worked in the contact centre, and the hundreds of staff designing the digital channels, remained unmet and without cake, despite running the channels through which the vast majority of service interactions, and the origination of new products, actually occurred.

If the bank was an army, it was akin to the officers obsessing about the needs of the cavalry and horses, while ignoring the emerging and more effective tanks and machine guns.

All in all, it was a great example of how difficult it is to change the long-held business models and traditional ways of doing things in a long-established industry, because it was not only the staff model, technology and business processes locked in old stone, but also the relationships, ego needs, and sense of nostalgia and human connection in both sets of staff that was very difficult to acknowledge, let alone dismantle.

Obviously, the COVID-19 pandemic has given all the big four pause for thought on their branch networks and how they'll rationalise. That's not my point. My point is that when a big bank — or any large corporation or organisation — has to strategically rethink something, it finds it very difficult to do so in a detached and unemotional manner because many of the observers, analysts and decision-makers are so heavily vested in the very scenario and orthodoxy that they're supposed to challenge.

Why it's important to understand the need for transformation

Obviously, there is no guarantee that all of the personalities described above exist within your company, or that all of the corporate factors mentioned in this chapter are present in your unique organisational context. However, forewarned is forearmed. It's only by fundamentally understanding why transformation is so difficult that you can embrace the mindset and mechanics you need to drive a successful and sustainable change program. That way, you will at least be on the lookout for, and ready to deal with, all of the corporate elements and personalities that can actively or passively resist change.

Key points from chapter 2

- The pace of disruption is accelerating, and we've not yet reached 'peak change'.

- Global forces such as the climate crisis, population growth and technology change — especially the rise of AI — will all wash over our companies and industries in the near future. It's unlikely that any industry will be immune, and these forces will create disruptions, opportunities and direct pressure for all organisations to transform.

- Organisations will have to contend with unique company-centric forces. Products may become obsolete due to technological change or evolving customer preferences. The deferral of investment and the resultant technical debt may crowd out the ability to invest exactly when needed.

- The skills demographics of your workforce, or the prevalence of 'bullshit jobs' that you've never addressed, may distract you and make launching a transformation program more difficult than it would otherwise be.

- Growing regulation and the need to remediate operations may distract management and delay investing in more growth-oriented projects that address the looming disruption to take the company forward.

- In the coming years, success (and, in some cases, survival) will be defined by the ability of leaders to understand and remain comfortable with all three elements of transformation:

  o They will have to identify and respond to the sometimes-weak signals of disruption that may threaten their business model and the profitability of their organisations.

- o They will have to develop cogent and pragmatic strategies that address these disruptive forces as they emerge and strengthen.

- o They will need to be able to take action confident that they can actually implement the strategies they develop.

- Leadership of these transformations will be very different from leading the more comfortable BAU operations of a company. Knowing that transformation is difficult is not enough. Leaders must understand why change is difficult so they can design transformation programs that have the very best chance of success.

- A company will stay in a state of rest unless acted on by a force. The organisation's status quo will therefore remain unchanged unless active and effective efforts are made to change it.

- It's inevitable that factors and people inside the company will actively resist changes.

- It will be difficult to identify potentially weak signals of disruption: the current investment slate may already be full and the current executives might focus only on what their direct competitors are doing.

- Unwritten cultural assumptions, existing high-profile projects with significant sunk costs, and talent focused on their careers and next job — rather than the company and its need to transform — will provide a powerful brake on any potential transformation program.

- The executives who have the most to lose from implementing change rarely lean back and watch idly as their power base and sphere of operations are eroded. They may form coalitions of like-minded people to actively resist the proposed change; or not be interested in challenging the status quo and shaking things up; or simply not be capable of making a meaningful impact or actually transforming anything.

CHAPTER 3

The mindset for great change

Inscribed in the forecourt of the Temple of Apollo at Delphi, ancient Greece, are the words 'Know Thyself'.

Leading transformation is different from leading BAU operations. Not better or worse, just different. It's therefore important that you consider the mindset you adopt when launching a transformation program so that you have the best possible chance of being sensitive to disruption, develop the right strategy and most critically that you can implement sustainable change. Your mindset will be critical to dealing with the myriad and competing interests of different stakeholders, and to how you're perceived as a transformation leader.

When you undertake a transformation role, it's good to take some time and reflect on how you think, as well as what you think.

It's likely — given you've been entrusted with leading a transformation — that you're already successful in your own right, you have solid experience in either your industry or your company (or both) and that you have a record of delivering business success. 'Let's entrust our most important transformation initiative to [insert name], because she has a record of failure in everything we've given her so far,' said no boss ever.

If we acknowledge that large-scale change is hard, and focus in on the human elements of why it's hard, we remember that transformation is made more difficult because of the different people involved — and you now know who they are, from the insights I offered in chapter 2.

Being positive about change, ambitious for your company, and of a generous nature towards your fellow executives and colleagues doesn't mean that you'll not be confronted by people who have none of these traits, interpret the world differently, or cannot (or refuse to) think critically or independently.

You therefore have to adopt a transformation mindset that enables you to simultaneously recognise all of the ways that different people may think and respond to transformation, while also understanding and acknowledging how *you* perceive, think and respond to the world around you.

Before proceeding, it's also worthwhile to pause and discuss 'experience' and reflect on the positives and negatives that it can bring depending upon the context in which it's being leveraged.

At the end of the day, what in fact is industry experience?

The Oxford Languages online dictionary defines experience as 'practical contact with and observation of facts or events'. Deep industry experience comes from operating within the existing or slowly changing patterns, forces and challenges associated with an industry for a prolonged period of time, after which it's hoped that the person with the experience can identify threats and opportunities to their organisation and identify patterns that accelerate thinking, and it ultimately helps them safely navigate through these. They also have experience in managing and leading people from within that industry, and intuitively understanding the academic, cultural and institutional (and maybe geographical) biases that permeate the workforce of the companies that they inhabit.

Experience is based on knowing what's likely to happen (i.e. you've seen it play out before) and how your people will respond (because you understand them deeply, and you're in fact one of them yourself) and using both these knowledge sets to successfully navigate your course forward.

So far so good. But what happens when disruption is unlike anything you've seen before? Clayton Christensen referenced the distinction between two different types of innovation and disruption that can emerge to challenge an industry in his book *The innovator's dilemma*. According to Christensen,

> *sustaining technologies improve the performance of established products, along the dimensions of performance that mainstream customers in major markets have historically valued. Most technological advances in a given industry are sustaining in character.*

An easy example of a sustaining technology could be the launch of a new credit card product offered by a major bank that provides more features — such as interest-free periods or frequent flyer points — and is superior to the credit card offerings of its competitors.

Deep industry experience is ideal for, or at least highly capable of, identifying and responding to sustaining innovation because it falls within the established set of experiences that leaders are familiar with. Their deep industry experience means they intuitively understand their customers' needs, their own product characteristics and the likely behaviours and cultural biases of their own companies.

But what happens when something comes out of left field that doesn't resemble what has gone before within an industry? Christensen defines these *disruptive* technologies as those that

> *bring to market a very different value proposition than had been available previously. Generally, disruptive technologies underperform established products in mainstream markets, [but] they have other features that a few fringe (and generally new) customers value [because they're] typically cheaper, smaller or are frequently, more convenient to use.*

An easy example of a disruptive technology could be the launch of a mobile payment offering that allows you to use your iPhone to simply tap instead of using a physical credit card (also known as Apple Pay). Apple Pay has already significantly disrupted bank payment systems and credit card/merchant revenues by eroding some of the merchant fees, and this is about to get worse for established mainstream banks if rumours are true and Apple is allowed to create a way of storing financial value within the iOS environment that eliminates the need for a bank-issued credit card.

In these circumstances, it's very tempting (and certainly very human) for leaders to look through their deep personal experience sets and established industry lenses when crafting potential responses. At this point deep industry experience can become a liability instead of an asset. Christensen believes that

> *most companies with a practised discipline of listening to their best customers and identifying new products that promise*

greater profitability and growth are rarely able to build a case for investing in disruptive technologies until it's too late.

Add to this the emergence of increasingly disruptive forces that are new or playing out in unpredictable ways for which there's no historical pattern of reference to draw on, and it's very easy to see a business environment emerging for which there's no established blueprint for leaders to follow, and the application of historical patterns of thinking and response are exactly the wrong thing required. In such an environment, the characteristics of curiosity, sensitivity, imagination and humility become far more valuable than the attributes of experienced certainty, authority, denial and potential hubris.

Adopting a transformation mindset means building on all of the strengths and foundations you've already acquired and built with the objective of making you and the transformation program more successful than it would otherwise be. The techniques and styles of thinking discussed in this chapter are therefore intended to improve and challenge your current ways of thinking so that you're more aware of the biases and experiences that you bring (especially subconsciously) to decision making.

Styles of thinking that most create an effective transformation mindset include:

- *curiosity*: empty your cup
- *sacred beliefs*: recognise that you have deep biases
- *shoshin*: maintain your intellectual humility
- *ambition*: remember that it's not only about you
- *kokoro*: get to the heart of the matter
- *kime*: focus all your energies on the heart of the matter
- *renewal*: know when to let go and try something else
- *urgency*: remember that the meter is running
- *trust*: don't lose it
- *humour*: it's a long day without a laugh

- *resilience*: find some, because you'll need it
- *get over yourself*: put things down by the side of the road.

Let's now run through what's meant by each of these, and illustrate why they're important and what you need to do as a transformational leader to demonstrate these mindsets.

| Curiosity: empty your cup

Nan-in, a Japanese master during the Meiji era (1862–1912), received a university professor who came to inquire about Zen.

Nan-in served tea. He poured his visitor's cup full, and then kept on pouring.

The professor watched the overflow until he could no longer constrain himself. 'It is overfull. No more will go in!'

'Like this cup,' Nan-in said, 'you are full of your own opinions and speculations. How can I show you Zen unless you first empty your cup?'

You may have heard this story (taken from Paul Reps' book *Zen flesh, Zen bones*) before. Instead of 'Zen', think 'transformation'. It's a mistake to enter into a transformation leadership role thinking that you have all the answers, or a definite view of how everything will play out. It's inevitable that a transformation program will be a rich opportunity for personal learning, development and professional growth for the individual, and of institutional challenge, ambiguity, frustration and ultimate pride for the company.

Admitting this truth up front will potentially save you and the company much pain.

| Sacred beliefs: recognise that you have deep biases

In this context, 'sacred' is not used in a religious sense. Instead, sacred describes those beliefs you have that are regarded as too valuable to be interfered with. We might also call them those things that you believe to be sacrosanct. These are the beliefs that have been laid down in your psyche since you were a kid sitting around the kitchen table listening to the adults chat, through to arguing with your fellow teenage friends at school or university, all the way to the present day around the executive or board table.

To illustrate the point, and to get your intellectual juices flowing, you might have a very strong personal belief in response to the following statements:

- The science on climate change is agreed on versus climate change is a hoax.

- Australia should be a republic versus Australia should remain a constitutional monarchy.

- Abortion should be illegal versus abortion is a woman's right.

- Rich people should pay more tax versus welfare payments should be reduced.

You'll probably have a reaction to at least one of these statements, and you'll respond to it with your own deeply held beliefs. These may or may not be the result of earnest research and introspection, but regardless, it's how you feel, and your mind is made up.

Just like you're likely to have had a strong *personal* response to at least one of these statements, when it comes to your job and your career, there are likely to be situations, issues and questions for which you have an equally strong *professional* response.

Remember in chapter 1, I discussed TV shows, sword fights and flower arranging? I introduced the concept of the 'way'. 'What does this have to do with modern businesses and transformation?' I hear you ask. Well, as it turns out, a lot.

All of the main executive roles in a modern corporation are clear and well defined. Decades of practical experience and organisation design theory have produced the roles we all recognise, from the chief executive officer role to the executive team, with roles such as chief operating officer, chief financial officer, chief information officer, and so on, running the functional units, and then specialists with deep relevant industry experience (think banking, mining, aviation, manufacturing) running the operating businesses.

There's a 'way' of performing these roles, based on the accumulated experience, expectations and requirements of each role. To be an effective CFO you must understand the role of finance in the modern corporation, covering decision making, financial and management accounting, budgeting, transaction processing—plus treasury, debt and equity mix, and corporate reporting functions. As a CFO, you might have come up through the ranks after first starting in an accounting firm, done your professional year qualification, joined a corporate and then been gradually exposed to all facets of managing the finance function. All the while, you've been developed and mentored by those who went before you.

Likewise, your other executive colleagues will have come on their own corporate journeys, coming up through the ranks in their own functional or industry operating disciplines. Pretty much all of you will have mastered your craft—or the 'way'—of being an executive in your chosen field. You intuitively and experientially understand the way of leading and managing the BAU aspects of your area of accountability.

Then, at some point, you might be asked to step outside this familiar role, where you fully understand what's expected of you, and the 'way' of running your division or function, and asked to lead a transformation.

'No problem,' you say, 'I've got this.' After all, you didn't get to where you are by not being ambitious, confident and driven. And so you set out to lead the transformation. 'How hard can it be?' you ask yourself.

Well, if you're honest, curious and a little humble, apparently it can be bloody hard.

Let's acknowledge that the mental models and experiences of all successful executives run pretty deep. In most cases these models are what have underpinned their success. It's therefore inevitable that if you're tasked with leading a transformation program, you may fall back on the comfortable or familiar. For example:

- if you're a CFO, you might immediately focus on the program's scope, budget, burn rate and what financial benefits are to be delivered

- if you're a CIO, you might immediately focus on the technology solution that's been selected (or will be) and how it's expected to run in the existing environment

- if you're a CMO, you might focus on the market impact and seek to influence the strategy and marketing mix objectives of the transformation

- if you're a divisional GM, you might focus on what this might mean for your division and how it delivers value within its industry segment.

All of these responses are valid, but none of them, individually, are enough. To lead a successful program you must consider all aspects of the transformation.

Just like all of the functional and industry roles within your company, there's also a 'way' of doing transformation, with its own set of principles, tools, techniques and pitfalls. And leading a large-scale transformation may now require you to set aside your familiar mental models, biases and ways of thinking — ironically those very ways of thinking that have served you so well and made you so successful — and adopt some new mental models.

To successfully lead a transformation may require you to think a little differently. If you're honest with yourself, such a role will take you into unfamiliar territory as you run into resistance from previously harmonious peers and colleagues, use tools and techniques that may be foreign to your experience set, work with people who are experts in jobs you didn't know were a 'thing' or even existed, and all while feeling the scorching bright light of accountability shining down upon you from the board, the executive team and rank and file of the company itself as you start your first few days in your new role.

In the following sections you'll find some of the mental models that I've found useful over the years as I've observed, participated in and led transformation efforts.

Shoshin: maintain your intellectual humility

'I'm the most humble person I know,' said no truly humble or self-aware person, ever. Humility is a quality that once recognised in oneself is, ironically, gone. However, that doesn't mean that we can't aspire to be a little humble.

There's nothing that gives you an instant dose of physical and intellectual humility more than entering a traditional martial arts dojo. First, they give you a white belt to tell you and everyone else that you know nothing about the journey you're about to embark on. From the moment that you and your white belt, new training *gi* and bare feet enter the dojo, you have entered a place where everything reinforces the fact that you know nothing. Regardless of what prior physical sports or activities you have pursued, nothing can prepare you for the systematised way that you're acknowledged as a beginner. From the time you bow in at the very end of the line of students, to standing at the back straining through the warm-up exercises and stretching, and then being taken aside as more senior students take you through the 'basic' techniques of blocking, striking and kicking. Also, you can see the higher grades, how they move, and the myriad techniques they can so effortlessly unleash when required.

Think about something that you're passionate about.

It could be an active physical pursuit or sport, playing a musical instrument or something entirely cerebral such as chess or bridge. Think back to your first encounter with that thing which has now become your passion. I imagine you were excited at the first encounter, perhaps grappled with its challenges, and then persevered with it until now it's a key part of who you are. And I also suspect that if you're truly passionate about this pursuit, then you're still learning and enthusiastic to be even better. In martial arts, it's customary to remember that you were once a white belt, and maintain *shoshin*, a Zen Buddhist term meaning 'beginner's mind'.

How do we maintain this intellectual humility and beginner's mind through time when it's so easy to self-reference as an expert and to inadvertently stop learning or getting better? And why is humility important in a transformation leadership context?

Well, there are several reasons, but the two most important are:

- a little humility creates intellectual doubt, and this doubt may lead you to be truly and authentically open to other people's views and alternative ways of achieving goals

- humility keeps your own role in perspective and helps you acknowledge and recognise the efforts of others, to put their needs first and to bring people on the transformation journey with you. Humility helps you avoid being an authoritarian arsehole.

Let's unpick each of these points.

When is the last time as a leader that you actively welcomed intellectual dissent, *and* truly and comprehensively changed your mind because someone constructively challenged your view and came up with a better approach or idea, *and* you then pursued that idea with all your energies and commitment, with no hint of irritation or jealousy, while giving credit for the idea to the team member who shared it with you?

If the answer to this is 'regularly', then awesome. If the answer is 'I can't remember' or 'never', then perhaps you have some personal reflection to do because you're either the 'cleverest person in the room' (possible) or you have stopped listening and learning (probable). In any case, odds are on that your transformation will be more successful and far reaching based on the more ideas and constructive challenge it's exposed to.

There's an old adage in the military that 'officers eat last'. This is intended to remind the leaders that their role is to look after the needs of the troops. Once the needs of the team have been met, then (and only then) the officers look after themselves. This adage is intended to generate an outward focus on others rather than an inward focus on oneself.

An example will illustrate the point.

It's 1 September 1939, and George Catlett Marshall has just become the senior serving general in the US Army on the same day that Nazi Germany has invaded Poland to ignite World War II. What a way to wake up to the realities of your new job! The subsequent Japanese attack that brought the United States into the war was well in the future, and up until then the United States was enthusiastically neutral. Marshall inherited a 'third rate' army of just 170 000 enlisted men, and just over 200 military aircraft.

At heart, Marshall was a transformation specialist, described by the likes of Winston Churchill as one of the key architects of allied victory. At the conclusion of World War II, the United States fielded an army (including the army air force) numbering over 8.2 million personnel (47 times its size in 1939). Marshall was the Chief of Staff of the Army and had appointed and/or mentored all the famous generals people still recognise, such as Dwight D Eisenhower, George S Patton and Douglas MacArthur. It's to his credit that these generals are more famous than he is.

He was an extremely humble leader who put the needs of his own boss (President Franklin D Roosevelt) and his country before his own personal ambitions and desires. For example, privately, Marshall wanted command of the Normandy invasion, but instead, he allowed it to be delegated to Eisenhower, his deputy, because Roosevelt famously remarked that he would feel more comfortable having Marshall at his side in Washington. Thus, Eisenhower got the job and was able to leverage his fame and success into a successful run at the United States presidency, becoming the 34th president in 1953.

Even at the time he died, in October 1959, Marshall had studiously planned to avoid the trappings of fame. Though he had planned formal military funerals for Presidents Harding and Roosevelt, and for General of the Armies John J Pershing, he stipulated that he did not want a state funeral for himself.

Marshall was the epitome of a good leader. Professional, strategic, capable, decisive and humble. There's a lot we can learn from someone like him.

By aspiring to be humble, you're likely to keep your ego in check, listen to others, and focus on the needs of others and the transformation project itself, rather than yourself. All of these are conducive to a successful transformation.

Some of you will remain unconvinced. Some of you may even yourselves be calling bullshit on the need for some humility because you still don't believe it's appropriate or needed. 'What about Steve Jobs and Apple?' you ask. 'He had no humility whatsoever. He self-identified as the cleverest person in the room, and created one of the most successful companies ever.'

Well, when you hear galloping hooves, think horses, not zebras.

'WTF?' you say.

In other words, sometimes someone brilliant, such as Steve Jobs, will emerge: someone who lacks humility and acts like (and is) the cleverest person in the room. They'll create something absolutely amazing. Sometimes — rarely — those 'hooves' will in fact belong to a zebra, and not a horse. But mostly, the person lacking humility will blow themselves and their transformation up. They'll be full of their own ideas, they won't listen, people won't follow them and they'll avoid accountability for the big decisions that need to be made.

And as a footnote, let's not forget that Steve Jobs was fired from his own company. Obviously, he was then hired back again, and rebuilt Apple into the company we know today. But when he tragically died in 2011 its market capitalisation was $340 billion, whereas now, under Tim Cook, its market capitalisation exceeds $2.12 trillion. We'll never know whether Apple would have been more or less valuable if Steve Jobs had continued to run it.

Anyway, to summarise, if you're leading a transformation, try to keep some humility about you. Be open to the ideas of others and don't believe or act as though you have all the answers. Look out for the needs of others and make sure they've got everything required to be successful before attending to yourself and your own needs.

Ambition: remember that it's not only about you

It's early 1982, and the ruling junta of General Leopoldo Galtieri is once again sabre rattling over the ownership of the Falkland Islands in an effort to divert attention away from the chronic economic and political problems Argentina was facing. The Falklands — 'Las Malvinas' in Spanish — remain a potent open sore in domestic Argentinian politics and society, and they've been the focus of ongoing and tense discussions between the British government and the Argentinian junta.

The rival claims to sovereignty are tricky. In his book *Who dares wins*, Dominic Sandbrook describes the convoluted political history of the Falklands as follows:

> *First visited by the English but first settled by the French, the [Falklands] changed hands several times in the eighteenth century, ending up with Spain. During the Napoleonic wars the Spanish abandoned them but left a plaque insisting that they still belonged to the Spanish crown. When Argentina declared independence in 1816, it claimed sovereignty over the Malvinas, and eventually established a small colony. However, the British had not abandoned their own previous claim and in 1833 moved in and re-established control. For the next 150 years the Falklands were British.*

In any case, pressure is building: Galtieri wants to reclaim the islands by January 1983, to mark the 150th anniversary of the British takeover. As Sandbrook relates it, Galtieri feels that 'taking the islands would be fairly straightforward: once their troops had landed outside Stanley, it would be easy to overpower the tiny garrison of Royal Marines'. Ironically, and unknown to Galtieri, back in London there's a growing mood — as Sandbrook recounts with humour — that 'most British politicians would have been delighted to return them'.

By Wednesday, 31 March 1982, it's clear that an enemy fleet would invade the Falklands on Friday. It is immediately understood back in Whitehall that it could not be stopped, and the Ministry of Defence declared that there would be no way of reclaiming the Falklands once they were seized.

But Prime Minister Margaret Thatcher has other ideas. Once made aware of the intelligence, she is crystal clear on her ambitions: 'If they are invaded, we have got to get them back.'

An Argentinian invasion force of 2500 troops duly lands near the Falklands capital, Port Stanley, on 2 April, and quickly overruns a token force of 79 Royal Marines. At 0925 the governor, Rex Hunt, orders surrender. The Falkland Islands are now the Islas Malvinas.

What to do?

Back in London, there's both anger and doubt. Anger at the temerity of Argentina to invade sovereign British territory and doubt as to what can be done about it. The Falklands are 12 870 kilometres south of the UK, and budget cuts have been steadily diminishing the power of Britain's armed forces. Planning, launching and supplying a taskforce to take the Falklands back will not be easy. Some say it's impossible. Many of Mrs Thatcher's ministers strongly doubted the wisdom of such a complicated operation. It's also apparent that even if Britain can form up a counter strike force, as it approached the Falklands it would be vulnerable to attack.

Prime Minister Thatcher is having none of it. Her ambition and determination to retake the Falklands remains steadfast. Although inexperienced in military affairs, she knows that Britain must retake them. As such, writes Sandbrook, 'Mrs Thatcher listened more than she spoke, always deferring to her [military] commanders on the details but remaining totally clear sighted about the wider objectives.' The Argentinian attack simply cannot be allowed to stand.

Throughout the conflict, Thatcher's ambition and determination never wavers. As she famously writes in her memoir *Downing Street years*, 'When you are at war, you cannot allow the difficulties to dominate your thinking: you have to set out with an iron will to overcome them.'

Likewise, her confidence in the British fleet and its ships, first-rate equipment and highly trained men provide the entire taskforce with a unity of purpose, clear objectives and support from the very top. Combined with this ambition, however, there is also a keen sense of taking accountability: 'Everybody knew that the stakes were higher than ever. In a matter of weeks, either she would be a national hero, or she would be finished', asserts Sandbrook.

Within less than a month of the Argentinian invasion, British forces are steaming south and retaking South Georgia, an island part of the Falklands group. Thus the opening shots of a short, sharp and violent war commences. By 14 June it's all over and the British accept the surrender of the Argentinian garrison. The Falklands are once again governed by Britain.

The toll? The UK suffered 255 servicemen killed, the loss of seven major naval ships and 34 aircraft. The Argentinians suffered 649 dead, nine ships sunk and more than 85 aircraft destroyed.

Reflecting on the complex and challenging events that had played out, the perceived doubts as to whether Britain could do anything in the face of Argentinian aggression, the difficulties associated with the military operation and the high risk of failure, Thatcher remained clear:

> *The Falklands proved that we could still do it, and do it superbly. There was a feeling of colossal pride, of relief that we could still do the things for which we were renowned.*

Thatcher's ambition for achieving big things in the face of adversity and challenge played a significant role in the overall success of the military operation. She was ambitious for three key outcomes: her country and its role in the world, the military operations and — unashamedly — she was also ambitious for herself politically.

Ambition is a massively positive part of the human condition. A strong desire to do something or achieve more and to advance one's circumstance has been the engine for human development since some early unknown hominid got so pissed off being cold in her cave, that she taught herself how to make fire with two sticks. On it went through human history with the invention of tools and agriculture, the domestication of animals, and the construction of villages, towns and city states as ambition drove people to seek better ways of doing things.

Ambition, however, requires balance. Too much ambition can lead to failure, and too little ambition may mean that success doesn't actually matter. When it comes to transformation, ambition needs to be considered across three dimensions:

1. ambition for your company
2. ambition for your transformation project
3. ambition for yourself.

Ambition for your company

Consider a couple of questions:

- What do you want for your company or organisation?
- How do you measure its success?
- How is it going in comparison to others?
- Is your company winning?

These are interesting questions for the leaders and employees of any company. However, inexplicably, these questions are not interesting for everyone. There are people for whom work is simply work, and who feel no personal connection to their company and its commercial fortunes. I've seen a few senior executives who seemed to have no fire in their belly for the company they work for. I suspect that you might even be thinking right now of someone in your own company. Someone you think is either disengaged, a little disinterested or just not quite up for it. At their worst, these executives only come in to eat the free biscuits, pay for their children's private school fees and afford their holiday house.

I've been fortunate to work with and for people who were massively ambitious for the companies and organisations that they worked for. They wanted to be number one in their industry, they knew the measures of success, and they strived each day to take the company forward. By doing so they created an amazing environment that was energising, full of opportunities and massively personally rewarding. We came in each day ready to compete and win.

A lack of connection to the competitive nature of your own organisation is quite sad, because real engagement in a company, its operations, its competitiveness and helping to set its ambitions is massively exciting and energising and lies at the heart of any transformation effort.

Ambition for your company means a relentless quest to be even better today than you were yesterday. And to do so while absolutely smashing the competition. Developing a strong ambition for your organisation and translating this ambition across the entire workforce from top to bottom is powerful. It brings clarity to everyone and context to their daily actions, and leaves everyone feeling just a little uncomfortable wondering how they'll achieve their goals and objectives.

Given Australia's love affair with sport, let's consider a simple example. Imagine your favourite sporting team. It could be netball, basketball, Aussie rules, rugby league, rugby union … It doesn't matter which. Let's now dissect preparation for the coming game.

First, everyone knows what game they're playing and how to score points. And when I say everyone, it's from the coach, down to the supporting staff and the players. Everyone knows the game they're in, and how you score and win.

Second, they know who they're playing. It might be an unknown team, or 'those bastards from team X', which means that you're in for a real grudge match.

Third, as game preparation continues, everyone is confirmed in their position. And their position matches their skillset and experience. It's the position that they train in and are expected to understand the required responsibilities and skillsets of. In rugby, if you're a winger, it's highly unlikely (in fact dangerously so) that you turn up and the coach says, 'You know what, Bob, today I think I'll play you at hooker.'

Fourth, you turn up to the game and you eyeball the competition. You look them in the eye, and you make it personal. You see your counterpart, and you know that they've trained and prepared for the game just like you have, and you know that when the referee blows the final whistle there will be a result. One wins, one loses.

Last, as the game unfolds, the players are allowed to play the game. Sure, the coach will send a couple of messages when the trainer runs on, or they may substitute some players because of injury or performance, but generally, the players just get on with it. They can do this relatively independently because they understand:

- what they're trying to achieve and what's important in doing that

- the competition, and what they're doing well, or what vulnerabilities are emerging

- their own role: the skills that are expected of it, and their personal accountability to their role

- what's happening in real time as the game unfolds, and therefore what adjustments are required to win it.

This is all very clear and simple. If you look at all the successful sporting teams, you'll see this simple set of principles in place. Sure, the coach will introduce strategies (player scouting, selection, acquisition, training), tactics (certain plays and moves) and culture (team expectations and rules) that make the best teams unique. But on the whole, sports contests are a great example for everyone having an ambition for their team and/or their club organisation and then being clear on all the details.

Australia has generally punched above its weight on the world sporting stage and this has created a national expectation that when our national sporting teams compete, we expect them to win. We should translate this ambition to our national corporates.

So, back to business — literally — because my hypothesis remains that we need to be more ambitious for our companies and organisations, both in their domestic performance and their relative performance on the world stage.

When it comes to your organisation: what's your ambition? Do your players, or employees, understand the four points I mentioned?

1. *What they're trying to achieve and what's important in doing that:*
   o How does this translate to your industry?
   o What are the critical success factors for your industry?
   o What opportunities and threats are emerging within your industry?
   o What are you trying to achieve or change within this industry?
   o What does winning actually look like?

2. *The competition, and what they're doing well, or what vulnerabilities are emerging:*
   o Who is your biggest competitor?
   o Is it really who you think it is? (Remembering that Kodak's biggest competitor didn't turn out to be Agfa.)
   o Who might be getting ready to cut your lunch?

3. *Their own role: the skills that are expected of it, and their personal accountability to their role:*
   o Are you fielding the best team?
   o Do all your executives understand what's expected of them?
   o Are all your executives actually up for the game?

4. *What's happening in real time as the game unfolds, and therefore what adjustments are required to win it:*
   o How do you know what's happening?
   o What metrics do you collect, and how regularly?
   o What must you change to win?

Being ambitious for your organisation or company means that you can read these questions and be at least a little curious as to how your company is going.

Asking these questions out loud can also create discomfort, as I found out first-hand. I once sat in on an executive session at a Byron Bay resort in which the company's executive team was discussing ways to reduce expenditure and be more competitive. ('Stop having meetings at Byron Bay resorts,' I wanted to say, but I held my tongue.) Anyway, they went around the room, each sharing ideas, and eventually they got to a position that I thought lacked ambition. I wasn't called on to speak. The executives then had a quick open discussion with one another on how they'd performed as a team, on how they'd discussed the tough topics and eventually landed at something they were all comfortable with.

I happened to be sitting next to the most senior person in the room, and after he'd canvassed the views of everyone in the room, I asked him, 'Would you like to hear what it was like for me sitting here as an observer?' He couldn't very well say no, so I asked my first question:

'If a representative of [insert competitor] was sitting in this room, what would they say upon return to their head office? Would it be "Holy shit, these guys are all over it, we're in trouble" or would it be "No worries, we've got this"?'

My role in the meeting was to call out 'false consensus', and I had every intention of keeping my part of the bargain. I could not in good conscience remain silent. As I reminded the executives present, every employee in the company relied on those present to set stretch ambitions for their company, and to then secure and allocate the resources to ensure that those ambitions became a reality.

After the meeting, my questions and comments were the subject of two kinds of feedback:

- 'Courageous questions that should provoke us to be more ambitious.'

- 'How dare he ask *us* those questions.'

We all get to choose how ambitious we want to be. For me, the thought of another company being better than mine is hateful. Yes, hateful. I know it's a strong word, but that's how I feel. As a leader, it's my job to be competitive with other industry participants, to understand what's required to be the best in an industry and to be working towards the number one position. Nothing will guarantee that this will all play out. But surely we'd all agree that you have to be prepared to give it a red-hot go, and not say to yourself and others, 'Gee, wouldn't it be awesome to be second or third.'

Let's all be more ambitious for the success of our companies.

Ambition for your transformation project

Okay, let's imagine you're the newly promoted CEO and you're looking to transform the company. You have a strong ambition for your organisation and you want to see it sensitively identify and respond to the disruptive forces playing out. You've developed a cogent strategy, and you now want to execute the transformation.

How ambitious should your project be across the various dimensions of the transformation, especially covering scope, schedule and budget?

There's obviously no correct answer here, because it's so dependent on context, circumstance and what you're ultimately trying to achieve.

First, as the CEO, and the ultimate sponsor, how would people characterise you? Do you fall into one of the twin evils of transformation, characterised as:

- the over-committed sponsor, who expects too much of their projects, micro-manages, wants to achieve ever greater objectives with fewer and fewer resources, and drives the team on a kind of death march to the end that burns people out and ultimately destroys value, or

- the under-committed sponsor that says all the right things and communicates the importance of the project, but then doesn't turn up to meetings, or when they do, they surf the web instead of engaging in conversation with how the transformation is actually going. They never assign resources and think that the objectives will be delivered through mental will rather than hard work and effort.

More importantly, how would you characterise yourself?

How do you think about the scope, schedule and budget of your own transformation program?

Are you contemplating transformation or incrementalism? Incrementalism is defined as belief in or advocacy of change by degrees, otherwise known as gradualism. It assumes that the disruptive forces at play in the world will provide your organisation with plenty of time to respond and react.

If you think this represents your industry, and that your competitors will likely take a similar view, then that might be appropriate. However, if you have ultra-competitive competitors, or the presence of hungry start-ups probing and stalking your markets and seeking to cut your lunch, then incrementalism may not serve you well.

Is the scope sufficiently ambitious that success will move the dial on creating shareholder value and setting up the company for sustainable outperformance, or is it defined so narrowly that even if successful, the so-called 'transformation project' will hardly matter. Does your project matter? Is it likely to collide with the established ways of doing things within your company, improve the current products and services, and mark out new markets and customers? Does it create friction among the current management team, and generate energised debate and argument about how best to move forward? Is it controversial or comfortable; are people relaxed (I've got this!) or challenged (holy shit!). As Muhammad Ali so eloquently put it: 'If your dreams don't scare you, they aren't big enough.'

Is the schedule sufficiently ambitious so that it will make a difference in an appropriate time frame? Is there urgency to actually get the big stuff done? It's so easy to forget the value of time in modern times, with our fortnightly payroll cycles, monthly accounting periods, quarterly reporting cycles and annual financial year. It may not always feel like the clock is ticking. What happened to thinking with urgency in terms of days and weeks?

Napoleon Bonaparte escaped the island of Elba on 26 February 1815 and arrived in Paris with his supporters on 20 March 1815. Over the course of the next 90 days, he took over the national government, designed his cabinet, assigned roles, raised and equipped a major army comprising 70 000 men, and then marched into Belgium as the head of that army to fight the battle of Waterloo on 18 June 1815.

Now there's a man who knew how to get big strategy done!

These days it seems to take 90 days just to design a new role description, brief a recruiter and get a shortlist of candidates to their first interview. Set an aggressive schedule and get at it.

Is the budget sufficiently ambitious or have you sand bagged it? Okay, take a breath.

You've set an aggressive scope, and you intend to move fast. So far so good. When setting the budget, you have to be realistic, but not skimp or gold plate things. However, as you think about your project, and the degree of transformation it's pushing, you have to budget for the inevitable friction you'll create (and its resultant impact on decision-making speed) and the fact that it will uncover unexpected challenges. In 30 years of transformation projects, I've never, ever, turned over a rock and found buried treasure. I've only ever found things more complicated, complex and change resistant than expected. So my advice is go hard on scope and schedule but be realistic on budget. And have a decent contingency that's unashamedly transparent to the governance committee.

So be ambitious for your transformation project, and set out to make meaningful change that matters. Otherwise, why bother? You should aim for transformation of the company, not the re-engineering of the accounts payable department.

Ambition for yourself

Personal ambition is good, and when coupled with a strong ambition for the company, and for the transformation project, it forms a powerful triumvirate for success.

Positive personal ambition on a transformation project looks like:

- willingness to take accountability
- using the challenges and requirements of a complex project as an opportunity for personal growth and development of new skills
- putting up your hand to make the hard strategic choices, to call out false consensus and/or lack of alignment, regardless of the personal risk associated with doing this
- seeking opportunity to work with the most senior people to watch and learn how they think and conduct themselves, and in turn for them to see how you conduct yourself and what you're capable of
- taking accountability for the wins and the losses that will inevitably flow; for providing aircover for the transformation team and ensuring that credit is given to all those doing the work.

Transformation initiatives provide an opportunity to pull all of these elements together in ways that working in the BAU operations of a company rarely do. Positive personal ambition will be the engine that propels you, and the project, when you face the inevitable difficulties, resistance and challenges that come with trying to change the way things work. Former US president Dwight D Eisenhower identified the combination of single-mindedness and selfless dedication to the task at hand as being perhaps the greatest of leadership qualities. 'Any leader worth his [or her] salt must of course possess a certain amount of ego, justifiable pride in his [or her] achievements. But to be a truly great leader, the cause must predominate over self.' More on this later.

On the other hand, negative personal ambition will eventually derail a transformation initiative.

Negative personal ambition on a transformation project looks like:

- deflecting accountability: success has many fathers, while failure is an orphan
- claiming the challenges of a complex project as an excuse for poor performance

- failing to admit the need for personal growth and development of new skills
- delegating (upwards or downwards) the hard strategic choices, failure to call out false consensus, and/or lack of alignment, and a determination to deflect all personal risk associated with the project
- seeking opportunity to ingratiate with the most senior people and for them to see how well you do everything
- deflecting accountability for the losses that will inevitably flow, claiming only the wins for themselves, while letting others get shot down should there be any failure.

I've developed a simple test for whether I think someone's personal ambition is at the right point. How ambitious for themselves are they, and what are they prepared to sacrifice on the altar of personal advancement? I call it the 'lifeboat test', and in essence I ask:

'If I was adrift at sea with this person in a lifeboat, would it be safe to fall asleep? While I was asleep are they likely to:

- throw me overboard to save space
- eat all of our remaining rations
- eat me
- hold a shade cloth over me so I don't get sunburn?'

When transformation projects get tough, and they will, I want to be hanging out with the latter people, and I want to be one of them myself.

In the next three sections, three interrelated concepts are described that, because of their importance, are at the very core of traditional Japanese martials arts:

- *kokoro:* heart
- *kime:* focus
- renewal: letting go.

Kokoro: get to the heart of the matter

In most corporations there's never enough time nor resources, and executives are expected to intuitively understand the trade-offs associated with their decision making. They're encouraged to focus on the important, not the urgent. To prioritise. To focus.

Kokoro is a Japanese martial arts word that describes getting to the heart of the matter.

In *The way and the power*, author Fredrick Lovret writes, 'Basically, it consists of eliminating all concepts that do not have a direct and positive bearing on the task at hand.' It comes from a fundamental need within martial arts to strip back everything that's not important and is periphery to a combat situation in which defeat could mean certain death. It can be assumed that nothing crystalises what's important more than a situation in which the consequences of getting it wrong are so high.

In our corporate lives, we may not be faced with life-or-death decisions; however, we are still accountable for the success or failure of the companies that we are custodians for. Getting to the heart of what's important remains — and will always remain — critical, as illustrated by one of my heroes, Barbara Jordan.

It's 17 June 1972, and five men have been arrested in the Watergate complex in Washington DC dressed in business suits and wearing surgical rubber gloves. Police have seized a walkie-talkie, bugging devices, 40 rolls of unexposed film, two 35-millimetre cameras, lock picks and tear gas pens.

Although current President Richard Nixon was ahead of the Democratic candidates in the polls by 19 points, just to make sure, a small group of Nixon loyalists felt it imperative that they illegally break in and bug the Democratic National Committee offices to get the inside scoop on their political opponent's presidential campaign plans and strategies. What would become known as the Watergate Scandal is off and running.

The story quickly breaks into the media, with the *Washington Post* grabbing hold of it like a terrier on a bone. By late August, the story is growing, with calls for a thorough investigation to be undertaken. President Nixon rejects a recommendation to appoint a special prosecutor, independent of the Justice Department. As far as Nixon is concerned, his counsel has already conducted an investigation that revealed no-one on the White House staff, or in his current administration, was involved in the incident. Move along people, nothing to see here.

Fast forward two years to February 1974 and, as described by Mary Beth Rogers in her 1998 book *Barbara Jordan: American hero*,

> *the House of a Representatives [has] voted overwhelmingly, 410–4 to direct the Judiciary Committee to investigate fully and completely whether sufficient grounds exist for the House of Representatives to exercise its constitutional power to impeach Richard M. Nixon, President of the United States of America.*

The House Judiciary Committee is duly formed, continues Rogers, with

> *not a particularly distinguished group of members of Congress, consisting for the most part, of obscure suspected second rates and partisan politicians. One reporter said, 'there was hardly a statesman in the bunch'.*

Over the coming months, the 21 Democrat and 17 Republican members of the committee question every procedural move, and jockey for prestige, influence or notice in the media. The Republicans are united in their belief that the whole scheme was a joint effort fabricated by the Democrats to put an end to Nixon and the Republican Party.

By late July the whole process has bogged down in procedure, partisan argument and counter argument, and no-one has been able to get to the very heart of the matter at hand, or frame things in a way that the average American punter can understand. Therefore, to help things along, it's decided that each member of the judiciary is to be given 15 minutes to publicly summarise their personal view of the proceedings and how they think it should advance. Each member speaks, blatantly ignoring the 15-minute rule, each full of passion and eloquence for the topic at hand, but falling neatly along party partisan lines. After two hours, only two speakers have delivered their remarks. It's become a talkfest.

Things are about to change though, because Barbara Jordan is scheduled to be the third speaker.

Born in Houston, Texas in 1936, she is a teenager through the 1950s and keenly aware of the challenges and prejudices of being African-American in the United States South. Because of segregation, she could not attend the University of Texas in Austin so she chose Texas Southern University. She's pushed against and breaks all kinds of ceilings as she studies to be an attorney, becomes the national champion debater while defeating all comers from Ivy League schools and graduates from Boston University School of Law in 1959. This is followed by being voted the first African-American state senator in Texas since 1883, and the first black woman ever to serve in that role.

At just 38 years old, Jordan is now the first African-American woman elected to the United States House of Representatives. As a relatively junior congresswoman, she finds herself on the Judiciary Committee deciding the future of the President of the United States.

Jordan takes her responsibilities on the Committee incredibly seriously, even visiting the National Archives twice to stand in line with the tourists to look at the Constitution in its airtight glass casement, to ponder its messages and her role in protecting it. In her own televised words, her faith in the Constitution is whole, it is complete, it is total.

She leans into the microphone and starts her opening remarks.

Rogers shares in her book that 'within a mere fifteen seconds, no more than fifty words into her text, both the sound and the content of her words began to engage, even captivate her audience'.

In contrast to every partisan speaker so far, Rogers continues, Jordan 'began to explain—in effect, to teach—what the whole crisis was about: the rule of law and a president who put himself above the rule of law'.

Jordan impartially, intuitively and decisively gets to the very heart of the matter. She lays out what impeachment for 'high crimes and misdemeanours' actually means. She lays out the criteria enshrined in the Constitution and case law and sets it in the context of what the president has actually done. She quotes James Madison, one of the founding fathers of the United States: 'A President is impeachable if he attempts to subvert the Constitution.'

She famously finishes her prepared remarks, taking only 13 minutes to completely eviscerate the actions of President Nixon, with a phrase that lays down a politically lethal challenge to all present:

> *If the impeachment provision in the Constitution of the United States will not reach the offence charged here, then perhaps that 18th century Constitution should be abandoned to a 20th century paper shredder.*

The effect is electric. The Committee's narrative has immediately changed. Rogers continues, 'After a year of Watergate revelations, resignations, details and denials, Americans clearly needed a voice of reason from "on high", and Barbara Jordan gave it to them.'

Within days, six Republicans join 21 Democrats in approving articles of impeachment. Rogers concludes by writing, 'On August 8, with the certainty that the House would vote to impeach him and that he would face a Senate trial, President Nixon resigned.'

Few of us will be called on to preside over such historical affairs as Barbara Jordan was. However, if you think about the organisation that you work for, there are likely to be one or two elements that sit at the very core of what's important. This is the *kokoro*. It's the very essence of what's important.

Getting to the heart of the matter is about knowing the essential thing within the context of your company and its need to transform. This *kokoro* or 'essentialism', as described by Greg McKeown in his book *Essentialism: the disciplined pursuit of less, is not about how to get more things done; it's about how to get the right things done. It doesn't mean just doing less for the sake of less either. It's about making the wisest possible investment of your time and energy in order to operate at your highest point of contribution by doing only what's essential.*

| *Kime*: it's all about focus

There's an important concept — perhaps the most important — in traditional Japanese martial arts known as *kime*. Like many Japanese words, there's no perfect translation, but the generally accepted one is that *kime* equals spiritual focus. In *The way and the power*, Fredrick Lovret writes,

> *The purpose of kime is pure and simple: power. By focusing your strength on one point, you greatly increase effective power. One pound of pressure spread out over a wide area is of little importance, but a needle driven by one pound of force will penetrate deeply.*

Said another way, it's usually better to drive two to three things forward a mile, rather than 10 things forward an inch.

In traditional karate, *kime* is the foundational physical, mental and spiritual goal. It has as its objective the harnessing of every part of your physical and mental capability and capacity into a single point, at a single point of time.

Together with *kokoro* (getting to the heart of the matter), *kime* (focus) is one of the most important mindsets required for effective transformation. Combined *kime* and *kokoro* mean that you're focused on the most critical things. It's important to remember — in the words of Stephen Bungay, author of *The art of action* — that

> *generating activity is not a problem; in fact, it's easy. The fact that it's easy makes the real problem harder to solve. The problem is getting the right things done: the things that matter, the things that will have an impact, the things a company is trying to achieve to ensure success. A volume of activity often*

disguises a lack of action. We can mistake quantity for quality and then add to it, which merely makes things worse.

There are two elements to this:

- organisational focus
- personal focus.

Organisational focus

Effective transformation requires focus. All of the organisation's resources and elements must be in alignment. Nothing is wasted and everything is coordinated and purposeful. Everything and everyone is working to deliver the same goal.

Sounds easy, so let's make sure everything is squared away and aligned by the end of the week. Yeah, right.

Focus is about putting maximum effort into only those few things that will have the greatest impact. In an effective transformation, it means that everyone understands the objectives and how they'll achieve them. From strategy, through to execution and project management, everyone is clear, and everything is geared towards the goal. Everyone is focused.

When thinking about transformation, if you can't describe the objectives in about three bullet points, then you probably don't have enough focus.

Another easy test of whether a large corporation is focused is to take a look at their capital budgeting and investment slate. If the investment slate cannot be grouped into a couple of themes, there's a good chance that they're not focused. If the strategy and the transformation objectives are clear, then most of the investment slate will be focused on these. Obviously, I hear you say.

Actually, it's harder than you think.

You may be surprised by the number of bids that will be made for the available investment funds in a company. From pet projects to regulatory requirements to replacing worn-out infrastructure: all will have a draw on the investment slate and reduce the focus on the transformation. An easy way to empirically gauge the level of focus is to add up the proportion of the investment slate that's absolutely and unequivocally directed at the transformation goals. The degree of spend — regardless of the rhetoric — describes what the real priorities are.

If you want to assess whether your strategy and capital investment budget are aligned and focused, ensure that each individual program of work is ranked in an absolute sense and a relative sense. Rank your individual initiatives in order of relative importance because this will force the hard conversations and build agreement about what's *most* important. Don't take the easy way out by saying they're all high priority. There can only be one thing ranked first in importance.

Obviously, all projects that get financed will be important in an absolute sense (i.e. they're internally logical and make strong commercial sense). However, they should be able to be ranked in a relative sense (i.e. they're ranked from most important to least important). Under this approach you must have a #1 initiative, and then a number #2, and so on. It's always too easy to claim that all your projects are high priority, which means in fact, none of them are high priority. As you make progress in executing against all of these priorities, the time will come — like an air traffic control exercise — when you'll have to determine which initiative gets the scarce resources ahead of its peers.

Personal focus

Let's now think about how you spend your time.

If you have 100 percentage points of effort, how should they be allocated? How many percentage points are spent on the transformation project? And of those, how much are spent on those few things that will most move the dial with regards to the transformation? If we're honest, we all waste at least a little time at work. Not all activity is progress. Being focused is about ensuring that most of your time is directed at achieving the objectives of the transformation.

It's not rocket science, but it's difficult, because there are always so many things competing for your time. That's also why it's so important to cut to the heart of the matter — the *kokoro* — so that you can spend every available minute focused on its achievement. It doesn't matter how talented, competent or hard working you are, you will eventually be overwhelmed if you try and do everything. And when you're strung out and exhausted, mind wandering and in need of a rest, your team will be overstretched, confused about what's truly important, and never complete anything. Operating and living like this is punishing. Instead, you must identify the essence of what needs to be done (*kokoro*) and then focus everything on executing against only that (*kime*).

Every now and then, you should also look back over your meetings and the pattern of what you've spent time on to gauge whether your focus is actually on the right things. Just like the capital budget is a useful indicator of the relative priorities of a corporation, your own personal diary is a useful yardstick that describes what you prioritise and deem most critical. You may be surprised at where you spend your time.

Renewal: know when to let go and try something else

I remember as a kid watching classic Hollywood action movies full of sword fights, and even then I was surprised at the choreography. Let me explain. The hero and the villain would be fighting, thrusting and counter swinging their swords, jumping over obstacles, and eventually, they'd find themselves face to face, their swords crossed and locked, spitting their hatred of each other and straining to push against the other's sword. You too probably recall similar scenes, because it's standard Hollywood fare designed to build drama and excitement in the confrontation.

My question, even as a kid, was why when the swords were locked, didn't the hero simply let go of his sword and punch his opponent in the face? Or in other words, why, when what he was doing wasn't working, didn't he abandon trying harder at the same thing, and try something new?

We all get fixated on what we are doing. In corporate life, this becomes even more common because everything is geared around doing things the same way. There's great benefit in the standardisation of processes (i.e. what we do), but less benefit in the standardisation of how we think.

It's important to identify the true essence of something — its *kokoro* — that's the most important thing that needs to change, and to then apply *kime* — or focus — on it to achieve results.

But sometimes neither of these two things is enough. Sometimes, you need to know when to let go and try something else. Don't fall into the trap of persevering and doubling down on tasks and approaches at the very time you should be taking a step back and detaching from the issue. Not all activity is progress.

Albert Einstein (apparently) said that 'the definition of insanity is doing the same thing and expecting a different result'. Equally, John Maynard Keynes recognised that when the facts changed, he changed his mind. Neither was the first to recognise that we have to maintain mental flexibility in the midst of our endeavours.

Let's face it, we can all become a little obsessed with our goals, and when we are not achieving them, it's easy to assume that we just need to work harder. We all know intuitively that we should avoid the insanity of doing the same things, and when facts change, we should also change our minds. The difficulty is having sufficient detachment to recognise these situations, because the price of focus is loss of peripheral vision.

This has long been understood in martial arts because the price of persevering with an inappropriate technique or approach was often defeat. As a result, there's a long tradition of acknowledging this dynamic, and in specifically naming the situation, and providing advice and guidance on what to do when it happens.

Miyamoto Musashi remains the most famous swordsman in Japan. He was born into a samurai family in 1584 in the middle of Japan's warring period, when multiple generals were seeking to unify the country and install themselves as Shogun, or military dictator. To say these were rough times would be an understatement: Musashi had his first duel at the age of 13 when he responded to a public challenge by a travelling samurai and killed his opponent. Musashi was undefeated in more than 60 individual duels, using everything, from the long sword, to the short sword, wooden swords, or even two swords simultaneously.

Just before his death in 1645, Musashi wrote what has become a classic on military strategy and philosophy: the *Go Rin No Sho* (*The Book of Five Rings*). In his book, Musashi calls out the need to acknowledge the danger of becoming fixated on things.

According to Musashi,

> *'to renew' applies when we are fighting with the enemy, and an entangled spirit arises where there's no possible resolution. We must abandon our efforts, think of the situation in a fresh spirit, then win in the new rhythm. To renew, when we are deadlocked with the enemy, means that without changing our circumstance we change our spirit and win through a different technique.*

Musashi also acknowledges the Hollywood sword fighting dilemma, when the two-handed samurai swords are locked, and the two opponents are fighting for their very lives:

> *'To release the four hands' is to know when to give up whatever you were aiming to do, and to win by another means. If there is a four hands impasse and a locked in situation, the first thing to do is to quickly discard the previous designs and come up with something [new].*

There are key takeaways from this nearly 400-year-old text that are relevant for us today: even when you're focused on the very heart of the matter, if you run into obstacles or resistance — both of which are inevitable in a transformation project — know when to step back and reconsider. Recognise that you might become so focused that you lose your peripheral vision right at the time when the facts have changed and it's therefore time to change your mind. Sometimes, it's time to renew your approach and try something different.

Urgency: remember that the meter is running

Transformation leaders must be urgent.

This doesn't mean that they're always rushing around, or thinking everything represents a crisis that must be solved today. Instead, urgency in this context means continually scanning the world around you to identify opportunities that need to be grabbed before competitors grab them, and threats that must be acknowledged and attended to before they can get out of hand. As Professor John Kotter maintains in his book *A sense of urgency*, 'Urgent action is not created by feelings of contentment, anxiety, frustration, or anger, but by a gut-level determination to move, and win, now.' Urgency means a desire to achieve more for the company, and to avoid kicking things down the road or waiting to see what your competitors do before you act.

And remember that urgency doesn't mean moving in an unsustainably rapid manner. You should go as fast as you can without rushing. Urgency means setting the pace.

Leading transformation is very different from running a BAU team because it requires more urgency.

BAU is — as it says on the tin — business as usual.

Everything is geared towards delivering the existing (or certainly past) objectives of the organisation. All the business processes — whether efficient or not — will continue to deliver their existing outputs unless an external force requires them to change. So too the underlying technology platforms, which were once hard wired to support the processes, together with the people undertaking the tasks to bring the various parts of the system together to deliver the outputs. The organisation will continue to operate as originally designed and staffed.

In such a system or environment, if the leader fails to make a decision, or doesn't turn up to work, the actual impact on that environment may well be low. This kind of complacency becomes pervasive partly because even smart and sophisticated people may not see it. People will continue to work as they did yesterday. If the process was efficient yesterday, it will likely be efficient today and tomorrow. People will default to their existing historical understanding of their work and keep doing it. And by doing their work, the organisation will continue to operate and is unlikely to do anything, in the short term at least, particularly wasteful.

Likewise, the cost of this existing system can also be accurately calculated. All the people involved — the equipment, the resources consumed, and so on — can all be tallied up to arrive at a cost per day or week, month or year. In reality though, this is rarely done. Many corporates and organisations typically do not think of costs in relation to the work actually delivered each day or week. At best, they'll make estimates based on the month, or the quarter, and they'll review them in that context as they seek to understand and identify areas for improvement. Eventually, the costs will be understood in the context of cost of goods sold, or the overheads associated with a support function such as finance. The outputs will also be expressed in a historical manner (e.g. units manufactured by quarter, or shift). This can be considered reasonable in many organisations, and in the short term the BAU managers are generally tasked with maintaining the status quo of the entire system so that it delivers consistent and predictable results.

Transformation leadership is different. Right from the very start of a transformation project, resources such as employees, management consultants and rental space will be allocated to the project. The employees will likely come across at cost, the fees of management consultants are clear and the different line items will quickly add up. It's very easy to then calculate the cost of the project team into a daily, weekly or monthly burn rate.

The burn rate is simply the cost of the project expressed as a dollar figure over a daily, weekly or monthly period. It's this burn rate that makes transformation so exciting, rewarding, frustrating and challenging all at once.

As a transformation leader, given all these resources, and the transparency of their cost, you'd better be getting something done. You need to be urgent. The meter is running, costs are being consumed, so you need to get something done. And that something must be valuable.

Because the proverbial meter is running, transformation leaders typically need to be more urgent than most corporate managers, because the nature and costs of a project are so transparent.

I've often been surprised — as both a management consultant and a banking executive — at the lack of speed, urgency and logical planning that some leaders have applied to their projects. This has then both burned costs (bad) while also having little to show for the costs that have been incurred (even worse).

For transformation leaders, never has the phrase 'time is money' been so important. So, have an urgent mindset.

Trust: don't lose it

To give no trust, is to get no trust.

Lao Tzu, *The Tao Te Ching* (c. 400 BCE)

Trust, once gone, is very difficult to restore. On the other hand, most people respond positively to being trusted. They typically rise to the occasion and work hard not to disappoint the person who has bestowed the trust. Sure, there is a tiny minority of dishonest people in corporate life, but I think most people appreciate being trusted and are unlikely to do the wrong thing.

There's a catch though: you need to, in no uncertain terms, tell the person that you trust them. And you have to back this with actions that show that you trust them. Over three decades, after having told people on my various leadership teams that I am choosing to trust them, I've never had a single one betray that trust. Sure, some might not have achieved their assigned objectives or always exercised the greatest judgement, but they've never maliciously taken the corporate equivalent of a cheap shot or betrayed my trust. And just because you trust someone doesn't mean you don't review their work. Bestowing trust is never an excuse for not knowing what's going on.

So, when was a time you actively chose to trust someone? Or when was the last time someone trusted you, and how did it make you feel?

I remember an early lesson on trust (and accountability). As a principal consultant I'd finished an eight-week business case for a client, and then written the follow-up proposal, worth $1.2 million (which back in 1999 was quite a big engagement) that was to go to the client. I placed it in front of my boss, the lead partner, and he looked at me and said, 'Are you happy with it?'

'Yes,' I replied. 'Don't you want to read it?' I asked as he started signing his name.

'I trust you,' he said, 'and after all, it's your job, and you have to deliver it.' He slid it back across the desk and I walked out of his office feeling 10-foot tall at being trusted, and very much on the hook for making the engagement a success. His trust in me created a massive sense of accountability, and I would have walked barefoot on broken glass to ensure the job succeeded and I didn't let him down. The job was a big success, and led to a very happy client and millions in consulting revenue. It also led to a long and productive working relationship with my boss, based on mutual trust and accountability.

Trust, when combined with clear direction, is a very potent dynamic for transformation teams. When people are trusted they're likely to feel confident in developing creative solutions to deal with ambiguity, a sense of ownership and accountability to get things done with urgency — and, critically, a strong connection to the objectives and their achievement. They're less likely to delegate upwards or sweat the unimportant details when faced with the inevitable delays and obstacles that will arise. Trust helps people get on with it.

It should also be remembered that most people respond positively to trust, and that our entire society operates efficiently and effectively because most people trust that everyone else will also follow the rules and obligations placed on them. More often it appears that trust is our default status: we tend to trust without thinking about it in most situations.

However, it's also clear that some people find it hard to trust people. 'You have to earn my trust' is an early refrain from many leaders as they set about recruiting and forming their teams. We must also acknowledge that many managers find delegating to others very difficult. After all, as Stephen Bungay rightly acknowledges,

> *In delegating authority for decision making one gives away power without giving away accountability. It implies trusting your people. If you have been brought up to believe that leadership is about knowing how to do something better than your followers, it's difficult to see the task of leaders as enabling followers to perform their jobs better than they otherwise would and admitting that they may know how to do those jobs better than you do.*

If we reflect deeply on the requirement of a boss for direct reports to earn their trust, it quickly becomes ironic. After all, why would you hire, or keep, a person on your team if you don't trust them? Enabling your team to get on with things, and to bring their authentic selves to the task, requires trust.

As *The Tao Te Ching* states so eloquently, 'to give no trust is to get no trust'. A truly transformational mindset requires trust. It requires that you both give trust to others and be worthy of trust yourself.

Humour: it's a long day without a laugh

A person without a sense of humour is like a wagon without springs. It's jolted by every pebble on the road.

**Henry Ward Beecher (1813–1887),
American slavery abolitionist**

To those who know and work with me, one thing is very clear: I am not a comedian. I laugh at my own jokes because I want at least one person to.

However, I do understand the importance of creating an environment of levity, of treating a serious matter with humour and a good old-fashioned joke or two throughout the day. Let's face it, we spend most of our waking hours working, and it makes for a very long day if everyone is deadly serious. Sometimes people need some light relief. How you frame situations can make them serious and stressful, or humorous and, therefore, memorable.

Humorous and serious are not opposites. We can take the achievement of goals, objectives and commitments very seriously, while also having some fun and laughter along the way. A transformation program doesn't have to be some kind of death march towards its ultimate destination. Maintaining your sense of humour, despite the inevitable setbacks, is critical. Transformation requires resilience (more on that later) and a sense of humour.

In my earliest days at NAB, I was working in a corporate centre role and I was proposing a new project to a senior technology executive in the Australian bank business. When I arrived at the designated meeting room in Docklands, Melbourne, it was already occupied by someone who introduced themselves, in a somewhat unfriendly manner, as 'Hi, I'm [their name]. I'm a general manager.' *Wow, your parents must be so proud*, I thought. We sat for a minute or two before the more senior person I was meeting arrived.

I made my pitch, which was all about the standardisation of project management techniques in the bank so we could define clear methods and approaches, have consistent stage gates and governance, more easily train our people, and, ultimately, take a portfolio view of what was going on with the investment spend. All pretty logical and reasonable. Not so fast. The two of them ripped into me, and my idea, and said that they'd never adopt it.

In fact, the meeting was so bad, it was almost comical. As I was walking back up to the Group Head Office in Bourke Street, I decided that I needed to turn the meeting outcome into its very own brand or anecdote and make it a little less dire and serious. I was determined for it to be memorable, for people to see the funny side of it and for something good to come of it.

Upon my return, my boss naturally asked me how the meeting went, to which I responded with a laugh, 'It was the three "Ds".'

'The three "Ds"?' my boss naturally asked. 'What the hell is the three "Ds"?'

I responded with 'Discredit, Descope and Defer.'

'Discredit me: how long have you been at the bank, what's your background and experience, etc. etc. Then discredit the idea: that will never work, we couldn't possibly standardise projects when they're all so different from one another, etc. etc. And finally, discredit Group: you guys sit up there and don't know the challenges we're facing, blah, blah, blah.'

'Then it was Descope: if we were to try it, let's use the methodology on a small project, the smaller the better. Instead of an entire project management methodology, let's just use some standard reporting.'

'Finally, it was Defer: of course, our investment slate is very full and we're very busy, so let's introduce the changes you'd like to make at the end of the next century, blah, blah, blah.'

While an accurate depiction of what had happened, I knew that it was only round one, and that this was the opening gambit. I also knew that by looking at the encounter through a humorous lens it would quickly do the rounds of the Corporate Centre (it did) because everyone was finding it tough to get things done and needed a little light relief and a chuckle. And, I knew that eventually it would get back to the two plonkers I'd met with (which it also did).

I know that this anecdote is not that funny (hey, I said right up front that I'm not a comedian) but it set a better tone than frustration or hostility. Eventually, we did implement a standardised and consistent project management methodology and approach across the company, which gave us better control over the investment slate, a clear view of project status and improved the training of our people. The benefits of the project clearly outweighed the resistance of its opponents.

According to Jennifer Aaker and Naomi Bagdonas, authors of *Humour. Seriously*, there's a growing body of research that reinforces the need for humour and suggests that a

> *lack of levity has dire consequences for our physical health (our workplaces are killing us), our relationships (the single driver of happiness at a time when we are growing more disconnected than ever), and our teams and our companies (which are struggling to compete in a rapidly transforming world).*

I imagine that we've all worked in environments that were a deep reflection of a leader or a prevailing culture that took itself too seriously, actively discouraged humour and required everything to be just so. The kind of place where they may require visitors to the corporate floor to put on a tie and jacket, put fancy linen table protectors under every carefully placed and measured crystal water glass, where people speak in hushed tones, and you are asked to submit your papers — along with your intended jokes — for their review a week before the meeting. In such a setting, how probable is it that constructive, energising, challenging and engaging debate is likely to take place?

I've found humour to be the lubricant for really constructive, serious and cerebral debate. Humour is the safety valve that lets out sufficient pressure to prevent the system or its participants blowing up, while allowing them to criticise, challenge and pursue the truth or the best way of approaching the work.

It's not surprising that the need for this safety valve or lubricant was clearly recognised throughout history, and that the royal crowns of Europe often employed the court jester to play this role. The role of the jester was to use humour and wit to speak truth to power, and to tell it straight. Even the king recognised the need for at least someone to take the piss out of him every now and then, and call bullshit when needed.

It's no different today. Aaker and Bagdonas suggest that

> *[t]oday's employees yearn for more authentic, human leaders. Humour is a powerful leadership strategy to humanise oneself*

to employees, to break down barriers, and balance authority with approachability... [Research suggests that]... [l]eaders who use self-deprecating humour are rated higher on measures of both trustworthiness and leadership ability by their employees. [Additionally] a culture that balances serious work with levity and play can actually improve team performance.

One of Aaker and Bagdonas' particularly interesting and (now) aspirational findings for me — obviously because I'm the only one who laughs at my own jokes — was that 'managers with a sense of humour (regardless of whether they themselves were funny) were rated by subordinates as 23 per cent more respected, 25 per cent more pleasant to work with, and 17 per cent friendlier'.

So, what now?

Well, as former Twitter CEO Dick Costolo puts it, 'You don't have to be the quickest wit in the room. The easiest way to have more humour at work is not to try to be funny — instead, just look for moments to laugh.'

The point here is that if you're leading change, you need to keep your sense of humour. Don't take it all too seriously. Find things to joke about along the way, otherwise you, and everyone else, will go nuts.

Resilience: find some, because you'll need it

Not everything in your transformation will go according to plan. When shit happens — and it will — how will you respond? As a leader, and in particular a transformation leader, it is your job to pick yourself up and keep going. You are the one who must make the choice to be resilient.

For me, the morning of 25 November 2010 was unremarkable. I was in a car with a colleague heading out to see the vacant lot we were getting ready to acquire for the construction of NAB's new data centre, the first purpose-built facility since the 1980s and long overdue. My telephone rang with the personalised submarine style 'action stations' ring tone, which meant only one thing: a major IT outage was developing. Apparently, we'd failed to complete the bank's overnight batch process, and we wouldn't be finished before the branches were scheduled to open in around 30 minutes. But I was told it should all be okay.

At the time, I didn't know much about the batch process, but I was about to learn a lot, and fast.

Imagine for a second, a bank's overnight batch process. For NAB it was like a huge digital 'bucket' into which all the computer channels poured all of the day's transactions. All day the branches, ATMs, retail merchant terminals, institutional bank payments, corporate payrolls, internet banking applications and internal account-keeping systems recorded all of the various debits and credits and poured them into a big digital bucket. At various times of the day, the major banks also shared huge payments files, moving hundreds of millions of dollars in and out of the accounts within the bank. Hour after hour, the digital bucket collected more and more transactions, totalling millions, then hundreds of millions, and eventually billions of dollars, worth of transactions.

At the end of each business day, this virtual bucket was emptied and cleared in an incredibly complex set of commands, with a special program controlling the tens of thousands of executable lines of code. This complex symphony of computer code ensured that all of the money and transactions — by now worth several hundred billion dollars of accumulated debits and credits — were posted to customer accounts and other banks so that an accurate record could be held in the bank's ledgers. Once emptied, the ledgers were all up to date, and the entire system was reset, ready to start the next day. It was a process that ran like clockwork to such an extent, and was so reliable, that pretty much everyone took it for granted.

In the middle of the night of Wednesday 24 November and into the early morning of 25 November, the batch had hit a glitch. A complex piece of historical code reached a point where there was a contradictory command, and to resolve it, well-meaning teams had tried to fix it on the fly. Long story short, they ended up duplicating some sub-batches, and writing over other files, which meant that when the batch finally did settle for the evening of 25 November, transactions were duplicated or missing, resulting in incorrect balances for millions of customer accounts. Millions of savings accounts, home loans, cheque accounts and personal loans were all showing incorrect balances.

For a bank entrusted with the hard-earned savings of our customers, the technical description for the current situation was 'complete shit show'.

I didn't realise it that morning as I was looking at a vacant lot, but the next two weeks would test my personal and professional resilience in ways that I could never imagine. As the chief information officer, I was accountable for understanding the problem and its cause, fixing it and making sure that it could never happen again. It was a case of 'it wasn't my fault, but it was certainly my problem'.

Still not understanding the scale of the problem, I returned from Melbourne to my home city of Sydney on the Thursday night, and landed to the news that, contrary to expectations, we still had not settled the Wednesday night batch, and here we were at risk of falling another day behind.

Friday saw me on the phone all day liaising and reporting our position to the Reserve Bank of Australia and the Australian Prudential Regulatory Authority. With NAB being such a big part of the banking system, and the largest business bank, this now had the potential to negatively affect the liquidity of the country. It was getting more serious by the day. Saturday found me on the early flight back to Melbourne to physically re-join my team.

Over the coming days the media had a field day reporting the issues, and some of our customers were going nuts. When a Queensland customer drove his bobcat excavator through the doors of a branch, it was becoming clear how seriously this could escalate. It was the perfect storm of pressure and real-world consequence for one of Australia's biggest banks, and potentially the entire Australian banking system.

For the next two weeks, I spent about 18 hours a day in the office, leaving only to catch a couple of hours' sleep each night in my hotel room. Although I was surrounded and supported by a superb team, and very supportive leaders, it was a lonely space feeling accountable for everything that was going on. Contact with my family was limited to quick phone calls, and with the issue raging, and feeling accountable — and professionally (would I get fired?) and personally vulnerable (I didn't have all the answers) — I decided early on that I would be resilient.

I decided that I would be the best leader that I could be for the bank, for my team and for our valued customers. I made a clear and deliberate choice to be resilient and to be the agent of hope in every meeting and interaction, displaying a confidence (that I didn't always feel) that we would get through this successfully.

Over the coming hours, days and weeks, this resilience translated into managing a set of simultaneous processes to:

- understand and fix the batch issue
- commence the project to reconcile all accounts and make good for our customers
- continue to run the bank's BAU systems.

We did this by running our team on strict eight-hour shifts, insisting people didn't burn out, formally prohibiting people from driving their own cars home late at night, and generally managing their emotional and physical energy levels, all while ensuring that everyone was productive and working on the right things. We supported our specialists to work the problem with clear guidelines and expectations, and appropriate aircover.

We took accountability for doing what was required for our customers with urgency, professionalism and sensitivity. Accountability of this sort, in this kind of public pressure cooker environment, can be tough, and it can be lonely.

I remember waking up one morning and immediately calling the team for an update. The team told me the debits and credits were still in error, and the numbers were so big I had to get them to repeat them as I wrote them down: each number had 10 digits. Another night, after only two hours of sleep, the submarine ring tone woke me at about 4 am. It was very lonely standing in a dark, impersonal hotel room, a long way from home, authorising the movement of billions of dollars in and out of customer accounts.

After two weeks we got on top of things, everything sorted and squared away, and I flew home exhausted. When I look back on this episode and all of its problems and stresses, while I certainly don't want to repeat it, I find myself strangely grateful for the opportunity to be involved in such a serious situation that tested my leadership under pressure, and asked questions of my energy and resilience.

I was put in a situation where I had a clear choice: I could either choose to be resilient, or I could choose not to be. Resilience, and being resilient, is a choice. I was lucky enough to find a part of me that simply didn't countenance giving in or not facing into the challenge.

Where does resilience come from?

Before we get too ahead of ourselves, let's acknowledge that the business world — even managing the resolution of a batch issue in a bank — is pretty benign when compared to other human endeavours.

Let's not any of us think we're too tough. After all, consider the great Keith Miller, veteran World War II fighter pilot and Australian test cricketer, who was asked by Michael Parkinson about the pressure of going out to bat before one of the victory tests played after the war.

'Pressure?' says Miller, 'There is no pressure in test cricket. Real pressure is when you are flying a Mosquito with a Messerschmidt up your arse.'

Nonetheless, the pressure in transformation can feel real enough. I made a conscious choice to be resilient many years ago, and I approach being resilient like anything else: I think about it as a kind of skill, I try to practise it and I seek inspiration in a range of things to help me be resilient.

I'm lucky to have a supportive family, and some great friends, but whenever I've been faced with challenges, I've always tried to reflect on my own role, and what I expect of myself. I don't always get it right, but I find these things useful:

- *Perspective*: I try to keep perspective on what's happening. If the spectrum is catastrophic and life threatening at one end, and mildly annoying at the other end, then I think about where I am right in the moment. Once I introduce perspective, it typically helps me find a way to navigate whatever challenge I'm facing. Business transformation is generally more annoying rather than being up there dealing with a Messerschmidt.

- *Expectations*: I've never expected everything in my life to be perfect or fair. Let's face it, shit happens, and I don't know anyone who has had a perfect life. Knowing this, it makes it easier for me to cope with setbacks, and I know that the day-to-day challenge or annoyance will eventually come to an end. This includes the expectations I have of myself: I know that I will not always live up to my expectations and the person I want to be. Sometimes I'll be less than what I aspire to, but hey, that's okay. Nobody is perfect.

- *Inspiration*: Ever since I was a little boy I've always been fascinated by history, and I use what I've learned to try to inspire me to be more resilient. I also draw on those close to me: my father was incredibly resilient, and my wife takes resilience to another level. In fact, my best mate asked me 'What's it like to have a wife who's tougher than you?' He's right, and the answer is 'lucky'.

- *Determination*: I've never liked being beaten, whether that has been in karate, sports, school class or business. I'm very competitive, and I don't like to even countenance being beaten.

- *Gratitude*: There's so much I'm grateful for, and this helps me be resilient. I feel lucky to live in Australia, have family and friends, and good health. Not everyone, including some of you reading this, may feel so lucky, and you may have challenges that I don't, so I certainly don't want to diminish these, but if we each look carefully, I'm confident that we'll each find something to be thankful for.

- *Pride*: We will all remember challenges in the past that we've overcome. Reflect on these, and how you felt during the dark days of that past challenge, and how you then found a way to overcome or cope with these challenges. Having done it once, you can do it again.

I came across a quote from author Mary Anne Radmacher saying that 'Courage doesn't always roar. Sometimes courage is the little voice at the end of the day saying, "I will try again tomorrow".'

This quote reminds me to focus on what's in front of me today — that there are different types of courage — and it makes me think of my dad.

When I was 18, my dad started to get very sick with a rare form of bone cancer. Despite the challenges and pain he felt, he never complained, and he tried to get on with his life as best he could. He went on walks with me, he went out for dinner, took us on holidays and he continued to go to work. Sadly, he died the next year, and it was not until I went in to his work and cleared out his office desk that I realised just how painful his last year or two had been for him. I found a bottle of prescription morphine in his office drawer that he had needed to use every now and then just to get through his day. He was always tough and resilient.

His courage was to say: 'Just get through today, and then maybe the next day.'

All these years later I still think about him a lot. He helps me keep perspective and inspires me to be resilient. I know that many of you will have family, friends and loved ones who also inspire you to be resilient.

Leading a transformation program is going to be tough. If it's sufficiently ambitious, then it's going to test your energy and professional resilience. Develop your goals and approach and keep pushing forward. Find your own sources of resilience and draw on them as needed. And as you get through each day, and achieve a little more, be thankful that you're not one of those soft and needy people who needs to get a ribbon for coming 8th in the school running race.

Get over yourself: put things down by the side of the road

Tanzan and Ekido were once travelling together down a muddy road. A heavy rain was still falling.

Coming around a bend, they met a lovely girl in a silk kimono and sash, unable to cross the intersection.

'Come on, girl,' said Tanzan at once. Lifting her in his arms, he carried her over the mud.

Ekido did not speak again until that night when they reached a lodging temple. Then he no longer could restrain himself. 'We monks don't go near females,' he told Tanzan, 'especially not young and lovely ones. It's dangerous. Why did you do that?'

'I left that girl there,' said Tanzan. 'Are you still carrying her?'

This quote, from Paul Reps' book on Zen stories, is another favourite of mine. It reminds me to be more philosophical when faced by the perspectives of others.

In corporate life, and especially within the context of a transformation program, the collision of ideas, hopes, fears, ambitions and aspirations for the company is inevitable. It will be impossible for everyone to agree all of the time. In fact, you don't want them to. A diversity of ideas and perspectives will make the transformation richer and more likely to be successful.

In such an environment, it might be easy to feel aggrieved if someone criticises your idea, or doesn't like how you do something or the decisions that you made. Remember that it's inevitable that you'll rub people up the wrong way, and that they'll rub you the wrong way. Don't be too fragile. If you want to be a leader, you're choosing to enter the arena where ideas and influence compete. Not everyone will like you or your ideas. Get over it.

A more modern story will help reinforce my point.

It's February 1990, and prisoner 46664 has been released from the solitude of his tiny cell on Robben Island after 27 years of imprisonment. The former political activist squints in the harsh sunlight, his eyes permanently damaged from decades of hard labour in the glare of the African sun.

After these lost years, where to now? How should he respond to his former captors? What revenge might be justified for the indignity, the beatings and the attack on his very humanity?

Nelson Mandela, the anti-apartheid revolutionary, is having none of it. Filled with hope, patience, love and kindness, he sets a path to become the first black president of South Africa from 1994 to 1999, and to serve as a dignified and unifying force for all of his country — even his former gaolers.

None of us will face the challenges that Mandela did, and if he can put 27 years of torment down by the side of the road, then we can put our transformation frustrations down too. Leading a transformation project — if you're truly trying to transform — will be a bruising affair. There's an old management consulting adage that if you're not creating resistance, then you're probably not pushing things hard enough.

Usually, people resist a transformation project and its objectives because they sincerely believe it's not in their own or their company's interests. Even the most die-hard loyal company person will still find it difficult to support an initiative that's bad for them. Sometimes, rarely, the people who resist transformation do so for a far simpler reason: they're arseholes. You've probably met the kind: no-one knows as much as them, works as hard or is as clever. Don't forget that for people like this, their beliefs are not based on facts, so no amount of facts will persuade them to change their mind.

Given the existing difficulty with a transformation program, and that your backpack is already full of hard work and tasks, deadlines and milestones, you don't need the extra weight of carrying the arguments, disappointments and resistance of others. Do not be like the young monk, Ekido, simmering on perceived wrongs or issues all day and carrying them with him as he walks in the rain.

Adopting a mindset of equanimity can be one of the most difficult things to do. Especially when you're dealing with arseholes. In the heat of a fierce debate and hot resistance it's hard to even remember to put things down, let alone to actually do so. Therefore, put your ego aside, address the concerns and resistance of others, accept the difficulties when that's the only option and put it all down by the side of the road. Keep moving forward.

Key points from chapter 3

- A positive, transformative mindset will help underpin success.

- Your personal mindset will impact how you perceive risks and threats, the quality and ambition of your strategy, and to what degree you are prepared to make the changes necessary to implement transformation.

- Be prepared to 'empty your cup' and be curious about the world: don't assume you are an expert who has little left to learn. Keep an open mind.

- Maintain *shoshin*, or 'beginner's mind', to help you identify potentially weak signals of industry disruption, to consider a broader set of strategic options, and to create an environment where the most creative ideas are heard and debated.

- Be ambitious for your company, its transformation and yourself.

- Make certain that your transformation goals are achievable.

- Ensure your ambition is positive: take accountability, seek personal growth, make the hard decisions and provide aircover to your team.

- Get to the very heart of the matter — the *kokoro*. This is that single essential thing that must be achieved to guarantee success.

- Once you know your *kokoro*, focus (*kime*) all of your attention and resources on achieving it to ensure you don't waste time on the unimportant things.

- Bad things can and probably will happen: be prepared to reflect and renew. Don't become so focused that you lose your peripheral vision or don't realise that you should change your approach and try something else. Let go, reflect and re-engage.

- Maintain ongoing urgency to get things done: time is money and the 'meter is running' on a transformation program because of the transparency of goals, milestones and highly visible resource consumption. Get at it and deliver results. Now.

- Acknowledge that transformation is difficult: this will help you build a safe environment in which people are prepared to work hard and take the necessary personal and professional risks.

- Actively find ways to trust people. Trust creates an environment where hard facts can be put on the table and debated rather than obfuscated or kicked into the long grass. Trust will make people work harder than you thought possible.

- Keep your sense of humour. Shit will happen. How you frame challenges and position the corporate personalities that will inevitably resist change makes all the difference. Have a laugh along the way and create an environment that is both energising and professional.

- When things really hit the fan, maintain your resilience. Be determined to press on and succeed and if necessary, get through today, and then the next day.

- Put things down by the side of the road. When you successfully transform your company, it's best if you're not burdened by distractions.

CHAPTER 4

The mechanics of great change

We've established that transformation is difficult and considered the different transformation *mindsets* (such as being curious, open, ambitious, determined and resilient) that can make your change program more likely to succeed. It's now time to consider the actions that must be taken to address, mitigate and overcome these inherent difficulties. These actions are the mechanics of transformation.

All three elements of transformation are difficult in their own way. It's sometimes difficult to identify the weak signals of disruption, and to then extrapolate their impact on your own industry or company. It can also be difficult to make choices and craft an appropriate strategy to address these disruptive forces. The transformation mindsets mentioned in the previous section are well suited to seeking to identify and understand disruption, and for the development of creative and innovative strategies to respond to and address the resultant opportunities and threats that these disruptions will deliver.

Ultimately, the transformation will create an inevitable collision between the power of the status quo, the active resistance of certain executive personalities and the inherent change inhibitors associated with the company and how it operates. It is, of course, the leader and team who suggest and then drive significant change.

With regard to transformation *mechanics*, there are many books on the current disruptive forces at play in the world, and there are a million books on how to develop corporate strategy. In my view, the world doesn't need another book on the development of corporate strategy, and certainly not one from me. Disruption and how to develop corporate strategy are therefore not the subject of this book. Instead, I will focus more on the third element of transformation: how to actually implement change. Because even when you successfully identify the disruption and craft a kick-arse strategy, it's difficult to implement it.

Let's quickly recall our modified version of Newton's Law of Motion from the previous section:

- *Law 1*: a ~~body~~ ***company or organisation*** continues in its state of rest, or in uniform motion in a straight line, unless a ~~force~~ ***transformation project*** acts on it.

In other words, transformation can only happen when action is taken.

And before we start, a word of caution. There are no silver bullets. There's no magic list of actions that, should you take them, are guaranteed to deliver a successful transformation. All these mechanics must be considered in the context of your own company, and its industry, at a certain point in time. These mechanics shouldn't be considered as a set of steps to complete in a linear manner. Instead, to borrow a sailing analogy, they should be used as a checklist to help you understand where you are on the ocean of change, and to help you trim the sails to course correct as you navigate towards full implementation of your strategy.

A simple set of mechanics for leading successful transformation comprises:

1. *do the work*: personal commitment of the leader
2. *make decisions*: choose, own and communicate a clear strategy
3. *build the team*: get the right people
4. *be thorough*: follow a proven methodology and approach
5. *keep score*: use KPIs to align and provide regular feedback.

In this chapter we will discuss each of these five mechanics.

1. Do the work: personal commitment of the leader

There are no bad armies, just bad generals.

Napoleon Bonaparte (1769–1821), French emperor and general

Napoleon was right: it's been known throughout history that the role of the leader is critical and that 'everything is leadership's fault'.[1]

The importance of the role of the leader in transformation cannot be overemphasised because if the leader is not absolutely committed, it's

---

[1] Attributed to Hopper, in *A Bug's Life*, Pixar Animation Studios for Walt Disney Pictures

probably best not to bother. To be truly successful, the leader must position themselves as the 'transformer-in-chief' and personally do the work. There are certain things in the transformation that simply cannot be delegated.

The leader as 'transformer-in-chief'

In my experience, the people in most companies all have quite sensitive 'bullshit meters' and they know when the leader doesn't believe in what they're espousing, or talks to them in corporate-speak that lacks authenticity or simple grounded messages. Equally, they know when a leader is determined, taking accountability and genuinely enthusiastic for the transformation. The personal ownership, commitment and inspiration of the leader is therefore the fuel that sustains the transformation. Once people know what you're trying to do, and that you're committed to it, they're far more likely to be engaged and themselves get behind it.

Successful transformation is dependent on a clear alignment of strategy across all levels of the organisation, from top to bottom, so that everyone is pulling in the same direction. Because of this, there's no substitute for the commitment of the leader to the development of the strategy and to its ultimate execution and implementation.

So, what should the role of the leader be in the context of a large-scale corporate transformation? Should they have a bias for retaining the BAU operations and delegating transformation responsibilities, or should they become the 'transformer-in-chief' and delegate the management of the BAU to their subordinates? How much should they focus on the sometimes-competing demands of each role? If they only have 100 points of effort, what's appropriate for each of leading the transformation and managing the BAU?

The leader as 'transformer-in-chief' should spend the majority of their time leading and managing the transformation because it sends a strong message about:

- strategic reality
- symbolism
- accountability.

Strategic reality

My definition of transformation covers identification of disruption, the crafting of a strategy and execution of the program to change the organisation.

Strategic logic would, therefore, suggest that failure to identify the disruption underway means that eventually, the organisation itself will become irrelevant as its industry changes, its product offerings lose relevance, and its customers take their business elsewhere. In the face of such disruption, it would seem illogical for a leader to retain accountability for managing the BAU and delegating the transformation to someone else. This is akin to rearranging the deck chairs on the *Titanic*. Under ongoing disruption, the BAU is itself under threat, and unless it changes, the company will fail.

In the face of this threatening disruption the leader should, therefore, spend the majority of their time on leading the transformation to safely navigate their company to a better and more relevant place within their industry.

Symbolism

It's important that someone is the actual and symbolic face of the transformation, and by doing so lends the weight of their role, reputation and energy to the successful achievement of the transformation objectives. This ensures everyone understands that it's a serious undertaking, that resources will be assigned, and that it receives appropriate oversight and governance. This symbolism will also help attract and retain the energies of the organisation's very best talent.

Non-involvement or casual engagement by the leader in the progress, detail and governance of the transformation will inevitably be interpreted by people across the company as the transformation not being important, the leader being uninterested and the project not being tightly aligned to the future fortunes of the company. All of these are deadly to a transformation project.

Accountability

Our landings in the Cherbourg-Havre area have failed to gain a satisfactory foothold and I have withdrawn the troops. My decision to attack at this time and place was based upon the best information available. The troops, the air and the Navy did all that bravery and devotion to duty could do. If any blame or fault attaches to the attempt it is mine alone.

Found on a handwritten note written by Dwight D Eisenhower (1890–1969), Supreme Allied Commander, D-day Invasion, 6 June 1944

It's June 1944 and great forces are stirring. After the culmination of years of planning involving the complex orchestration of millions of men working within the air forces, navies and armies of a coalition of allies including the UK, United States, Canada and others, the invasion of the French coast at Normandy is about to begin.

Operation Overlord remains the largest amphibious military assault in history, involving thousands of ships, aircraft, tanks and vehicles, together with a supply chain and logistics organisation extending back to the UK and across the Atlantic to the United States, all requiring coordination and control. In the end, one man's accountable: General Dwight D Eisenhower, the Supreme Allied Commander.

In his sleepless hours before the D-Day launch, Eisenhower penned a handwritten note to be read in the event of failure. The simple note started with him acknowledging the unthinkable: that because the amphibious landings in the Cherbourg-Havre area had failed to gain a satisfactory foothold, he had withdrawn the troops.

His note went on as an almost perfect example of taking accountability:

> *My decision to attack at this time and place was based upon the best information available. The troops, the air and the Navy did all that bravery and devotion to duty could do. If any blame or fault attaches to the attempt it is mine alone.*

Luckily for our modern freedoms and liberties, the invasion was successful, and his message was never needed. It remains, however, a powerful symbol of a leader taking full and unequivocal accountability. Eisenhower leaves no room for ambiguity. All blame or fault attaches to him, and to him alone.

Real leadership requires taking ownership and being seen to take ownership.

The leader taking authentic and unambiguous accountability means that the transformation is relevant and closely aligned to their success. In the face of disruption, it should be impossible for the leader to be professionally successful and receive incentive payments for managing the BAU operations while a strategic threat to the organisation's very existence emerges for someone else (namely one of their delegates or successors) to address.

Should the leader delegate this existential accountability *solely* to a subordinate executive, it weakens the resolve of all concerned, and inadvertently creates a potential wedge between the newly minted transformation executive and the rest of the leadership team (including the leader themselves). When difficult decisions arise — and they most assuredly will — the conscientious transformation executive will be pitched against all of those executives responsible for (and potentially comfortable within) the status quo. The leader will then be in the unenviable — and preventable — position of having to arbitrate between the different forces and factions created by the difficult choices driven by the transformation.

It's easy to predict that in such a situation, the rest of the team will lobby their boss hard, both for and from their positions, making all kinds of arguments for how the project should proceed, or how their business unit should go last... blah, blah, blah... so that it will be almost impossible for even the most well-meaning leader to make sense of it all.

The easiest way to avoid this is for the leader to take clear accountability at the outset, to immerse themselves in the nature and threat of the disruptions, and to understand the trade-offs associated with the selected strategy and the broad approach and detailed steps contained in the execution plan.

It's important for the leader to put their name and accountability to all decisions, especially the hard ones.

I've been amazed to see during my consulting and executive career, leaders who don't want to put their names to the hard decisions. The hard decisions are typically those decisions that mean people lose their jobs, and let's face it, most transformation projects create winners and losers. The winners get new, better or more interesting and satisfying roles. The losers are those who are demoted, or outsourced to a third party or whose roles are made redundant and they consequently lose their jobs and livelihoods.

Do not be one of those leaders who wants to be popular and loved by the very people who you're making redundant, by offering false platitudes or trying to make out that it was not your decision. Or worse yet, you do this all while seeking loopholes to enable you to pay these redundant people even less than you should be paying.

In their book *Extreme ownership: How US Navy SEALs lead and win*, Jocko Willink and Leif Babin emphasise that leading a transformation is not a popularity contest:

> *On any team, in any organisation, all responsibility for success and failure rests with the leader. The leader must own everything in his or her world. There is no one else to blame. The leader must acknowledge mistakes and admit failures, take ownership of them, and develop a plan to win.*

Instead, turn up, own the decision and make it clear that you made the decision, outline and communicate your reasons for doing so clearly to everyone, and better yet, try to pay those affected a little more than they're entitled to. It will help settle those who are leaving, but more importantly, those who are staying.

Doing the work

It's March 1945 and the allied armies are smashing their way east toward Berlin. Resistance is savage as the Germans fight tenaciously for every inch of the fatherland. General George S Patton is at the front of his 3rd Army, driving it forward through the ambiguity and fog of war. Toward the end of March his attack is stopped by the mighty Rhine River, and his officers delay, wondering how to get across, given that all bridges in their area of operations have been bombed into pieces.

General Patton returns to his command post, points to the map and says 'let's cross here'. One of his officers responds with 'General, we'll probably have to make a bridge and we don't know the local conditions and whether that's even possible.'

Annoyed, General Patton says firmly, 'We will cross here, every man can walk across, and the tanks will be able to drive across too.'

'But general, how can you be so sure?', asks the officer.

'Look at my wet pants,' says Patton. 'That's how deep the water is. I've already walked across and returned, so get your men and get them across now!'

If we're honest, how often do we see a new chief executive officer hire a team of management consultants to help them work out what needs to be done. As a former management consultant, I appreciate how useful this can be. It's useful for figuring out what should be done to drive the company's performance, and for identifying what opportunities exist and what performance across different business units might be like.

However, management consultants aren't a substitute for the personal involvement of the new transformation leader. Outsourcing this critical process solely to third parties runs the risk of missing an opportunity to make a significant impact and create foundations and relationships that will be invaluable. Use consultants sparingly to augment your work and not as a substitute, because the objective of this initial consultation is for you to immediately grab hold of the business and really connect with its people to understand what's going on, and why. It can't be outsourced. It's also critical for building credibility in the delivery of your messages via the report back, which should come after this consultation report.

The feedback gained from these interviews is invaluable for quickly understanding what's going on, and an excellent way to get a feel for the people in each of these groups as you start to evaluate who's who in the zoo.

The importance of the leader 'doing the work' and getting out to the frontlines of their business early in their new role to see what's going on with their own eyes, even if they get wet pants, cannot be overstated. Looking at business operations and talking with the people actually doing the work will both build your knowledge and your credibility, and send a message to everyone in your company about what is important.

And a note to remember: while you zealously evaluate the personalities, character and skills of people around you, it's easy to forget that the most talented and best performers are doing the same of you. Do you listen? Are you curious and open? Approachable or closed? Do you already know it all? Do you do most of the talking? While you're assessing people through the lens as to whether you want to keep them, they're assessing you through the lens of whether they want to stay.

Let's face it, all of the people you interview will immediately go back to their desks and be asked by their colleagues, peers and bosses: what was she/he like? Be clear on what it is you want them to report back. If you truly want to commence building employee engagement and start into a transformation, you definitely *do not* want them to say:

'Doesn't listen, thinks he knows it all.'

2. Make decisions: choose, own and communicate a clear strategy

MEN WANTED for hazardous journey, small wages, bitter cold, long months of complete darkness, constant danger, safe return doubtful, honour and recognition in case of success.

Advertisement in *The Times* newspaper, London, 1 August 1914.

Now there's a job ad that calls a spade a spade.

Described as a masterpiece of understatement, this advertisement was placed by Sir Ernest Shackleton to identify and recruit men for his 1914 Trans-Antarctic Expedition. More than 5000 applicants responded to the ad, and Shackleton departed England soon after with a crew of 28 hardy (and clearly optimistic) hand-picked men on board his ship, the *Endurance*.

If you think Shackleton's description of the job conditions was direct, his overall strategy was equally clear: make the first land crossing (comprising approximately 2900 kilometres over four months) of the Antarctic continent from the Weddell Sea to the Ross Sea via the South Pole.

Shackleton set his expedition objective, described what it would be like to actually be involved and then communicated it clearly to all. There was no high-brow corporate speak, no jargon. No long-winded boring presentations with irrelevant clip art. Just a simple message clearly and passionately delivered. No-one was left wondering about his personal ambition and what it would be like to be involved.

Long story short, soon after arriving in the Weddell Sea, the *Endurance* got trapped by the sea ice in January 1915, forcing the crew to endure the bitterly cold Antarctic winter. The *Endurance* was eventually crushed and it sank in November 1915. This forced the crew to abandon the ship (and their expedition objective) and set up camp on the ice. With the ice drifting north across the Weddell Sea, a decision was made in April 1916 for the entire group to sail to Elephant Island in the lifeboats they had salvaged from the *Endurance* across the rough waters of the Southern Ocean. From here, a select number of the crew, led by Shackleton, attempted to sail two small boats to the closest land, a whaling station on South Georgia, some 1300 kilometres away.

After successfully navigating to (apparently the wrong side of) South Georgia, Shackleton and his men were then faced with trekking across the interior of the island — a journey that's still considered an amazing feat of determination and skill to this day — to finally raise the alarm and seek help. Shackleton returned to pick up the rest of his crew from Elephant Island in August 1916.

Shackleton's positive and inspirational leadership is credited with keeping every single one of his crew alive over their harrowing two-year odyssey. He remained clear and direct throughout. And he certainly didn't disappoint when it came to fulfilling the conditions described in his original ad.

When it comes to transformation, being unclear on what you want to achieve is a recipe for widespread employee disengagement as people mentally pull back, wait to be told what to do and voluntarily remove their discretionary effort. All of which can slow or kill a transformation effort.

This book is not about how to develop a corporate strategy, but it's important to touch on some of the aspects of its development that relate to the role of leading transformation. It's critical that you choose a strategy with simple goals that you can communicate.

The following checklist is a guide to the role that you should play as the leader of a transformation. You must be able to:

- be decisive: choose well
- have a strategy
- clearly and succinctly describe the transformation
- communicate a compelling case for change.

Let's take a look at each of these points.

Be decisive: choose well

'Choose' is an active word that requires the leader to actually *do* something. As General George S Patton Jr stated, 'A commander will command.'

No organisation can do everything, so at some point, choice will be required.

You — as the leader — will have to make a decision, and by doing so, own the strategy. The leader as strategist is an important concept that should drive transformation leadership, writes acclaimed professor at Harvard Business School, Cynthia Montgomery in her excellent book, *The strategist: Be the leader your business needs*:

> *The strategist is the one who must shepherd this ongoing process, who must stand watch, identify and weigh, decide and move, time and time again. The strategist is the one who must decline certain opportunities and pursue others. A consultant's expertise and considered judgement can help,*

as can perspectives and information from people within an organisation. But, in the end, it's the strategist who bears the responsibility for setting a firm's course and making the choices day after day that continuously refine that course.

I recently listened to a great podcast by Emile Sherman called 'Can we put a value on human life?' that was a debate between an economist and a philosopher about solving poverty. At one point, the moderator asked the philosopher about the need to choose between funding two extremes. The philosopher didn't like being put on the spot and so responded that they'd prefer a world with sufficient resources to do both — if only the government provided more money... Unfortunately, there will never be sufficient resources to avoid making decisions. Companies are no different. No matter the depth of their resources and the size of their investment slate, there will always be more requests for funding than can actually be met.

This is where the adults are needed. At some point, after much discussion and debate, a decision will need to be made, and often it's a choice between two 'right' options. Someone has to make the decision. And don't mistake consultation with consensus — *you'll* have to make a decision. You'll have to differentiate between the many people who have an opinion and those few who have a vote.

And let's agree up front that there's no such thing as 'no decision'. If someone actively avoids making a decision, 'yes' or 'no', then the decision made is of course 'no'. The status quo prevails, because it's the only option that has momentum and never has to argue its case.

People can avoid making a decision because:

- no-one is really clear on what the objectives are, or why options are even being evaluated
- the options aren't clear: not enough work has been done to flesh out alternative options
- there's not enough information: events have yet to play out to inform the decision
- they don't yet know enough: they haven't taken sufficient time to soak into the decision

- something else is happening: there might be a problem that requires resolution
- they have personal ambition and a fear of failure: they're afraid of taking accountability.

The first four reasons can be addressed through hard work or patience.

Clarity of objectives can be confirmed. After all, what are you actually in business for? Even a cursory reference to last year's corporate goals will provide some guard rails in this space. If these objectives are not clear, then you have other, even bigger, problems.

A broader analysis of the options available to achieve the objectives can always give rise to more detail, the identification of risks, and the financial and commercial consequences. Each option can be fleshed out in more detail and assessed against the objectives to determine what adds the most value or makes success most likely.

Clear milestones can be defined when sufficient information will be available and a decision can then be made.

If objectives and options are known, then the leader needs to invest sufficient time to actually understand the differences between options, and the absolute and relative merits and costs of each. Again, this requires real work and should include in-depth questioning so that each option is fully understood.

The fifth reason is legitimate. There may well be something that's affecting the context in which a decision needs to be made, and this must be resolved first.

The last reason is the most worrisome. When leaders do not want to make a decision despite understanding the objectives, the options available and the relative merits of each, it points to a potentially more sinister dynamic: that the leader is looking to cover their own butt.

There's no place in a successful transformation program for a leader who cannot, or will not, make a decision. When faced with options — and with the financial meter running (see 'Urgency: remember that the meter is running' in chapter 3) — a decision must be made. If the discussion leads to commentary such as 'let's do some more work and make a decision next week', then obviously that's the decision. It is always active, never passive. There's no such thing as no decision.

It's important for the finances, momentum, symbolism, credibility and success of the program that decisions be raised, escalated and decided upon in a transparent and timely basis. This is self-evident, but on challenging, large-scale transformations, it's rarely the case.

As a quick aside, a key principle to maintain momentum is to clearly communicate to everyone on a project that you expect the people closest to the decision to actually make the decision (within the original scope and financial boundaries of the project) and if they cannot make it, to escalate the decision to someone who can. Not being able to make a decision should be noted as an impasse, and the maximum time before an impasse is escalated should be 24 hours.

This doesn't mean that a decision will then always be made immediately — that's not the point. But it does mean that the need to make a decision is noted with a degree of urgency.

If you aspire to be a leader, you need to embrace the need to make decisions, and have the courage to actually make them.

Have a strategy

Again, this book is not intended to be about the development of strategy. There are already many excellent books on the development of strategy, and there are people who have dedicated their entire careers to a study and development of all kinds of strategies.

I'm not one of them, so instead, this book is predominantly about transformation, or in essence, *implementing* the strategy. That said, the two concepts are obviously related. The easiest way to think about this is to describe the 'means' and the 'ends'. This seems obvious, because the 'ends' is typically what you're trying to do, and the 'means' is how you intend to do it.

Let's elaborate. You head to your closest Bunnings Warehouse hardware store because you want to buy a drill bit. Is this the ends or the means? Clearly, it's the means. The 'ends' is that you want a hole. Despite the simplicity and obvious nature of these two concepts, corporations can get them mixed up, especially when it comes to projects that involve re-engineering business processes and implementing new technologies.

At the start of a typical project, one might define each of these two concepts as follows:

- *ends*: 'we'll generate increased shareholder value by significantly simplifying our business and reducing costs by 20 per cent'

- *means*: 'we'll do this by re-engineering selected business processes and implementing a new ERP system'.

So far, so good. However, over time, large transformation projects tend to forget the difference between the means and the ends. They can morph into a business unit in their own right, and then, as costs mount, time goes on, and people come and go on the team, a large transformation project will somehow evolve from being the 'means' to becoming the 'ends' in itself. The leader must therefore own the strategy over time and remember that the strategy isn't a destination or a solution. It's also not a problem that needs solving and settling. It's a journey that needs constant, uninterrupted leadership.

Said another way, these big projects evolve from the statement above towards a different view of things:

- *ends*: 'we'll generate increased shareholder value by significantly simplifying our business and reducing costs by 20 per cent' *becomes* 'we'll try to re-engineer our business processes, but failing that, we'll implement a new ERP system that tries to automate how we've always done things'

- *means*: 'we'll do this by re-engineering selected business processes and implementing a new ERP system' *becomes* 'we'll do this by putting in place ever greater governance, reviewing the project burn rate to ensure that we don't spend more than is absolutely necessary, and we'll bring in some new consultants to help us get out of this shit show as soon as possible'.

When you hear the language change from delivery of the original business benefits to delivery of technology, with example statements such as 'Let's just get something implemented, we'll get the benefits later', you'll know that there's now confusion between the 'means' and the 'ends'. Or, in other words, you've gone to Bunnings to buy a drill bit, and you can't remember why.

Clearly and succinctly describe the transformation

We all know what 'clear' means, and we recognise it when we see or hear it. We also recognise the opposite of clear, which might be opaque, complicated, confusing, complex or full of shit. A successful transformation strategy should be capable of being clearly communicated in a couple of sentences. If it can't be easily communicated, then odds are it's not clear.

An easy way to test whether it's clear is to fill in the blanks of the following sentences:

> Because of *[insert a, b and c (drivers of change)]*, our company is embarking on a transformation project to *[insert strategic objective (the ends)]*. We will do this by *[insert build/ acquire/implement methods (the means)]*. This critical work will be led by *[insert name (accountable executive)]*. We expect the project to take the next *[insert time period]*; however, we won't know the exact duration for certain until we finish *[insert phase]*. We will know that this program has been successful when *[insert measures of success (metrics)]*.

Let's test how this works with an example of a big endeavour (noting that it works with any project with a start and a finish).

Imagine an automaker trying to launch an electric vehicle capability:

Because of the emerging consumer trend towards electric vehicles, and our own aspirations for a cleaner and carbon neutral planet, *our company is embarking on a transformation project* to protect the future viability of the company via entry into the electric vehicle market. *We will do this by* developing, manufacturing and marketing a range of electric vehicles. *This critical work will be led by* 'Bill Smith'. *We expect the project to take the next* five years; *however, we won't know the exact duration for certain until we finish* our initial design phase over the next 12 months. *We will know that this program has been successful when* we are manufacturing and selling a minimum of 50 000 electric vehicles per month, we are steadily reducing the manufacture of internal combustion engine vehicles and we are decommissioning our legacy internal combustion engine production lines.

You can use this format for any project, big or small, if the components are clear.

You have to keep the essence — the *kokoro* — of the strategy simple so you can communicate it. The strategy must be able to be communicated in a clear and memorable manner that resonates with the people impacted. It should sound like a story or narrative that you can polish and deliver so that everyone 'gets it'. If you, as the leader, present your message and subsequently no-one remembers it, then that's on you. No matter how well you think you spoke, or the quality of your slides, or the quality of the venue, if the message isn't memorable then you've failed. Communication 101 is that the onus of ensuring the message is heard is on the speaker, *not* the receiver.

One of the best examples of a clear strategy and masterplan is Tesla. Notwithstanding Elon Musk's unusual foray into the purchase of Twitter, the achievements of Tesla remain massively impressive. So far, they've developed two masterplans.

Masterplan part 1 (released by Tesla in a shareholder letter from Elon Musk on 2 August 2006) was a simple bulleted list:

- Build sports car.
- Use that money to build an affordable car.
- Use that money to build an even more affordable car.
- While doing above, also provide zero emission electric power generation options.

Masterplan part deux (shared in another shareholder letter on 20 July 2016) was just as simple and read along the lines of:

- Create stunning solar roofs with seamlessly integrated battery storage.

- Expand the electric vehicle product line to address all major segments.

- Develop a self-driving capability that's 10× safer than manual via massive fleet learning.

- Enable your car to make money for you when you aren't using it.

The main point here is not whether Tesla has delivered on these points, but instead to illustrate how clear and effective it is when you can communicate the strategy in such a succinct and simple manner. Tesla was able to communicate the very essence of its strategy over a decade in under 80 words. Their plan was clear, measurable and concise, with absolutely nowhere to hide with regards to achievement. Each bullet point is easily measured as either green (achieved) or red (not achieved).

Communicate a compelling case for change

Once you've completed the initial consultation, you have the credibility and the knowledge to report back to the organisation what you've learned.

The easiest way to do this is using in-person sessions to get in front of as many people as possible. The objective is to show everyone that you have spent the time trying to understand what's going on, and sharing some of what you've been told. You do this so that the transformation effort is grounded in reality and you're perceived as connected and representative of it.

Don't forget to list all the people you've consulted. It's human nature that many in the audience will seek to find their own name on the list. They'll inevitably recall the meeting with you and go over what they told you in their mind. They'll listen for their feedback as you proceed, and when they hear it, they'll feel good for having shared it, and for you having heard it. Both build engagement.

This list is also a very visible reminder to everyone present that what you're about to share with them was not made up but is instead a reflection of what you've been told. And just quietly, because you've seen so many people, it's also an opportunity for you to take a little poetic licence and slip into the presentation some of your own intentions or hypotheses. After all, the consultation process has bought you some credibility and the right to speak your mind.

Now, how to communicate what you've heard.

First, even if the current state of the organisation deserves it, do not shit-can the past. Blunt messages just piss everyone off. The least engaged people will feel justified in being disengaged, and you'll risk losing the most engaged people, who are the very people you now need.

Instead, be honest — there's no need to sugar coat — but use nuance and turn your communication into a positive. The easiest way to do this is to use the approach of 'a strength, when overdone, becomes a weakness'. This allows you to acknowledge the positive things people are doing, while also being direct and clear about what needs to be addressed.

Call out the strengths that you've observed. People will see these things, take pride in their own involvement and recognise the strengths that they know to be true. Summarising them builds rapport with the audience and shows that you listen and are balanced. But also summarise the impact of a strength being overdone. It must be explicit, there must be real examples and you can go hard. If you do this well, you'll see members of the audience quietly nod in acknowledgement that not everything is perfect.

I've used this approach several times, including in new roles at NAB, and again at NSW Land Registry Services when I first stood in front of the newly privatised company soon after it had transitioned from a New South Wales government department to a private operator. The privatisation had been very unpopular with stakeholders, and many of the employees had enthusiastically joined demonstrations against privatisation outside the New South Wales Parliament House.

It's always important to be honest, but also not to annoy or alienate everyone while doing so. Table 4.1 gives some examples of when 'a strength overdone becomes a weakness'.

Table 4.1 when strengths become weaknesses

Some of our STRENGTHS ...	... when overdone can become WEAKNESSES
Having great pride in what has been achieved over many decades	*We may take criticism personally, get defensive, or not see the need to change and improve.*
Having a strong strategic view	*We can become strategic purists who don't deliver short-term improvements or will only deliver 'perfect' solutions.*
Being very cost conscious to hit our budgets	*We act like supermodels who only get out of bed if we can charge $10 000; we do business with ourselves, and transfer money back and forth between business units.*
Building consensus around ideas	*We can disperse individual accountability, find it hard to make decisions or undermine change initiatives — all of which makes change harder than it needs be.*
Sorting things out well in a crisis	*We celebrate the heroes who solve crises instead of those who work strategically to prevent crises developing in the first place; and we address the current problem again and again instead of fixing the root cause.*
Having the freedom to personalise our workspace	*No agreed-upon standards means that we've got some of the most untidy and cluttered office space I've ever seen.*
Concern for employee working arrangements	*We can be inefficient or allow employee costs like overtime and flex time to go unmanaged.*

Second, remember the golden rule of communication: it must be compelling and connect with the audience.

According to British psychologist Kevin Dutton — as quoted from the 2022 podcast titled 'The next big idea — Book bite #14: Are you a binary thinker in a complex world' — the rules are:

- 'frame a message so that it appeals to a person's self-interest
- construct an argument so that it makes people want to be part of something bigger than themselves
- put over your point of view so that people feel that it's right to support you, or follow you ...'

Let's pick apart each of Dutton's rules.

Appeal to people's self-interest

When engaging with the audience about the transformation to be undertaken, it's critical that you have sufficient empathy to understand how people might be feeling, to acknowledge this and to paint a picture of how people could benefit. This doesn't mean that you bullshit or tell lies.

Let's face it, in many transformations, there's likely to be an element of improvement and rationalisation that results in cost reduction, and that cost reduction is often driven by reducing the number of jobs. People know this. It cannot be glossed over, repackaged or dressed up as something that it is not.

Surprisingly, despite the fact that everyone always knows that jobs will be lost, I've seen leaders try to pretend that everything will be fine, and that no jobs will be lost. Claiming that no jobs will be lost is dishonest and wrong. This is not appealing to people's self-interest.

Instead, when launching a corporate transformation, you must acknowledge the disruption in the world, link this disruption to the local situation and lay out the case for change. While being honest about the certainty of job losses, you also need to explain:

- that all the jobs that remain will be safer because the company will be transforming to meet the challenges of its industry or market. It's likely that the optimists will assume that they won't be one of the people being made redundant, and so their self-interest will be addressed via potential job security

- all of the newly created roles and opportunities resulting from the transformation. When you do this, a large number of people, especially the most engaged individuals, will immediately start to think in terms of what those opportunities might mean for them. New roles, new skills and moving between different parts of the company are all opportunities driven by transformation and change. For those less engaged, by being honest about the certainty of job losses, you may even appeal to their self-interest by offering a redundancy cheque.

Make people want to be part of something bigger

Many people want to feel part of something bigger than themselves. When communicating the transformation, it's certainly easy to link the message to the importance of your company's survival or its desire to grow and succeed. Generally, people within an organisation will feel at least some connection to their employer and to the company's success. Pitching the need for transformation through the lens of safeguarding, growing or improving the company can be a powerful force.

It might also be possible to link the transformation to the very essence or purpose of the company and its success in the face of change and disruption.

Purpose has always been powerful, and it's becoming even more so.

In a 1970 essay for *The New York Times* titled 'A Friedman doctrine: The social responsibility of business is to increase its profits', Milton Friedman introduced the hypothesis that businesses that exist only to create profits for their shareholders seem out of touch with commercial reality. While this is certainly important — in that it's impossible for unprofitable companies to be purposeful or useful for long — profits are only part of the equation. Many people are not inspired by shareholder value. Instead, they want to get out of bed in the morning and feel inspired to create something better for society, to help people or to make the world a better place. This all complements the generation of profit.

According to Harvard Business School Professor Ranjay Gulati (from his book *Deep purpose: The heart and soul of high performance companies*),

> *Purpose is a unifying statement of the commercial and social problems a business intends to profitably solve for its stakeholders. This statement encompasses goals and duties, and it succinctly communicates what a business is all about and who it's intended to benefit.*

Find a way to link your transformation message to something big.

Make people feel that it's right to back you

Most people can sense when a message is honest, clear and realistic. Likewise, they can tell when someone is being shifty, dishonest or not levelling with them.

This is why it's important to:

- build credibility with the audience via what you do rather than only what you say. As mentioned earlier in the chapter (in the section 'Do the work: personal commitment of the leader'), it's important that you get out and consult people so that you know what's going on. Make it clear who you have spoken with. Demonstrate an understanding of what's going on and own the message. While they may not all like you, and may even resent your arrival or approach, people will at least acknowledge the work you've done

- be honest about the disruption and challenges the company is facing. No-one likes being patronised or spoken down to about the changes that are happening in the world. Tell it like it is, treat people like adults and level with them. They may not like the message, but they'll appreciate the honesty and authenticity

- communicate the transformation in terms of what's best for the company. Explain how it will improve the organisation and make it better suited to a changing world, or more able to deliver its purpose, or to be more financially successful so it can invest in better products and services that meet the needs of its customers.

Get up in front of everyone, be your authentic self and deliver an honest message. Never bullshit.

3. Build the team: get the right people

The first thing one does to evaluate the wisdom of the ruler is to examine the men that he has around him; and when they are capable and faithful one can always consider him wise, for he has known how to recognise their ability and to keep them loyal; but when they are otherwise one can always form a low impression of him, for the first error he makes is made in his choice of advisors.

Niccolò Machiavelli

At its very essence, transformation is about getting the right people, getting them aligned around the transformation objectives, and then using their skills, energies and temperament to take the entire organisation on a journey. Transformation should leave the existing status quo in its wake and introduce a new way of being that's measurably different and better.

As the leader of the transformation, it's your job to select the right people and to get them aligned. When selecting your team, you should be aware of a few elements:

- we are judged by the company we keep
- look for temperament and skills
- not every kid gets a prize.

To help in managing these dynamics, this section offers several tips for evaluating people. It also introduces some examples of the positive corporate characters I've met along my career journey so far, together with some of the psychopaths and narcissists that inhabit some companies.

First, let's address these three elements.

We are judged by the company we keep

Our parents were right: we are judged by the company we keep. As leaders, let's agree that we are continually assessed on the quality (skills, capabilities and character) of the people on our team, especially our direct reports.

Quite simply, the people you select will make or break the transformation.

Ideally, you'll select people with hard and soft skills: they have the intellect and experience to make sound business decisions to drive the transformation forward, and the awareness, empathy and humility to take people on the journey and to be personally curious to find better ways to do things.

Professor Gulati described a paradox via the simultaneous holding of different positions in transformational leadership. Gulati described leaders as having to balance being decisive and flexible; realistic and optimistic; and directive and empowering.

Above all, they must continually model the behaviours and transformation mindset necessary to actually get things done, and equally, believe in the objectives of the transformation that's being undertaken.

A great way to assess whether a company is truly behind its own transformation effort is to look at who is assigned to it. Be in absolutely no doubt that people across the company will gauge the seriousness of the transformation program, together with its probability of success, by looking at who is assigned to lead and be involved in it.

In my experience there are generally three types of people sent into the transformation effort:

- *The talented*: the companies most serious about transformation put their best people on it. You should ask your executives for the names of the one or two people who they can least do without in their business, and then assign them to the project (if they have a passion and ambition for the company and its transformation, and some ability in performance improvement and project management).

- *The new recruit*: this is that enthusiastic new person recruited because of their special skills relevant to the transformation. It might be their industry experience (they've done a similar project for a direct competitor) or their technology or project management skills. They can quickly complement and build out the project team to help build momentum — however, they shouldn't be relied on exclusively. They must be supported and blended in with the internal talent already assigned. Without this balance, the project will be disconnected from the actual company and appear to be doing the project to the company rather than with the company.

- *The journey(wo)man*: I've seen many companies assign a person to a transformation project who is likeable, only mildly competent, but knows the company well because at some point long in their past they had a more senior role than they actually do now. You know the type: they've been around a million years, they've been gradually restructured further and further down the food chain from their past peak, and they may even have a live redundancy letter in their shirt pocket. They refuse to resign and hope to inhabit the corporate or group office, which has become some kind of 'elephant graveyard' where those people who once had big jobs in the past go to die. However, their greatest superpower is that they're available to start now. Right now. As in immediately. That's because their current boss is always willing to let them go at short notice. As you can imagine, transformation programs led or staffed with these people are not off to a good start.

To be successful, ensure that you resource your transformation project with lots of talented people complemented by some new recruits. Avoid the journey(wo)men. They may be available, but there's a reason for this. A transformation project resourced primarily by the people who are most available is not off to a good start and is unlikely to deliver the outcomes required or desired.

Look for *temperament* and *skills*

A simple model useful for assessing who should lead and be on a transformation project is based on two dimensions, each of which represents a broad spectrum covering: temperament and skills.

Temperament, or character, is typically innate. Character traits include attributes such as courage, integrity and honesty at the positive end of the spectrum; and authoritarianism, dishonesty and cowardliness at the other end. By the time someone comes to work in your company, odds are on that they're fully 'baked' as humans, and these attributes are deeply set within their personality. These attributes are representative of who they are and form the lens and sacred beliefs and behaviours through which they view the world. It's a very safe bet to assume that they're unlikely to change.

Corporations are filled with every kind of person with every kind of attribute. Some attributes are more suitable to successfully leading and driving transformation than others. What's clear is that temperament is critical. When it comes to transformation, 'whether someone is the "right person" has more to do with character traits and innate capabilities than with specific knowledge, background and skills', as Jim Collins writes in his book *Good to great*.

Skills, by contrast, are not fixed. You can — if open and motivated — learn new skills throughout your life. Within the corporate world, we know that careers typically commence with a narrow set of skills, generally grounded in an undergraduate degree, and then develop over time based on the experiences, challenges and environments encountered. These skills are obviously massively diverse and driven by the myriad combinations of industries, companies, operations and functions in which people work. This is obvious.

What's also obvious is that some skills lend themselves to involvement in transformation more than others. For example, a chief economist in a government department may be expert at leveraging their considerable skills to determine what's happening in the world, and the emergence of disruptive factors based on real life data. Equally, they may not be as skilled at converting this insight into a strategy, or at pulling the right levers to effect change across a corporation.

There's no perfect position on either of these dimensions, but rather, there are attributes that make someone more or less suited to leading and participating in transformation. Tables 4.2 and 4.3 list some of these attributes.

Table 4.2   transformation temperament

Less suitable	More suitable
Closed and fixed	Open and curious
Rigid and authoritarian	Flexible and empowering
Careerist, ambitious for self	Team player, ambitious for the cause
Arrogant and divisive	Humble and inclusive
Ambivalent about results	Highly driven to achieve results
Unfocused	Highly focused

Table 4.3   transformation skills

Less suitable	More suitable
Predominantly BAU experience	Predominantly business change experience
Career experience limited to single industry	Broad industry experience
Career experience limited to single function	Broad functional experience
Line management experience	Project management experience

It's unlikely that potential candidates will fit neatly at either end of the spectrum on every dimension. That's not the point. This model is only intended to promote thought, discussion and debate about who should play a leading role in the transformation effort. Too often, participants are selected based on the fact that they have deep 'BAU' industry or functional expertise in the area or function being transformed, or worse, based on their relative seniority.

Tables 4.2 and 4.3 show how consideration of potential transformation leaders against these two dimensions should help identify those most suitable by virtue of their temperament and their skills.

At the end of the day, when it comes to temperament, if you want to successfully drive and ultimately deliver transformation, you need to ensure that you appoint people who are best suited to the dynamic nature and ambiguity of a large-scale project. It's that simple and that difficult.

As already discussed, leading and managing transformation is different from running BAU activities with all of the associated and existing processes, technologies, structures and metrics. People respond to transformation objectives and the ambiguity associated with them in either of two ways: they are suited to it, or they are not.

At the most basic level, those who are suited to it are curious, ambitious, urgent, focused and sufficiently self-confident to deal with ambiguity and intellectually navigate to the heart of the matter. They also know when to let go and try something else if things aren't working. They're engaged, competent and they can get shit done. They quickly appreciate the strategy and overall objectives (the 'what' and the 'why') and let their imagination and energies start to shape the 'how'. They have a bias for action and realise that a good plan executed with energy today, is better than a perfect plan next week. They get at it.

Broadly, those temperaments that are not suited (rather than resistant, as described earlier) to the ambiguity associated with transformation fall into two broad categories:

- the 'Care Free': those who wait to be told what to do
- the 'Authoritarians': those who can't wait to tell everyone else what to do.

The 'Care Free' is that breezy and cheerful person who's happy to do whatever you ask of them. They'll follow procedures, complete an entire checklist or tick off every task on the 'to-do' list. The problem is that they don't do any of these things until directly asked. You've probably seen one of these people in a restaurant. They seem magically oblivious to someone reaching awkwardly across the table to grab the salt-shaker, even though it's within an inch of their own hand. They'll happily pass the salt, but only if you ask them directly. By name. With a written request via email. Keep them off the team unless you want to re-introduce carbon paper memos and make every request in triplicate.

By contrast, the 'Authoritarian' is that bossy person who thinks they're at their best and most inspirational when telling others what to do. They think the role of a leader is to tell everyone else on their team, their company, or indeed their country, what do to in every circumstance. No-one can do things quite as well as they can, and they must micro-manage every element of everyone's job. They do this because they know deep down that no-one except themselves can be trusted. The only one they don't tell what to do is their boss, because their respect for hierarchy, formality and rules makes them the ultimate conservative unwilling to imagine a better way of doing things, let alone implement one. Keep them off your team for the sanity of yourself and everyone else.

Your role as the leader is to choose and field the best team. As Peter Drucker (in his book *The effective executive*) reminds us,

> *It is the duty of the executive to ruthlessly remove anyone — and especially any manager — who consistently fails to perform with high distinction. To let such a man stay on corrupts the others. It is grossly unfair to the whole organisation. It is grossly unfair to his subordinates who are deprived by their superior's inadequacy of opportunities for achievement and recognition. Above all, it is senseless cruelty to the man himself. He knows he is inadequate whether he admits it to himself or not.*

In summary, when forming your transformation team, you need to seek out and identify those who are more naturally suited to it, while avoiding or removing those who have upward delegation tendencies, are too authoritarian or are simply not up for it. This will make your life much easier and give the transformation the greatest chance of success.

Not every kid gets a prize

I acknowledge that it's *my* generation who invented the award of ribbons to children for coming eighth in the school running race and seems to have decided via a United Nations special resolution that every five-year-old kid playing 'pass the parcel' at a birthday party had to get a prize.

I remember hosting my son's fifth birthday and getting ready to play all the various kids' games. Pass the parcel was a natural choice. A simple game in which a small present is wrapped in paper and then wrapped in multiple layers of newspaper. To play the game, kids sit in a circle, the music plays and when it stops, someone unwraps one layer of paper, until after several rounds, some kid triumphantly wins the final present. Great.

Not so fast. Apparently, things had evolved significantly since I was a kid, because now, instead of one present at the very end — for whoever was randomly lucky enough to be holding the final parcel — there had to be a present under every layer of wrapping, and it was like a Mensa test to not only remember which kids had already had a turn at unwrapping, but also, which kid had already won a prize in any of the earlier party games. Every kid had to win at least something.

As you know, in corporate life there are winners and losers: not every kid wins a prize.

Let's say you've just been appointed the CEO or the executive leader of a major transformation. You no doubt celebrate, you're excited and you get ready for the new role, because you want to make a positive impact and build strong momentum in your first 90 days (see chapter 5).

And of course, everyone in the new organisation — especially the senior cadre of executive leaders — is over the moon with your appointment: they're excited, they sincerely believe that you were the best choice, that you'll be far better than anyone else they know, and frankly, they simply cannot wait for your start date. In fact, they wish you were starting tomorrow: 'Let's get on with this transformation.'

Yeah, right. Absolute bullshit.

As you enter the new role as the transformation leader (because you got to peel off the last wrapper and open the last parcel), you need to be aware of the context in which you were appointed. You may be a new CEO (as in new to the organisation) or you may have been selected among some former colleagues to lead the transformation within a company you already worked in. In both cases, you need to be aware of the feelings of others, who else might have been in the running for the role, and the motivations, resentments and impacts that all of this could (probably) unleash.

That's not to say that no-one will be excited at your entry. There will be people who are realistic and see someone new to the organisation injecting new perspectives and ideas as good. Alternatively, if it's an internal appointment, some of your colleagues may be sincerely and authentically excited for you because they've seen your capabilities and qualities, they know you as a person and they think you'll take the organisation forward.

The point here is that it's unreasonable for you to expect that *everyone* is going to be excited and supportive. Not everyone will get a prize as a result of you getting your new job: there will inevitably be winners and losers. To assume otherwise would be naïve.

Additionally, if you are truly committed to transformation, then it's inevitable that some managers and employees will be better off and some will be worse off. Beware of any corporate initiative (and especially a public policy launch by a politician) that is launched with a simultaneous announcement that no-one will be worse off. As if. We all know instinctively that an initiative or policy is dead before it starts if it promises this. For any truly material or significant change to an organisation, there has to be at least someone made worse off. There have to be winners and losers — otherwise it's not called 'transformation' it's called 'tweaking'.

As the leader, it's your job to be discerning and ensure that, hopefully, the right people are better off, and the right people are worse off. Or if good people are negatively impacted, then they're treated in an honourable and civilised way (see section on managing redundancies on page 222).

So, regardless of whether you're new to the organisation or not, you need to tread carefully and take some time to understand the current landscape and truly evaluate people. Above all, continue to treat everyone with empathy and respect, remembering this timeless advice from Machiavelli: 'And anyone who believes that new benefits make men of high station forget old injuries is deceiving himself.'

You should also keep in mind that there are two ways that 'injuries' can be inflicted, and you need to be aware of both of them. Injuries occur:

- *before* you even arrive in your role, and they're inflicted — or certainly that's the view of the recipient — by whoever appointed you to your role, and by so doing, overlooked an incumbent or another executive who coveted your new role

- *after* you arrive in your new role, and they're inflicted by you on the recipient based on how you treat the senior people around you, the actions you take and the way you communicate.

Injuries inflicted by others

In these cases, the damage is done before you arrive. Someone internal to the company or division may have wanted the role that you've been given, but for whatever reason, the decision maker went with you.

If poorly managed during the selection, and then afterwards upon your entry, this has the potential to create an 'injury' in the mind of the unsuccessful candidate. Very real human emotions such as disappointment, disbelief, jealousy, rage, depression and disengagement can all arise in people when they miss out on the job they covet. These emotions might be nonexistent (great, but unlikely), fleeting (hopefully/probably) or they might burrow in and make themselves right at home in the mind of the aggrieved executive (disastrous).

While this type of injury is not your fault, it certainly is your problem, because left unmanaged, the executive with the disastrous combination of professional jealousy, disappointment or frustration can easily become resistant and disruptive to the transformation agenda, and 'white ant' you (see the section 'Corporate characters: the good, the bad and the psychopaths' below) and your agenda.

I've spoken to many people who've been appointed to CEO and senior executive roles and had to form new teams, and always, literally always, I've heard them express regret for not taking immediate or early action on the inherited 'white ant' in their team. 'I'm really glad that I let [*insert name of 'white ant'*] stay on my executive team to obstruct and erode the transformation project,' said no-one ever.

Having said that, we all love tales of redemption. Who hasn't sat watching a movie and then cheered when the evil protagonist finally acknowledges their negative ways, owns it and then moves on to sunlit pastures to do good. It's a great thing when someone admits that they were wrong, puts things down by the side of the road and gets back into gear. While undoubtedly great, it's also exceedingly rare.

There's no excuse for not dealing with the 'white ant' because:

- everyone in and around the executive team typically knows that [*insert name of white ant*] is in fact eating the foundations, or is likely to
- if you leave them in place, everyone will perceive you as being indecisive and weak, or at best, naïve and 'nice'
- by leaving them in situ, you're saying that they, as an individual, are more important than the collective organisation and the pressing need to transform and address the disruptive forces it faces.

None of these are good reasons, and all put the success of the transformation at risk. It's therefore likely that you'll have to take action to ensure you have the right team in place to drive the change required. And as Machiavelli references, no amount of future reward or recognition is likely to make good on the injury that the recipient feels has been heaped on them. The white ant simply has to go.

Injuries inflicted by you

You're in a hurry, you've come into your new role, you've got lots of ideas and you're already drawing some clear conclusions. You've got to get everything ramped up, and you can see what needs to be done in a way that others can't. It's busy, there's not enough hours in the day and pressure is building for results.

Take a breath and remember that we've all sat in the shade of trees we didn't plant, drunk from wells we didn't dig, and been warmed by fires we didn't light. Be respectful, because this is the time you can inadvertently create an unnecessary injury in the minds of the very people you need to help drive the transformation.

A casual word, lack of care, a sense of arrogance or dismissal can all reduce the engagement of the executives who will be needed to deliver the transformation. You might not give them the recognition they feel they deserve, you might unwind their pet project, fire their best corporate friend or move a part of their role to someone else and reduce their sense of prestige or power. There are a million ways that you can potentially piss someone off.

This doesn't mean that you shouldn't do any of these things. It merely means that you do them carefully, and give due consideration to the impact that they'll have across the executive team and each individual. You just need to be aware that your actions could give rise to friction and an unexpected reaction, and this could grow into a sense of injury or disengagement from your agenda. And this lack of engagement could become resentment and resistance as you try to lead the transformation.

Tips for evaluating people

Of all the manifestations of power, restraint impresses men most.

**Thucydides (c. 460–400 BCE),
Athenian historian and general**

Transformation requires a continual constructive challenge of everything to do with the business and the program to adjust the effort and to deliver the best possible outcome. Filling your executive transformation team with 'yes-people' or sycophants is a sure-fire way to stuff it up right from the start.

So, how should you evaluate people when the business world is filled with such fascinating and diverse characters?

As you come into a new transformational leadership role, it's easy to make snap decisions about the executive team who report to you. You watch what people say and do, you rely on first impressions and you ask the opinions of others.

Remember that even the senior people you meet may be nervous or off their game as you come into the team. Not everyone is extroverted and/or confident in expressing themselves to their new boss, and it's easy to mistake the emotions and style of people until you get to know them. It's important to collect actual empirical evidence of how they think, what they deliver and how they behave.

It's useful to assess people across several dimensions. For example:

- Are they demonstrably proud of, and ambitious for, the company?
- Do they demonstrate basic professional substance and competence?
- Can they actually get something done?
- Do they display good behaviours/work well with colleagues?
- Can you work with them and help them develop?
- For executive roles: do they enjoy the confidence of the board?

As you come into your new role, a very easy way to evaluate the existing team using these questions is to create table 4.4 and then add handwritten notes for each executive. Keep it close to hand and fill it in after you observe each executive in action. Use facts and empirical evidence. Watch how they respond to ambiguity, or how they treat their colleagues and guests to the executive team. What have they achieved in the company? What work do they have underway, and how is it going? You'll be surprised at the level of real insight you can gather in a very short time.

Table 4.4 first 90 days executive assessment sheet

Do they exhibit pride and ambition for the company?	Do they have professional substance and competence?	Do they get things done?
Observations	Observations	Facts and evidence
-	-	-
-	-	-
-	-	-
Do they work well with colleagues (behaviours)?	**Can I work with them and help them develop?**	**Do they enjoy the confidence of the Board?**
Observations	Gut feel and instinct	Facts and evidence
-	-	-
-	-	-
-	-	-

While it's important to give due process, let's also acknowledge that sometimes it's appropriate to make snap decisions because someone is clearly an absolute superstar, or equally, it's clear that they're a toxic corporate psychopath, set to undermine the project as soon as they can.

Corporate characters: the good, the bad and the psychopaths

In the opening line of *Anna Karenina*, Leo Tolstoy writes, 'Happy families are all alike; every unhappy family is unhappy in its own way.'

The same appears true with executive and transformation teams.

I've been lucky to work on some great teams, with extremely positive role models who have been patient, encouraging and exceptionally supportive of me. The team dynamics of great teams have all been similar. The team members have been somewhat alike, in that they were intelligent, personable, passionate and ambitious for the success of their company, while simultaneously diverse of background, gender, sexual orientation and perspective, and at once sensitive to each other's needs *and* constructively challenging and provocative with regard to overall performance.

We've now looked at the importance of temperament and skills, and some tips for evaluating people's suitability to be on a transformation team. This next section brings to life many of the personalities who make a positive contribution to a transformation, or by contrast are likely to sabotage (whether directly or indirectly) the transformation effort, or even kill it dead in its tracks.

Your job as the CEO or leader of the transformation program is to choose the strongest team possible with regard to temperament and skills. In the end, it's pretty simple: select more people with positive executive traits and fewer people who exhibit negative traits.

Positive executive personalities

You already know these people. I suspect that these are the people who you too have noticed in your career in different companies, teams and circumstances. As Tolstoy referenced, the positive and constructive qualities of these people are probably very much alike. They're adept at understanding the corporate context in which they're working, drawing on the deep well of experience and leadership styles they've developed, and providing the right leadership at the right time. These positive corporate characters include:

- *the 'Nike'* are excellent at telling their people the 'what' and the 'why', and then getting the hell out of their way so they can just do it. Your people should be careful what they wish for because the Nike will give them all the rope they want, and then expect results

- *the 'plastic man/elastigirl'* is that person who is always looking to give their people stretch. They continually take them out of their comfort zone and help them realise that they can do far more than they ever thought possible

- *the 'coach'* does, well, what the label suggests — they coach. They give their people honest feedback, they tell it as it is and give them advice and wise counsel, all with the goal of making them better. They're at once tough, uncompromising and they set high standards, while simultaneously being caring and supportive

- *the 'sensei'* just knows stuff: they've seen it all before, and they've walked down the path your team aspire to be on. They're always prepared to share their knowledge and experience freely and constructively

- *the 'Zen master'* is unflappable. No matter what happens they remain calm, goal focused, human and empathetic. They ask their people questions so they can figure it out, instead of telling them stuff. Their quiet, insightful questions are so much more powerful than someone else shouting answers

- *the 'yoga teacher'* is endlessly flexible and is prepared to change or adapt to achieve the objective. They'll find or make a way, all while remaining grounded, composed and caring

- *the 'fire chief'* is always ready to extend a ladder. They make it a point to develop and pull their people up through the organisation and help get the members of their team promoted

- *the 'witness'* is that person who always sticks to the facts. No gossip, no 'he said' or 'she said', only the facts. And they use the facts to make good decisions, ask good questions, hold their people accountable and importantly, to assign credit to others

- *the 'air traffic controller'* understands that ambition for the company and the transformation comes with risk, and they're prepared to ensure there's a safe — but demanding — environment to get big things done. They look after their people when things get tough and provide solid air cover

- *the 'admiral'* ensures that all boats make it to shore. They create a collegiate team environment where everyone knows their role, are supportive of one another, and all appreciate what needs to be done to successfully navigate all executives and business units safely home to their destination

- *the 'Red Bull'* understands workloads and tough deadlines and is prepared to turn up and help at all hours, and, with Red Bull cans in hand, to provide leadership, energy and sustenance to their team

- *the 'cricketer'* is always prepared to go in to bat for their team: their ideas, project, or pay rise. Endlessly supportive, they recognise value and are prepared to put their money (or at least their budget) where their mouth is

- *the 'concierge'* makes everyone feel welcome. They greet everyone and welcome them to the meeting without regard to seniority or hierarchy and are determined to create an environment where the best ideas flow.

Negative executive personalities

At the other end of the spectrum are the complete narcissists and psychopaths who are unpredictable and damaging as they rampage through the organisation creating completely toxic corporate cultures. Unlike the positive characters who are somewhat alike, each of these psychopaths is negative in their own distinct way. Not surprisingly, these characters are the easiest to recall, the most humorous to observe, the most interesting to describe and absolutely *the* worst to work with or for. I suspect that you've already met several of them so far in your career, and you've maybe even left your job or company because of one of them. (Yes, it's true: people do indeed leave their managers, not their companies.)

The sooner you can identify these psychopaths and get them working for your competitor, the better.

The bad and the ugly

As mentioned earlier, as you enter the organisation, or commence a transformation, you may need to think a little differently, and this new perspective should extend to the people you choose to surround yourself with. Different lenses you can use to check whether people are the right fit for your executive team, or to lead your transformation, include:

- humility and curiosity
- decisiveness and willingness to take accountability
- team player and work-with-ability
- general executive competence.

With that said, let's now introduce some characters from each of these four lenses (and let me 'fess up: they're based on real people, and if we ever get a chance to chat over a beer, well, I'd be happy to elaborate).

(A lack of) Humility and curiosity

Okay, let's start with those people who in their own mind are full of ideas, constructive criticisms, strategies and gems of knowledge, but really, are seen by others as being full of, well, you know what I mean.

- *The 'you're all shit'* is that new executive who thinks everyone doing the work is, well, shit. Facts and results don't distract them, it's all instinct. They have sensitive antennae, and they just know stuff. No one around them is clever, hardworking or committed. Except them. And maybe the 'Smithers' (see below) they brought along with them.

- *The 'thank God I'm here'* is closely related to the 'you're all shit' but with a bigger ego. And more experience. You know the type: they claim to have fought and died in three world wars and seen and done more in their careers than anyone in the history of careers. And it's lucky for you, the division, the company and in fact the country, that they've arrived.

- *The 'fundamentalist'* believes that they're fundamentally right and that you are fundamentally wrong. Their beliefs are not typically based on facts, so no weight of facts will change their mind.

- *The 'iceberg tip'* is that person who knows a little, or has heard of, just about everything, and can opine at length on it all. But not enough to either make sense or make a difference. They can't get anything done despite their strong opinions. In a nod to Paul Keating's famous characterisation, they're 'all tip, and no iceberg'.

- *The 'Nostradamus'* knows definitively what will happen in the future. They lean back in their chair, and with an air of superiority and trumped-up gravitas, share their wisdom. 'Mark my words, here [insert subject/event] is what will happen.' Okay. Let's write that down and put it on a poster in the board room, and we can all come back to it in a couple of months to see how things played out.

(No) Decisiveness and willingness to take accountability

Then there are those people who seem to thrive and succeed by not putting their name to anything. They cruise through the corporate year determined to go around, above and beneath any obstacle without addressing it, and to leave no wake in their path. You can't see what they've done or what they've stood for. They are literally Teflon-covered executives off whom slide the everyday details of commitments, milestones, decisions and agreements.

- *The 'statesman'* is not gender specific but is that annoying executive who lets everyone speak first on a topic, because they don't have any clue. Instead of being honest about it, they then try to sum up and present their wisdom to the group. They're exasperating when they also have 'thief' and 'plagiarist' tendencies (see below).

- *The 'brand manager'* views every decision, interaction and role through the lens of their own personal brand. Nothing — and I mean nothing — is allowed to negatively impact people's perceptions of them. When required, the company and its shareholders, customers, suppliers, employees and their colleagues will all be willingly sacrificed on the altar of their personal brand.

- The *'Waylon Smithers'* agrees with their boss, regardless of topic. 'Yes, yes, Mr Burns, 2 + 2 can sometimes equal 5, under the right circumstances.' More common at bonus time, the boss-praise can reach stratospheric levels. The rise of the 'Smithers' sycophant typically plateaus when their boss is promoted, fired or moved, because everyone else knows that they're both useless and a suck-up.

- The *'Switzerland'* is the executive who stays neutral and won't take a position except to maintain their existing wealth and borders within the organisation. Anything can happen around them with no effect but stray into their area or responsibility and they come out swinging.

- The *'down the road'* is that person — closely related to the Switzerland — who won't make a decision that could put them at professional risk. Despite the many reports from the many different management consulting firms that have already studied the problem, there's just not enough data to make a decision. So, unfortunately, we're going to have to do another study. With another consultant.

- The *'Chicken Little'* is that executive who, when faced with stress or an unexpected situation, immediately jumps to the worst possible conclusion. In the face of a business threat or ambiguity, they insist on modelling zero revenue, standing down staff and cutting costs — all before morning tea. The sky is literally falling, or about to fall, at every team meeting. They were especially prevalent during the early days of COVID-19.

- The *'someone just told me'* is that overly credulous person who vehemently believes the last thing they heard or read. It doesn't matter how outlandish or unsuitable it might be for their own organisation — if they just heard it, it must be true. Even better if they read it in the *Qantas* in-flight magazine. Deadly to reasonable decision making when coupled with *'tourist'* tendencies (see page 174) and they're just back from a trip to Silicon Valley.

- *The 'hill charger'* pursues a new idea every day. Don't worry about yesterday's unfinished idea: move on and stop being pessimistic. These people are all activity, no progress.

- The *'lolly shop'* is closely related to the 'hill charger' and is like the proverbial unsupervised kid in a lolly shop. They just want to shove every new idea down the company's throat as quickly as they can.

- *The 'look over there'* is an expert at deflection. When faced with inconvenient truths, their solution is to simply quote different 'facts' that move the conversation away from the subject at hand, while simultaneously presenting themselves in the best possible light.

- *The 'novelist'* makes the 'look over there' seem pedestrian, because when confronted by inconvenient facts, they simply make shit up.

- The *'tonight's the night'* is deadly when combined with 'lolly shop' tendencies. This is the executive who operates with an idea-generating stream of consciousness, all of which must be completed and on their desk by first thing tomorrow morning, so they can eventually look at it the week after next.

- *The 'late to the party'* is that executive who waxes lyrical on the latest business topic and why the company should adopt it. They make a compelling case for the why, what and how. Except the company has already adopted it. Years ago.

- *The 'fabric softener'* seems to be growing in numbers. This is the person who has to remove the hard edges of decisions and messages by softening and diluting. They believe that it's not right to 'tell'; you have to 'guide'. Instead of saying 'you're fired' they're more likely to ask, 'Do you think it's necessary for you to come in to work tomorrow?'

- *The 'snout in the trough'* is that executive who likes the finer things in life and is convinced that the company was put there to pay for them. Regular fine dining, good wine, team dinners, chauffeur car home and that's before the offsites. You just think and perform so much better when you helicopter in to exclusive and remote island resorts, and sleep on thousand thread count cotton sheets.

(Is not a) Team player and easy to work with

Although you might feel exasperated and exhausted doing so, you can generally get on with those executives who lack humility and curiosity, or who are determined to kick every decision down the road. By contrast, this next set of people are definitely not the kind that you'd want to be stranded on a desert island with. They are prickly, self-satisfied and delusional, and cannot possibly believe that the agreed rules, social norms and human etiquette of society (let alone the company) apply to them too.

- The *'white ant'* is that special executive who, having missed out on the top role in the organisation that they claim to love, is now prepared to eat its very foundations if that's what it takes to prove that they should have got the job. Deadly threatening to a transformation, the only thing that stops them is a dose of pesticide. They illustrate the point that sometimes, to be successful at change management, you have to change the management.

- The *'chameleon'* is that executive who is perfect at blending in with those equal to or above them in the corporate jungle, but simultaneously direct their deadly carnivorous behaviours to anyone below them. They are renowned for kissing upwards and kicking downwards and will continually change their colours to impress the boss.

- The *'Frank Sinatra'* cannot help but do things their way. It doesn't matter what was agreed in the meeting: the minute they step outside it's as though they're in a Tokyo karaoke parlour and channelling 'old blue eyes'.

- The *'you wouldn't understand'* is typically an engineer or technologist, but sometimes an economist or markets trader, who is so full of the complexities of their own knowledge that they just know us mere mortals simply won't get it. It's an unfortunate fact that most are male, and if knowledge is power then they see themselves as god … or at least an unaccountable monarch.

- *The 'thief'* seems to increase in numbers, the more senior the meeting. If the 'thief' had an original idea or thought it would blow their head clean off their shoulders to roll across the conference table. They have risen through the ranks by stealing the ideas of others and presenting them as their own. Bullshit artist credit-stealers.

- *The 'plagiarist'* is sometimes mistaken for the 'thief', but they're slightly different. They take someone else's idea and repackage it, dressing it up and changing its colour, before they finally present it as their own. Just as bad.

- *The 'assassin'* is especially prevalent at human resources round tables when the performance of direct reports of colleagues is discussed. They'll attack each lower level manager in turn, with each becoming the brunt of an unwarranted attack. Of course, all of their own direct reports wear capes, and underpants on the outside, because they're superheroes beyond reproach.

- *The 'Grenadier Guard'* is that person who is absolutely blank and humourless. If they smiled, their face would crack. Whether the news is good or bad, or the person they're talking to is young or old, senior or new, they treat them all with equal equanimity and the same lack of passion, humour or humanity. Absolutely deadly when encountered in the long silence of a lift between floors. Lighten up mate, no-one just died.

- *The 'Dale dug a hole'* (inspired by the movie *The Castle*) is that executive who can craft a compelling story about even the smallest achievement. Today the intranet, tomorrow the AFR, and hopefully next week a Harvard Business School case study. Nothing is too small to be communicated, celebrated and held out as a global benchmark. Always motivated for more publicity, they'd go to the opening of an envelope if it gave them more coverage on social media.

- The *'hollow log'* is that executive who hoards the company's resources for a rainy day. They're the kind of person who has 'Office of the (x)' on their stationery, and that particular office is full of assistants, entourage, heavy spans and layers, and plenty of fat in their operating budget. They only just make their plan each year regardless of what's happening in the outside world, and their division is full of bullshit jobs.

- The *'Sgt Major'* turns every subject into a parade so that they can stand in front of it. Every conversation is gently shepherded back to their core expertise so they can monopolise the meeting. Please, for all our sakes, shut up and listen for once.

- The *'tourist'* is that executive who is almost never at home. There's always another study tour to be had. Europe is good, India not bad, but Silicon Valley remains the gold standard, especially if it includes meeting some of the venture capital firms that financed Uber or 'Clash of Clans'. No matter that nothing ever changes in their company or division as a result of their trip, except that they return to Australia a newly converted religious zealot (more on this next). And we all know there's no fanatic like the convert.

- The *'religious zealot'* is that person we've all seen who simply cannot contemplate using a sentence that doesn't contain the latest buzz words. In years past they'd argue the toss between KPIs and KRAs or TQM and Six Sigma with religious fervour … nowadays, they can't finish a sentence without including 'agile' or 'tribe'. They sincerely believe that if they talk about it enough, it will miraculously happen. Complete tossers.

(Poor) Executive competence

When I was leaving university, I just naïvely assumed that all senior executives must be amazing in order to justify their seniority in the corporate landscape. Now, some 30 years later, I'm a little more realistic. I now know that there's a special breed of senior executives who represent an amazing arbitrage opportunity. By that I mean that the opportunity to buy them for what you think they're worth, and then subsequently sell them for what they think they're worth, represents a considerable positive financial spread. Or in other words, there is a group of executives who are simply not that competent.

- The 'journalist' can report on any issue no matter how esoteric and can't help themselves from sharing stories and anecdotes at every meeting, regardless of whether they're relevant, true or of any value whatsoever.

- The 'late bloomer' simply cannot turn up on time. They're always late. They sit down, unpack their mobile, then their laptop, power cord, then mouse. They then plug in said mouse, duck under the desk to plug in the cord, and 10 minutes after arrival they're ready to roll, just as the meeting is coming to an end. Turn up on time and bring an iPad for fuck's sake.

- The 'slogger' is that executive who is just always so busy. Simply run off their feet, with never enough time. You know the type: despite claims of being flat out, they don't actually get much done, and they can somehow cram a week's worth of normal deliverables into a month. Stop complaining and get something done.

- The 'juggler' is always on the laptop, iPad and iPhone at once, while simultaneously talking *and* listening. They want to give the impression of being highly engaged and clever, when really they're just on the smh.com.au website looking at share prices.

- The 'whiteboard' is that especially artistic executive who cannot communicate without a whiteboard and coloured markers. Everything in the company, the industry and indeed life, can be expressed as geometric shapes. Boxes, circles and triangles are great, but freehand 3D cubes and hexagons impress the most. Sometimes (rarely) they'll even stop talking to the whiteboard, turn around and actually look at you.

- The 'exhausted' sits in the corner of the meeting, quietly nodding off because they got up at 4 am to get in their triathlon/swimming/running/cycling/yoga/second job/ illicit affair activities. By the time the meeting starts at 9 am, they're ready for bed.

- And finally, as mentioned in the introduction to this book, there's *the 'self-righteous'*: that special executive who simply can't believe they could possibly show any of the traits I've described. As if!

In summary, choose the people who are going to grab hold of the transformation opportunity in front of them and actually get something done — and who will do so while not pissing everyone off. Pretty simple, really.

A note on creating diverse teams

Justifiably, there's currently a lot of discussion about diversity because we don't have enough of it.

It's important to clarify what's meant by diversity, and why it's critical to effective transformation. Let's reconfirm our definition of diversity (according to *Oxford Languages*) as:

- the state of being diverse, variety
- the practice or quality of including or involving people from a range of different social and ethnic backgrounds and of different genders, sexual orientations, etc.

And if we recap the three critical elements of transformation as being (1) identification of disruption, (2) development of strategy and (3) taking action, it is clear that diversity of thought will enhance all three of these elements. In fact, an argument can be made that diversity absolutely underpins transformation, and its absence is likely to severely impede the scale, ambition, scope and effectiveness of any transformation program.

The absence of diversity of thought will significantly limit the identification of disruptive forces within a business or industry because it means that everyone is likely to be thinking the same way or viewing the potentially disruptive forces through the same lens. When a team is diverse, people are far more likely to consider potential disruptions through their own experiences and draw different conclusions. This is obviously highly valuable. Without diversity, and the intellectual rigour and debate it generates, disruptive forces may well be mistaken for 'stuff that's happening' rather that those things that may well threaten the very existence or profitability of the company.

Likewise, when considering how to address these disruptive forces, a variety of perspectives and diverse imagination are likely to generate a far wider set of options than those put forward by a more similar group. Evaluation and challenges of these ideas will in turn also be more robust as the members of a more diverse team pressure test and argue the advantages and disadvantages of the potential strategic options through a variety of their own different perspectives and frame of reference.

When implementing actions and considering the implications of the strategies on the company and its employees, customers and stakeholders, a diverse set of views is guaranteed to develop a more inclusive and comprehensive plan that best reflects all potential stakeholders and acknowledges their requirements.

If you truly want to promote the best possible exchange of ideas and constructive challenge of options, a more diverse team is better than a less diverse team. This diversity of thought also reinforces the transformation mindset already described earlier, including elements such as:

- *curiosity*: the greater the variety of people on your team, the greater the degree of collective curiosity there will be

- *sacred beliefs*: the more diverse your team, the less likely that you'll all coalesce around the same set of 'sacred beliefs' that limit the quality of your intellectual debate and discussion

- *kokoro*: people with different backgrounds will inevitably look at the same situation through their own frame of reference, which means that a diverse group — after rigorous discussion — is far more likely to identify the very heart of the matter than a more homogenous group. This means that a diverse group is far more likely to be working on the right things and taking all necessary views into account

- *renew*: knowing when to let go when something is not working and try another approach is more likely to be called out by a diverse group, because the individuals within that group are going to have different tolerances for success and failure, and for the speed of progress.

All in all, if your transformation team has people of the same industry background, the same educational achievement, gender, age, ethnicity and sexual orientation, then odds are that the transformation project will be less effective and is off to a bad start.

Yes, some readers might say, 'but there's simply not enough diversity — for example, women in my industry — and that's why my team looks the way it does'. This might be true: some industries are notoriously non-diverse. For example, within the surveying industry, only 3–4 per cent of registered surveyors in New South Wales are female. However, if you're truly trying to transform an industry or company with such a ridiculously skewed demographic, the last thing you need is another person deeply ingrained in that industry. *You* have to create the change. This is the whole point of creating diverse teams because they'll contain people who ask the hard questions, challenge the dogma of the industry that created such a skewed result and promote an alternative.

In essence, diversity of team membership will create diversity of thought.

Some easy questions to ask yourself about the composition of the transformation team you're forming includes how many people are there:

- from different genders?
- from different sexual orientations?
- from different age demographics?
- from different geographical or ethnic backgrounds?

- with deep industry background and skills?
- with deep skills in another industry?
- with deep functional skills?
- with deep transformation skills?

If your goal is sustainable transformation, then you're going to have to invest in diversity. This may mean that you take a chance on very talented people, with the right skills and temperament, who are missing one or two elements, but who inject the diversity that's likely to generate a better outcome. And that you invest in the creation of a set of arrangements (which might include formal education, coaching, mentoring or on-the-job learning) that will then develop the extra elements you'd like and need. This investment in diversity will pay itself off many times over through the constructive challenge and wider frame of thought that's brought to bear on the transformation.

You've decided. So what now?

There are two sides to the coin of leadership. One side is all about telling people that they got the job; and giving promotions, pay rises and bonuses. The easy and energising conversations. The other side is doing the hard stuff like telling someone that they'll be losing their job.

If you like telling people that they've lost their job, then you're probably a psychopath. Removing someone from their job is a big thing. They may struggle to explain it to their spouse and/or kids and friends, they'll likely have financial commitments, it will be disruptive to their life, it might negatively affect their mental health, and so on. It should be a last resort. However, sometimes there's no option. Recognise the gravity of what you're doing, and the impact on people's lives, and try to make a bad situation as constructive as it can be.

Table 4.5 (overleaf) lists some of the do's and don'ts of giving someone the bad news.

Table 4.5 the do's and don'ts of firing someone

Do	Don't
• Be determined—once you've decided, push through to completion. • Be kind—ensure that the person losing their job is treated fairly and with respect. • Own it—'I've decided...' • Be clear and concise—'... that you'll be finishing up with the company'. • Be discreet—choose a place in the office that's private. • Have HR with you—once you've delivered the news, they can stay behind to explain all of the exit details such as pay, logistics, communications etc. • Be prepared—work out the severance pay and have it at the meeting (the $ amount can sometimes remove some of the sting, and the letter itself adds to the finality of the conversation). • Do be clear—clarify who has been appointed into the departing executive's role.	• Be triumphant—don't become an arsehole just because you're firing an arsehole (treat them well for the sake of those who remain). • Be talked out of it—ignore promises of future change, appeals to others or 'but what will I tell my kids?' • Delay it—schedule the meeting for as soon as practicable.

If possible, ensure that you deal with all the people exits in as short a time as is practical. In this way, you can honestly communicate to the team that you've taken action on those you need to and let everyone left in place now settle down to the business of transformation without them wondering who might be next. While it might feel brutal and eventually be referenced as some kind of infamous 'night of the long knives' episode, it will quickly remove the people least likely to support and contribute to the transformation and provide significant opportunity for the promotion and movement of people most likely to make the whole program a success *and*, critically, it will show that you're here to drive transformation.

Again, Niccolò Machiavelli said it well in 1532 when he wrote (with a couple of minor tweaks):

> *Wherefore it is to be noted that in ~~taking a state~~* **entering a new role** ~~it's conqueror~~ *the incoming executive should weigh all the harmful things he must do and do them all at once so as not to have to repeat them every day, and in not repeating them to be able to make ~~men~~* **people** *feel secure and to win them over with the benefits he bestows upon them. Anyone who does otherwise, either out of timidity or because of poor advice, is always obliged to ~~keep his knife in his hand~~* **watch their back**; *nor can he ever count upon his ~~subjects~~* **workforce**, *who because of their fresh and continuous injuries, cannot feel secure with him. Injuries, therefore, should be inflicted all at the same time, for the less they are tasted, the less they offend; and benefits should be distributed a bit at a time in order that they be savoured fully.*

4. Be thorough: follow a proven methodology and approach

We don't rise to the level of our expectations, we fall to the level of our training.

Archilochus (c. 680–645 BCE), Greek poet

When embarking on a transformation program it is essential to be thorough and to consider your strategy and implementation approach from all angles. Taking a multifaceted approach doesn't reduce your focus. Instead, it means that you will approach a difficult task in a comprehensive way. It also means that you approach transformation in a disciplined and systematic way — using a logical methodology — that can be honed and improved over time based on your own experience.

The importance of a comprehensive approach

It's mid 1918 and the Western Front in France and Belgium has been in stalemate for the last four years. Traditional approaches to military operations involving brutal frontal attacks have delivered a butcher's bill of needless death and destruction. Countless lives have been squandered by ordering brave soldiers to directly attack machine guns and barbed wire. And the generals on both the German and allied sides appear to be out of ideas.

Well, not everyone is out of ideas.

There is one — an Australian general who in peacetime was an engineer, lawyer, businessman and army reservist — who brings to his role a curiosity, confidence and scientific systems engineering approach that had never been seen before. He develops his plan, talks it over with his team to pressure test it, and then when ready, he unleashes it on an unsuspecting enemy. And by doing so, he transformed the manner in which battles were fought for the rest of 1918, resulting in the allied victory and a knighthood for himself.

The Battle of Hamel was launched on 4 July 1918 with the objective of taking the town of the same name that lay on a gentle hill and formed part of a bulge that earlier German offensives had pushed into the allied lines.

The battle is now famous because General Sir John Monash was the first modern general to pull multiple levers from multiple branches of the military organisation and use them in concert to achieve his objectives. There are many firsts involved in this battle, and now, so many years later, it all seems so logical, but at the time it was considered extremely radical. Monash was the first general to simultaneously coordinate all the following levers:

- Australian and Royal Artillery units had, for several days before, pounded the German trenches with high explosives and gas shells, with an objective of conditioning the enemy soldiers to an expectation of a daily gas attack.

- Royal Air Force aircraft flew low over the battlefield to mask the sound of approaching tanks.

- Australian and Royal Artillery units delivered a short initial bombardment, which caused the Germans to put on their gas masks in anticipation of a gas attack that never came (noting that it was claustrophobic and difficult to fight effectively with gas masks, thereby reducing the effectiveness of the defences).

- Canadian and British aircraft attacked and strafed the enemy trenches.

- The Royal Tank Corp then attacked the German trenches, closely supported by Australian infantry.

- Specially modified British 'supply' tanks also followed in reserve carrying machine gun ammunition and equipment ready to supply the advancing infantry.

- The Australian infantry aggressively attacked, and having achieved its objectives, quickly dug in and prepared to defend against the inevitable counterattack.

- Canadian and British aircraft attacked, dropping extra supplies by parachute to keep the infantry resupplied and ready.

By the time the dust had settled, Monash had achieved his objectives within 93 minutes, three minutes longer than planned. And his troops gained an incredible four times as much territory as any other equivalent-sized force had achieved up until that time in 1917/1918. By co-ordinating all of the different levers simultaneously — including artillery, tanks, infantry and aircraft — from four different sovereign countries including Australia, Canada, the UK and the United States, Monash captured Hamel from the Germans and inflicted 2000 killed and 1500 captured (many of the prisoners were still wearing gas masks) — which was a huge haul for such a small battle — for the loss of 1400 killed and wounded.

The Battle of Hamel became a textbook example that was documented in pamphlets and distributed to the general staff of the British, French, Canadian and US armies to help them plan combined operations and coordinate the different levers available. It became a blueprint for transforming warfare.

There's also a blueprint for transforming organisations. Leaders of transformation must use all of the levers available to them and know which levers to pull when to create the biggest positive impact and change.

Early in my management consulting career I came across two different methods for assessing and improving businesses that have guided my approach to transformation ever since. I've reflected on and added to them over the years, and both work in most business circumstances. They're timeless. And I've not yet come across anything better. The two methodologies are:

- the 'levers of change', first mentioned in *Better change,* a book by the Price Waterhouse change integration team
- 'shareholder value drivers', from the book *Creating shareholder value* by Alfred Rappaport.

Let's take a look at these two methodologies as they relate to leading transformation and preparing a blueprint for change.

Price Waterhouse's levers of change

Give me a lever long enough and a fulcrum on which to place it, and I shall move the world.

Archimedes (287–212 BCE), Greek mathematician, engineer and astronomer

Back in the day, when I was embarking on my management consulting career, the Price Waterhouse team (this was before the merger with Coopers & Lybrand) identified six 'levers of change'. They are:

1. *markets and customers*: how you segment and view your customers and the markets they inhabit

2. *products and services*: what you provide to these customers that forms the basis of your business and revenues

3. *business processes*: how you transform business inputs into commercial outputs

4. *technology*: the applications, networks, infrastructure and hardware that underpin and deliver your business processes and products

5. *people and culture*: the skills and workforce that deliver the business model, and the behaviours, culture and characteristics that are acknowledged and rewarded through time

6. *organisation and facilities*: how people are organised into roles, business units and divisions, and the facilities and spaces used to house all of the people and operations.

My 10 levers of change

Price Waterhouse's six levers of change were developed a long time ago, and since then the business environment has changed significantly. I've adjusted them to become 10 in total, divided into two types of levers: strategic and operational.

Here are my 10 levers of change.

Strategic levers

My strategic levers include the following.

1. *Customers and markets*

   The customers are the set of people or organisations that ultimately consume or value the company's products and services. They're the final arbiter of value for money and they decide the success or failure of the company via their purchasing decisions. If they value the product or service, they keep paying for it. The market is simply a grouping of customers by similar need or requirement, served by a set of organisations seeking to fulfil these needs and requirements. Markets can be defined as broadly or narrowly as suits your purposes.

2. *Products and services*

   The product or service is obviously the output offered for sale or consumption by the company or organisation. The output might be a tangible product (an aircraft or a cup of coffee) or an intangible product (an insurance policy or bank account). Or it might be a tangible service (such as health care or surgery) or an intangible service (such as legal advice). The product or service is the final result of all of the combined activities, ambitions and intentions of the company or organisation that produces it and is at the core of why it exists at all. For this reason, it has a huge bearing on how all of the other levers of change are established, organised and changed.

3. *Platforms*

A platform is a newly emerged lever that combines customers and markets with products and services in a distinctive way. In their book *Platform revolution*, the authors describe it as follows:

A platform is a business based on enabling value-creating interactions between external producers and consumers. The platform provides an open, participative infrastructure for these interactions and sets governance conditions for them. The platform's overarching purpose: to consummate matches among users and facilitate the exchange of goods, services, or social currency, thereby enabling value creation for all participants.

4. *Alliances*

An alliance is an association or coalition of two or more parties with the objective of co-creating a product or service to take to market. This lever is becoming more prominent because of the emergence of platform business models, the disaggregation of products and services created or manufactured by more traditional businesses, and the deep specialisation that's required to be successful in many markets. Example alliances include Starbucks and Barnes & Noble combining to make a more compelling retail coffee experience. Red Bull and GoPro work together to create compelling awareness and branding that benefits both. Tesla and Spotify have combined to create a better in-car entertainment experience.

Operational levers

My operational levers include the following.

5. *Business processes*

A business process is simply the collection of different activities and tasks, organised into a logical and related sequence, that converts inputs into outputs. At its essence, a business process describes how the company or organisation gets its work done. The inputs can be physical (such as raw materials) or virtual (such as digital data). Likewise, the activities and tasks can be performed by people (providing their physical and intellectual labour) or by technology (such as computers or robots). The outputs are a product or a service.

6. *Technology and data*

The technology lever encompasses all of the computing, connective and enabling technologies that underpin the business processes and the creation of goods and services. Technology therefore covers the entire technology 'stack', incorporating the employee desktop, online digital channels, through the applications layer deep into the network and infrastructure layer. It also includes technologies such as robotics and artificial intelligence. Data has increased in importance due to its underpinning of digital businesses, the creation of new innovative products and services, and compelling customer journeys. Data encompasses all the various pieces of information (internal and external to an organisation) that's collected, catalogued and stored, and then made available at various points, to enhance a company's products and services, and to improve the efficiency and effectiveness of its business processes.

7. *Organisational structure*

The organisation's structure reflects how roles and jobs within a company are arranged to perform the business process activities and achieve the goals of the company. The spans and layers of the structure define the number of typical reporting relationships (spans) that are in place, and the level of hierarchy defines the depth of the structure (layers) between the top — that is, the chief executive officer — and the frontline. Each job within the structure is described to detail the responsibilities associated with the role, and the skills required to fulfil the obligations of the role.

8. *People and culture*

This lever covers the spectrum of people who work in the organisation, including the quantum of individuals, the skills and experience that they each bring, and the behaviours, beliefs and symbols that they value and exhibit across all parts. These behaviours, beliefs and symbols may be implicit, in that they're developed organically based on the personality of the founders and/or existing executives and leaders within the company ('the way we do stuff around here'), or they can be explicit, by which they're carefully defined, communicated and rewarded via formal scorecards and incentives programs (i.e. formal performance management processes.)

9. *Facilities*

This covers the physical space and property within which the company conducts its operations, including everything from large factory spaces, corporate offices, retail shops, mine sites, warehouses, and now because of technology, the remote working locations of staff. It doesn't matter whether the space is owned, leased or borrowed, the facilities lever covers how and where people are housed to do their work, and the impact that this has on their productivity and culture.

10. *Outsourced providers*

Outsourced providers have emerged as it's become evident that no company can be the foremost expert or world's best practice in everything they do. As companies learn to focus on what's most strategic to them, they can then purchase or rent the remaining business services they require from others. And in turn, the companies offering these services — which may include cloud computing services, payroll, manufacturing, logistics, cybersecurity, workforce management and a range of others — have in turn focused all of their energies and expertise into providing these services, thereby improving their quality and reducing their cost.

Pulling the 10 levers of change

In the context of transformation, not all levers are the same, and different levers play different roles. If we recap, our definition of transformation encompasses the three elements of:

- identification of disruption
- development of a strategy
- implementation and taking action

… then it becomes apparent which levers must be pulled at what time.

The strategic levers are usually the subject of disruption. For example, your products and services are under threat by those of a competitor; the needs of your customers and markets are changing or being met by new means; or the industry you're part of is changing because of the emergence of a new platform business that now threatens your existence.

Uber is an example. To disrupt the traditional taxi industry, Uber pulled the strategic levers to:

- maintain the core traditional taxi industry output as defined by conveying a passenger from point A to point B ('service' lever)
- disrupt the traditional taxi engagement or 'hailing' process via the use of highly personalised and mobile technology ('customer' lever)
- broaden the market and attract new non-traditional or irregular taxi users ('market' lever)
- create a platform to directly connect Uber drivers with Uber customers ('platform' lever).

Uber, therefore, redefined the market and customer experience for personal conveyance and in the process disrupted the traditional providers of this service.

As it says on the tin, the strategic levers are therefore closely associated with disruption and the strategic response to the disruption. They're most relevant to the first and second elements of our transformation definition. In response to disruption, a typical corporate strategy will define how the levers should be pulled in different ways that significantly and measurably alter the product and services offered; the customers and markets targeted; the way in which the overall proposition is established (as a platform); and the alliances and partnerships struck to enhance the customer value created even further.

The easiest place to start when considering the strategic levers is with the first two of my 10 levers of change: customers and markets; and products and services.

1. Customers and markets

It's 2011 and Adobe's CEO Shantanu Narayan is about to embark on a fundamental change to Adobe's popular creative cloud product, and with it, transform the entire company. He's decided to shift the product away from Adobe's traditional model of selling customers its suite of products through a one-off licence transaction, to a subscription model that requires them to pay by the month, each and every month. It essentially moves the software purchase from a perpetual ownership model to a rental model, which has since become better known as a 'software as a service (SaaS)' model.

The shift is not universally well received. Adobe has built its business on a loyal following of customers who love their product, and now more than 30000 of them are sufficiently annoyed that they've signed a petition demanding that Adobe reverse the shift to the subscription model.

Narayan persists with the transition because he's confident that over time it will deliver a better customer experience, and it will make Adobe more money. He's proved correct on both counts. Offering the software as a service allows Adobe to continue to update and improve the software, roll out new upgrades and better functionality far quicker, and create more virtuous feedback loops that has them incorporate customer requests into the product quickly and effectively. The new subscription model does, however, also mean customers are paying higher lifetime costs.

The transformation to a subscription model was not just about changing how customers buy the product. Transitioning to a subscription model affected every aspect of Adobe's business: how it engineered the products, its operations, its go-to-market activities and its business models.

All this effort and transformation was worth it: the shift to a subscription model delivered significant shareholder value. Within four years of converting to the cloud, Adobe's luck changed for the better. According to McKinsey Digital, its stock price more that tripled, overall revenue growth climbed to double digits and recurring revenue soared from 19 per cent in 2011 to 70 per cent of total revenue in 2015.

2. Products and services

The profitable creation and delivery of goods and services to customers lies at the heart of value creation for every organisation. This is so obvious, and the products, services and customers of different organisations are so widespread, that it's impossible and unnecessary to go into too much detail on this particular lever here.

However, in the spirit of completeness and having a thorough approach to developing your transformation blueprint, there are a couple of universal and basic principles that remain relevant to all organisations, including considering questions such as:

- *Who is your customer and do you truly know them?* In some cases this is obvious (such as business to business); however, in other cases (such as business to consumer, through some kind of third-party distribution channel) it is not so clear.

- *Why does your customer need you?* It's critical to understand the reason why they buy your product, and the value that it provides to them. Understanding whether demand for your product is elastic or inelastic is critical to pricing decisions.

- *What alternatives exist?* Are you familiar with the alternatives and substitutes for your product? The folks at Kodak found out the hard way that a mobile telephone with a camera was a substitute for their core product.

- *What additional value might they need and be willing to pay for?* Understanding whether the customer has expressed a desire for further functionality or features requires a disciplined process for ongoing engagement with them to best understand their needs.

- *How do you price your products and services?* There are many ways organisations can price their products and services. For example, cost plus, whereby the price is a function of the cost of manufacture plus some kind of margin (for example, a loaf of bread); or value based, whereby the price is a function of the value that the customer gets from consuming it (for example, investment banking advice).

- *Are you potentially leaving value on the table?* Understanding where you add value and what alternatives exist is a pathway to better pricing, because ultimately most companies will want to maximise their revenue and profits. Even if you're the least-cost provider in your industry, you may not wish to leave too much money on the table.

- *Could you change the entire transaction?* Adobe was able to transform its business model and engage its customers with a completely new SaaS business model. This delivered significant gains to the customer and to Adobe.

The number of answers to these questions is nearly infinite given the variety of different industries and different business models available. Asking them may lead you to identifying new market adjacencies that are not yet served, re-pricing your products to capture more value or volume, or changing how your customers interact and buy from you.

To truly transform an organisation, and objectively address the disruption occurring within your industry, you'll need to consider the products and services you provide, the markets in which you sell them and the customers who pay for them.

This will lead you to considering the next two strategic levers: platforms; and alliances.

3. Platforms

It's 2015, and after 17 years of marriage, I find myself newly single. Lonely, daunted, a little confused and disappointed, I wonder whether I'll ever be happy again. Determined to meet someone else, I consider my options. I'm clear on who I am and what I want, and aspire to cut through the potential bunny boilers and vacuous women to find authenticity, intelligence, inner beauty and purposefulness.

What to do? Local bars? Introductions facilitated by my close friends? Tinder?

I land on RSVP. It boasts thousands of users and I'm confident that I'll at least get a start into this. I register myself, create a profile as 'Barefoot Runner' and pay $100 to buy credits for reaching out to prospective dates. The platform boasts thousands of users, and like a kid in a lolly shop, I scroll through profile after profile as they pop up on my screen. I'm away.

I'm on the platform for five minutes when I'm lucky enough to be pinged by 'BKBK', whose profile says she'd rather wrestle a sabre-toothed tiger than go shopping. Intrigued, we start messaging each other in the app, and with a newfound sense of excitement, we head out for what's my first ever RSVP date.

Long story short: we're now happily married, and RSVP got to bank my unused hundred bucks.

Platform businesses such as RSVP are based on a combination of technology systems, compelling brand propositions and business processes that, when combined with an existing and growing customer base, create powerful network effects for their users. These network effects create more marginal value for each additional customer in ways unlike other traditional businesses. Network effects are powerful, and they can help your business grow exponentially or to evolve into a platform.

Establishing your business as a platform at the centre of a network has become the holy grail of modern business and deserves deep reflection, as do opportunities to take advantage of an already established platform to transform your own business. Platforms warrant consideration as a distinct lever of change.

The main advantage of a platform business is that every new user who joins makes the platform even more valuable for those who already use it. This in turn attracts ever more users, who then add yet more value. A telephone network is an easy way to understand the power of a platform; after all, the second telephone added more value than the first.

The evolution of a platform business doesn't happen overnight. Xero is an online accounting software business that's well on the way to delivering on its original ambition to be a small business platform. By an inspirational combination of accounting software that enables small businesses to complete their financial accounts, it has quickly attracted the addition of new small businesses to the platform, which helps highlight new features to improve the underlying software, while also making it increasingly attractive for eco-system partners to write Xero-compatible add-on software that enhances its functionality. This includes detailed management reporting, online connections to actual bank accounts, and point solutions for procurement, staff rostering, treasury management and many other small business use cases. The product has evolved from its original software incarnation to now encompass a platform for small business owners to monitor and manage their businesses. Anyone who has used Xero will know that it delivers against its promise of being 'beautiful accounting software'.

Other examples of platform businesses include:

- *Facebook*: the addition of new customers continues to increase the potential number of connections that can be facilitated on the platform, adding value to each customer already on it. This in turn increases the analytics and intelligence that can be gathered about the user base, which can then be monetised via targeted advertising.

- *PEXA conveyancing platform*: PEXA has automated the land conveyancing process to facilitate the sale and transfer of land across Australia and has established a network of subscribers who can now connect to each other on a single workspace. This enables lawyers and specialist conveyancers to subscribe to represent their own clients confident that the third party on the other side of the transaction will also be represented on the platform.

It's important to note that a platform business is not the same as a natural monopoly. The water distribution and collection network for a big city is a natural monopoly because the cost of the underlying infrastructure, the lack of substitutes and the nature of the product make it so. As such, it's highly likely to be heavily regulated by the government to prevent excessive economic rents being charged on the city population.

A platform business is different. No-one forces you to use Facebook. Its economic moat comes from the fact that millions of users voluntarily register and connect with the platform each day, and a growing number of businesses set up their online presence to attract customers and provide goods and services from within the platform. Alternatives exist, including other social media sites, so it will be interesting to see whether the power and reach of the Facebook platform remains intact over time.

Clearly, Facebook is not a natural monopoly, but it will be difficult and expensive to supplant it. Every new competitor has to build a more compelling platform, and then attract new customers away from the established platform to use the new. This can prove tricky as the new customers have to forgo the promise of existing network effects with the old platform, on the promise of improved features and potential network effects from the new platform.

Notwithstanding the challenges, platform businesses based on network effects will remain attractive business models into the future, and therefore warrant thorough consideration within any transformation effort.

4. Alliances

Alliances have been used by people for millennia to achieve more with others than they could ever have achieved alone. Arguably, we are hard wired to collaborate with others to pursue opportunities and repel threats. Building alliances seems to be part of the human condition.

Alliance creation warrants its own consideration as a lever of change.

The emergence of new business models, digitisation, technology integration and data have made the creation of alliances easier than in the past. Because of new technologies, and their power to facilitate instant and live connection, organisations can now collaborate in real time on a range of different creative, contractual and customer fulfilment efforts that would have been difficult or impossible just a decade ago. This new ease of collaborating therefore makes it simpler to combine products, to assess usage results and to ascribe benefits in ways that would have been difficult if not impossible in years past.

An alliance is defined as an association or coalition of two or more parties with the objective of co-creating a new product or service to take to market, that's based on their respective final products. It differs from an outsourcing partnership arrangement because it's the combination of two final or distinct products or services to make a final integrated product or experience, rather than one product being a key input to the other.

Outsourced providers are somewhat different and are considered separately under their own lever of change. If we consider the creation of an Apple iPhone, Foxconn is the outsource provider that provides manufacturing and final assembly services. No doubt Apple and Foxconn will have a mutually beneficial contractual relationship, but one is a key input to the other without which the iPhone cannot be created.

Alliances are therefore about the discretionary enhancement of final products and services by creating relationships with other final products and services.

That said, we shouldn't get too worried about the distinction between outsourcing and alliances, but instead focus on what opportunities might exist to complement your transformation efforts.

As you think about your own industry and strategic positioning, how could you work with others to further your own success or profitability? What business alliances might make your business — together with an alliance member(s) — even more valuable than if they only worked alone?

Many businesses have opted to enter formal alliances designed to create synergy and incremental value. Examples include:

- *McDonald's and Disney*: many new Disney movie releases are accompanied by a tailored marketing campaign delivered in conjunction with McDonald's. Toys and figurines from each movie are combined with menu items to attract children to eat in the store. Or, if already eating in store, they're presented with Disney advertising that compels them to see the movie.

- *Tesla and Spotify*: the two have combined to create a better in-car entertainment experience. Tesla vehicles come with Spotify already integrated into the in-car entertainment experience, with Tesla having prepaid the usage fees. Spotify benefits from increasing its users, many of whom may open accounts for their own use once they've experienced it in their new electric vehicle. Tesla can boast of the best in-car experience by including Spotify as a feature.

When contemplating transformation and looking out into the market opportunities and threats that exist in your own organisational context, it will be beneficial to consider different companies that you may work with to create an even more compelling customer experience.

停

This book is not about how to *identify* an industry disruption or craft a corporate strategy in response. Instead, it's about how to get big stuff done, which draws more heavily on the operational levers of change to actually *implement* the changes to the organisation required to address the disruption.

The operational levers of change are those that will create lasting and sustainable change to actually address the disruption and bring to life the strategy that's been developed. In summary, as an easy rule of thumb, the strategic levers relate to the 'what' and the operational levers relate to the 'how'.

5. Business processes

At the most basic level, a business process is what transforms inputs provided by suppliers into an output consumed by a customer. The customer can be internal or external, but at some point, hopefully, there's someone who values the process outputs — otherwise, turn it off immediately and go home.

Re-engineering business processes remains a very potent approach to transformation and is the best starting point for improving performance, especially when it's considered and applied to the other levers of change. In a nutshell, it's easiest to think of ideal business processes as being efficient (as in, the conversion of inputs to outputs requires the least amount of effort, time and cost) and effective (as in, the outputs of the process are valued).

You can apply this framework to any business process, from making an aircraft to launching an advertising campaign.

As a junior management consultant, I spent hours and days documenting business processes for clients. I mapped the 'as is' business processes of industrial product manufacturers, fast-moving consumer goods, retailers, supply chain participants, and the finance, HR and other support functions for organisations across the business and government spectrum. This was then followed by challenging every process step, deciding what could be eliminated or removed and what could be automated, until the design of the 'to be' process emerged. There was a significant investment in understanding the process before the subject of technology and automation was introduced.

The analysis of business processes has evolved further into customer journey mapping whereby the experience of the customer at all points in an overall interaction with a business is identified and understood. The technologies they use, the number of screens they see, the simplicity of the underlying business process and the entire experience are reviewed and/or designed to be as customer focused as possible. Apple does this amazingly well and has made every detail of the experience of buying its products — from the unwrapping of them from the box through to their set-up and use — as simple and elegant as possible.

Once work is broken down, understood, documented and standardised, it can be improved. Continuous improvement then becomes a way of improving individual jobs and employee engagement. Documented processes also allow people to take accountability for the outcomes they produce and for improving the processes and systems that produce them.

Without documentation and standardisation of business processes, improvements cannot be sustained over time, and performance will inevitably tend to decline.

Which business processes should you analyse?

It's impossible to predict which business process should be re-engineered as part of your own transformation, because of the unique scope and objectives that underpin it. However, that said, it's important to think broadly about business processes and how they must change.

Let me explain.

Asian philosophies acknowledge the duality of life and thought through many texts and devices now familiar across the world. The concept of yin and yang, for example, is well understood to define the somewhat binary nature and difference of certain things such as light and dark, good and evil, or inhalation and exhalation. The traditional device or motif used to describe yin and yang, however, also acknowledges that things are not truly binary because there's something of the other contained in each of the halves.

The philosophy and curriculum of Gōjū-ryū Karate-do built on this ancient concept of duality and was first encapsulated in the *Bubishi*, an obscure martial arts text from the island of Okinawa. Within the *Bubishi*, 'Go' is taken to mean hardness, or those techniques — mental and physical — characterised by decisive, distinct and independent action. In a physical sense, a karate practitioner delivers a hard technique *to* an opponent.

By contrast, 'Ju' is taken to mean softness, or those techniques characterised by blending, rhythm and dependent action. A soft technique is done *with* an opponent.

The concept of Go and Ju is well entrenched in these traditionally Eastern philosophies and has relevance for how we think about transformation. For these purposes it's helpful to think in terms of hard and soft, or direct and indirect.

For example, when leading change, it's important to focus directly on the core levers of change relating to your goals. This might mean redesigning products and services, re-engineering the business processes that underpin the go-to market strategy, together with implementation of the enabling technology stack, individual roles and organisation structure. This all seems pretty clear and direct, and in the context of 'Goju' would encapsulate predominantly the 'Go' or hard aspects of the philosophy relating to the direct *implementation* of the change.

What's less clear, but no less important, is the need to identify those indirect levers, the 'Ju' or softer aspects that must be pulled to *sustain* the transformation. These may include adjusting business processes such as budgeting to ensure the changes are financially supported into the future, how HR processes identify, recruit and retain talent, or how executive scorecards and management reporting are adjusted to ingrain the changes and ensure their sustainability.

By pulling both the hard/soft or direct/indirect levers together simultaneously, you give yourself the greatest chance of successfully implementing change and sustaining the change into the future. True transformation shouldn't be a one-off event in the present driven by a personality or team. Instead, it should be a sustained change adopted and holistically embraced by the organisation well into the future.

6. Technology and data

How many times have you heard an executive tell everyone that they need to automate everything?

- 'We need a new system.'
- 'If only those two systems talked to each other.'
- 'We need to upgrade.'
- 'Can't we automate that?'
- 'Blah, blah, blah.'

Many businesses have set out to automate their existing business by migrating to new systems. This type of project can give everyone a sense of progress as they select new systems and providers, talk about agile tribes and the like, move their systems into the cloud, and leap, swimming goggles in hand, into the new data lake.

In my experience, implementing new technology across old business processes and practices will typically make what were already shit processes go faster, or be more reliable than they were in the past. In some cases, the new technology actually makes things worse because the project teams cut corners and don't actually address all of the existing business requirements that they should have. On its own, the new technology rarely delivers the transformation that people were perhaps expecting, because they often don't address the actual way that work is done according to the existing business policies and processes, let alone designing new and better ways of doing things.

Let me give you an example. Soon into my time at NSW Land Registry Services we were looking at how we dealt with customer requests for an extension of time on responding to a requisition. A customer had lodged a transaction, the examiners had found some kind of error or problem with the lodged document, and so had 'requisitioned' it, which meant it was pulled out of the process until the customer corrected the error. Apparently, no-one really knows why, the customer was given two weeks to respond, and if they didn't, they had to request a formal extension of time.

This is where the fun begins. The customer request was assessed via a workflow that took it across the organisation to a succession of people. There were something like 27 different steps, and now we were getting ready to automate the system to make it digital. And the kicker? Never in living memory had a customer request for an extension of time ever been refused. You can't make this shit up. Every customer who had ever asked had been granted the extension they requested. So instead of automating this terrible process, we simply eliminated it. There's no longer a policy, and no longer a process: customers can take as long as they want to fix their requisitioned transaction. After all, it's their transaction.

This is why technology—on its own—is not the answer to transforming the organisation.

This is certainly not to say that technology is not an important lever. In many industries technology is *the* most important lever. What I am saying is that technology should enable your strategy and your business processes and not be designed, configured or implemented for its own sake. Technology is always the 'means' and never the 'ends'.

As mentioned previously, we're living in the most exciting times with regard to technological change, dynamic business conditions, and opportunities to lead and be involved in transformation. It is truly incredible. The pace of technological change, and the resultant opportunities to rethink and refocus business models, processes and operations seems unprecedented. Over the past 30 years we've seen the implementation of personal computers, connection to the internet—the resultant .com boom and bust—the rise of iPhones, cloud-based computing, ultrafast chips, data warehouses, APIs and myriad other technologies that have opened a wealth of opportunities for business change.

We've not yet reached the peak of technology change. The coming years will unlock even greater change as we push further into machine learning, artificial intelligence and even deeper analytics. And as 5G telecommunications takes greater hold, virtual reality becomes mainstream and all kinds of business knowledge workers — from doctors and lawyers through to accounts payable clerks — have their jobs augmented by personal process robotics. It's going to be bigger. Far bigger.

Over the coming years, the emergence of new technologies, the need to manage and refresh existing technologies well, and to operate the entire technology stack so that it delivers competitive advantage at an optimal cost point is going to grow in importance. It's very real, and it's very exciting.

In this changing technology environment, every leader is going to require a working knowledge of technology. They won't need to be experts, but they'll need to be engaged, informed and interested.

There are two broad concepts to consider when pushing the technology lever: the technology stack's individual components, and how you run these components. These require decisions on aspects such as:

- enterprise architecture and deciding where you're going and why
- whether to buy or build software applications
- managing functional and non-functional requirements.

Enterprise architecture and deciding where you're going and why

Many years ago I undertook a comprehensive review of the challenges and opportunities associated with a bank's IT function. The review found that a standard home loan mortgage in the Personal Bank touched 42 different IT systems. It therefore took a long time to originate a mortgage. As an aside, I'd hosted a group of banking executives to visit the Boeing factory in Seattle, Washington state (yep — I've been a 'tourist'). We met with the project director of the 767 aircraft series, who proudly told us that Boeing could assemble a 767 and have it fly off the lot in about 23 days. That was far faster than the time we could originate and process a single mortgage application. Crazy bad.

The complexity was the result of technology people actively and sincerely trying to respond to business requirements but doing so without taking an 'enterprise' perspective, or actively trying to decommission old technology. The complexity and culture of the bank's application development function had been built over 40 years by being attuned to the special things the business wanted. Everything had been treated as a special case, with a focus on satisfying the individual special needs of the business sponsoring the program of work.

In some cases, existing third-party applications had been so heavily customised that there were now more lines of customised code than the original source code, making the application unwieldy, unreliable, difficult and expensive to test, and practically impossible to implement standard technical upgrades when they were provided by the vendor.

Individual project decisions continued to exacerbate the problem. Projects were free to select new technologies and implement them into the business. In some cases, business units did this without the involvement of the technology function itself (more on business managed IT a little later). Projects were never held to account for decommissioning old systems, which meant that the bank had become a little like Noah's Ark: it had at least two of everything. This led to inefficiency, high cost, and frontline staff frustration because of the number of systems that they had to learn and use.

The degree of specialisation and customisation had also created a technology environment that was difficult to manage from a skills perspective. The vast array of bespoke applications led to a diversity of special skills to keep the environment going. In many cases these applications were written in old languages and created key-person risk associated with their operation and maintenance.

In summary, it was a mess. An absolute renovator's delight. And as the chief renovator, it was my job to stop the proliferation, to unravel the complexity and to reduce the technical debt. The solution was to introduce some enterprise architecture standards, protocols and governance.

Enterprise architecture is like the town planning function for your business (any business), and you want to be less like the roads in The Rocks, Sydney (laid down without any plan or vision) and more like Canberra (lovingly designed by the architect Sir Walter Burley Griffin). You get the picture.

Over time, enterprise architecture, well executed, will save you significant time, resources and treasure, and deliver far better customer outcomes. In today's highly paced technology-driven world, it's key to extracting the best outcomes you can get to optimise the business and simultaneously deliver better business and customer results.

In a nutshell, you should consider enterprise architecture as the vision or roadmap you want to create, and the individual projects as the earthmoving equipment to lay them down over time. This requires centralisation of certain decisions and contemplation of more questions when you're designing and implementing transformation projects.

First, it requires the business to think in terms of the business outcome desired. Instead of 'I want to implement X' they must say 'I want to increase the effectiveness of my business process' and leave the discovery of the technology options to the architects. If they do their jobs well, the architects will probably include X in the option evaluation, but they'll do so only after looking at all options available that suit the existing technology environment and the aspirations to be better, cheaper and less complex.

Second, individual projects shouldn't be allowed to make individual architecture decisions.

Third, all projects should include a detailed, formal and fully costed plan to decommission the technology applications that they're supposed to replace. The project shouldn't be considered complete until the new application is fully implemented, the benefits are flowing, and the old technology is fully decommissioned and ripped out of the technology environment. The sacrificial destruction of an old server to symbolically acknowledge the full decommissioning of an old legacy system is a nice touch to formally close the project.

Whether to buy or build software applications

The operating applications comprise the software that enables the core business processes. They're either commercial off the shelf (COTS) or customised applications.

COTS applications are developed by specialist software providers, such as SAP (enterprise resource management (ERP) applications such as financial reporting, procurement, human resources and payroll) or Salesforce (specialist sales and customer relationship management (CRM) software). These are the systems designed and created by many of the high-profile technology companies that have become household names across the business world. The design process typically involves the technology company's specialist staff consulting to industry or functional experts, analysing and benchmarking business processes and then using these best practices to drive how the software and the underlying processes work. This 'outside-in' approach means that they're objectively designed to work efficiently and effectively across a wide range of clients and industries (i.e. an audience of many).

Once selected, the COTS application is typically installed in the customer's organisation by the systems integrator (a specialist consulting or technology firm) that confirms the business processes to be used, configures the COTS software and implements the application into the technology stack, thereby connecting it to all of the other elements such as the network, data centre or cloud.

By contrast, customised applications are typically designed and written for a company's unique business process. This typically involves specialist consulting and technology firms documenting and/or designing the business process and then writing the operating application to match these use cases. It can therefore be considered an 'inside out' process and is by definition designed for an audience of one.

Sometimes, a COTS application can be modified — or customised — so extensively that it more resembles a customised application than a COTS application. This is not typically a good thing because it starts to limit the benefits (such as standardised approach, clear documentation and upgrade path) associated with a COTS application and collects the negatives associated with custom-built systems (such as reliance on specialist resources, falling further behind the latest versions).

There's much debate about whether it's best to implement COTS or customised applications. Here are some things to consider:

- What's the business outcome you're trying to achieve?

- Is the underlying business process actually unique to your company? If so, does it truly need to be unique (i.e. is it a source of competitive advantage) or could you use a more generic process?

- Is your company in an industry for which COTS solutions have not yet been developed?

In the past, many organisations in industries as diverse as banking and financial services, telecommunications, mining and retail, all developed customised applications because there were no COTS applications available.

With the passage of time, many of these original applications have now become legacy. When you hear legacy application you should simply think, 'highly customised and old'. And with legacy software come several challenges including:

- *It's old*: the computer code it's written in is likely to be old. There have been multiple computer languages come and go. If the legacy application is sufficiently old, it may mean that accessing people with skills in that particular language is very difficult and will become more so with the passage of time. Just like young kids don't typically want to learn old languages such as Latin at school, they also don't want to learn the old computer languages. It will become harder and harder to find skilled specialists familiar with the older computer languages because such specialists are not only retiring, they're now dying of old age.

- *There's no upgrade path*: its customised nature means there's no upgrade path, which means that its existing functionality rarely gets any better. Change only happens when in-house specialists (typically your older IT employees who may have been involved in its original implementation) make ad-hoc modifications to solve business problems. And making these changes can be risky for the business because the documentation associated with the legacy applications is not typically well maintained, and the associated testing scripts and testing environments are also out of date. In many cases, the changes will not be able to be truly thoroughly tested until they're implemented into the production environment.

- *Risk of cyberattack*: the legacy applications may be at greater risk of cyberattack because there's no third party responsible for the development and distribution of patches to protect against contemporary cyber threats.

- *It's free*: because of age, most legacy systems are fully depreciated. This means that their original capital cost has been written off, and in many cases, the company that owns the legacy system has enjoyed a period of reliance on the system at no cost. This 'sweating the asset' means that when there's a project to replace the legacy — which undoubtedly will come with a decent price tag — it will seem even more expensive as there's no cost saving to offset it against because it introduces a cost where previously there was none.

- *Hardware challenges*: the use of legacy systems may limit the hardware and cloud infrastructure that you're able to use because the legacy software was not designed or architected to run in a cloud environment. In extreme cases, it may only run on old hardware, which itself becomes legacy. You might be surprised at how many large corporates have had to find hardware spares on eBay because their hardware assets are old and no longer supported.

- *Integration challenges*: the use of legacy systems may limit what you're able to integrate. In this case, the legacy cannot easily leverage APIs or integrate to other systems, which then limits the underlying business process design, or limits the transformation or commercial opportunities you can pursue.

Software as a Service (SaaS) is emerging as a very strong alternative to legacy applications and traditional COTS software. In simple terms, SaaS allows you to purchase software via a subscription model (for example, based on the number of licensed users, or the amount of computing power consumed, such as the number of customers you have on the platform). SaaS models are extremely flexible and have the following characteristics:

- *They're cloud based*: the SaaS provider runs a cloud-based model that enables you to access the software without hosting it in your data centre.

- *They're scaleable*: you can typically control the number of users you have licensed for the software, and you can also control the number of modules or access to varying levels of software functionality based on this user base.

- *They're efficient*: you only pay for what you use.

- *They're secure*: the SaaS provider typically invests in the latest cyber protections and patches to ensure that their offering is very secure.

- *They're reliable*: the SaaS provider runs a sophisticated service management regime that ensures maximum reliability, and in the event of an outage, the system is typically up and running again very quickly.

- *They're standard*: SaaS models are highly standardised, but also configurable to match your business processes. SaaSs are inevitably going to require you to make changes to your own business processes because they're next to impossible to customise.

- *They're continually improving*: the SaaS provider is typically investing in material improvements to their system, and these are made available to the customer on a regular basis. These improvements typically reflect improvements in industry business processes and better integration with other products.

Purchasing SaaS from a third party should make it more difficult for the software to eventually become legacy.

Managing functional and non-functional requirements

It's late 1939. War has broken out in Europe and General George Marshall has just been appointed the senior US Army Chief of Staff. Soon after his appointment, Marshall lobbied President Roosevelt for an increase in the size of the US air force. This was a time when the US was still neutral, there was considerable political and popular opposition to the US joining in the war, and the current state of the air force was woefully inadequate.

After some initial fact finding, Roosevelt himself proposed an appropriation of funds to purchase 10000 new aircraft. Feeling very confident, Roosevelt solicited the opinions of all the senior military and political advisors, all of whom acquiesced because this came directly from the president himself. Not Marshall: 'Mr President, I am sorry, but I don't agree with that at all.'

Many thought the Washington career of the newly appointed Chief of Staff would be short lived because he had so directly and publicly disagreed with the president.

Marshall saw disagreement as a critical part of his duty. He was obliged to disagree. He then made it crystal clear to Roosevelt that appropriations to purchase 10000 aircraft were useless unless there were also funds to pay for new runways, hangars, maintenance and armament programs, together with all the pilots, mechanics and armourers to make the aircraft useful over time. Without this expenditure and management, the introduction of the new technology — the aircraft — would be pointless. An example of 'amateurs talk strategy, professionals talk logistics'.[2]

Many modern technology transformation projects are still like this: the project focuses on the design and implementation of the initial technology, and ignores the costs and resources associated with the maintenance and operation of the technology into the future.

---

[2] Attributed to General Omar Nelson Bradley, 1893–1981, Chairman of the Joint Chiefs of Staff, United States Army.

Like Marshall, whenever you're discussing a project, think about the actual aircraft (functional requirements) but also about the pilots, mechanics and hangars (non-functional requirements), and the costs that will be incurred to pay for these specialist resources and maintain their productivity.

Data as a lever of change

Data has emerged as a critically important lever of change, and we are surrounded by it in increasing volumes.

I bet, like me, you've been talking about something with a friend, searched it on Google, and then, hours later, you're served an advertisement related to your search. This is an early, and very simple, example of the use of your data. And it's just the tip of the iceberg.

The prevalence of the cloud, as mentioned earlier, together with Moore's Law and the disruptive power, and reducing price, of technology means that the storage and crunching of data is only just beginning.

According to Statista, the amount of data created and stored in 2013 was 9 zettabytes (a zettabyte is a unit of information equal to one sextillion (1021) or, strictly, 2 to the power of 70 bytes). To use the technical term, a zettabyte is an absolute shit-ton of data. A zettabyte is the equivalent of 30 billion movies or 7.3 trillion songs. At the time of writing, it is estimated that by 2025, 181 zettabytes will be captured, copied and consumed. And that's in addition to the 147, 120, 97 and 79 zettabytes captured, copied and consumed in the years 2024, 2023, 2022 and 2021 respectively.

The description 'big data' doesn't feel, well, big enough, to describe the amount of data that's now out in the wild. And remember, it's the least amount of data there will ever be. It will only grow.

Traditional business models based on information arbitrage have already long ago been disrupted and in some cases destroyed by online models. Think about the traditional 'rivers of gold' classified ads in newspapers, or the used car market, or the employment ads that are now all gone.

The best-selling book *Moneyball*, by Michael Lewis, combined with the film of the same name starring Brad Pitt, illustrated how the collection and analysis of data could revolutionise the selection, recruitment and management of professional baseball players. In *Moneyball*, the Oakland Athletics baseball team manager, Billy Beane, ignores all of the established norms of talent scouting and selection and uses analytical and evidence-based statistics to forge an unlikely winning team. Unlikely because the resultant team included players considered past their prime, those who didn't look like traditional ball players and those rejected by mainstream teams. In the end, the Oakland Athletics team, with a player roster costing approximately $40 million a year, was regularly competitive with the New York Yankees, whose roster cost more than $120 million a year. Oh, and the Oakland Athletics won more than 20 games in a row — one of the longest winning streaks in the history of baseball. Data analysis can be powerful.

We've long seen the collection of your activity and clicks around the internet, with increasingly sophisticated 'cookies' tracking your every move, and either using this information to craft personalised ads and offers, or selling it to the highest bidder.

We are at the start of a new wave of business process and business model disruption. Take banking, for example. Automated credit scoring has been the holy grail of banking credit risk management for years. Banks have sought to automate the collection of data, and then pump it through models such as FICO (Fair, Isaac and Company), which use a collection of data about payment history (35 per cent), debt burden (30 per cent), length of credit history (15 per cent), use of different credit instruments (10 per cent), and recent searches and applications of credit (10 per cent) to determine a final score. This final score, based on all of the data pulled together, provides a universal (at least to most financial services companies) expression of your credit worthiness, and will help these institutions determine whether you're a good credit risk.

As they say, when it comes to banking, if you can prove that you don't need the money, then the bank is sure to lend it to you. As a prospective borrower, you fill in the bank's credit application form, and they then pump it into their FICO model to work it all out.

However, change is coming. New scoring models based on big data are emerging. Upstart is a new AI lending platform that partners with banks and credit unions to provide consumer loans using non-traditional variables, such as education and employment, to predict creditworthiness. Instead of just filling in an application form, the AI models trawl all kinds of personal, employment, social and financial data — big data — to form a detailed picture of your financial life and propensity to pay. According to Upstart, its AI models — drawing on analysis of massive amounts of data, and big data feeds — utilise more than 10 billion data points to predict the probability of default for each individual applicant for each month of the loan. Time will tell regarding the increased accuracy of new Upstart models over traditional FICO models, but the use of big data is just starting. The impact on highly paid banking credit specialists whose entire jobs might be made redundant by companies such as Upstart is also just starting.

It's impossible to say how big data will play out for companies and their business models, but what's possible to predict is that there's going to be a lot of disruption and a lot of transformation.

Existing data

With the right technology tools in place, the depth and breadth of insights to be gained from your existing data sets can help you be truly transformational in the following areas:

- *customers and markets*: indicating who your customers are, their behaviours, propensities and characteristics, and their potential demographic groups
- *products and services*: how your products are used, in what contexts and what product or service gaps may exist
- *process failure points*: such as when a customer going through an online purchase drops out of the process, indicating that the underlying business process may need redesign or simplification
- *cost behaviours*: what's happening with your variable and fixed costs, and how margins could be improved.

Classic data analytics techniques can help you to identify problems, insights and trends with empirical evidence that can then form the basis for resetting or refreshing your strategy and for understanding what needs to change. It's probably fair to say that if your transformation strategy is not grounded in business insights based on deep and broad data foundations, you may be setting up for failure.

Future data

As you identify the disruptions affecting your industry and your organisation, it's worth asking yourself whether you have all the data you need. Consider:

- What questions about the industry, your company, or some part of it, can you not answer?

- What new data sets do you need?

- Where might this data reside, either internally or externally?

- How can you make sense of this data?

- How and where is data stored and kept secure, and how is it accessed?

- How do you get accurate data into the hands of decision makers in time to make better decisions?

In summary, data has become one of the most powerful levers of change. It helps shine a light on what you actually know, and the incorrect assumptions that you're unknowingly making. Make understanding your company's data needs and capabilities one of your transformation priorities.

7. Organisational structure

Take a guess as to when the following quote was written:

> We trained hard—but it seemed that every time we were beginning to form up into teams we were reorganised. I was to learn later in life that we tend to meet any new situation by reorganising, and what a wonderful method it can be for creating the illusion of progress while actually producing confusion, inefficiency and demoralisation.

It was written by Petronius Arbiter, a Roman courtier, during the reign of Emperor Nero, and he wrote it *more than 2000 years ago*.

It's hard to say it better. Organisation restructures were recognised as overused even back then. I'm amazed that many executives and especially chief executive officers are so obsessed with designing new organisation structures, and yet cannot maintain them and keep them stable over time. I've heard countless times the need to restructure the organisation with excuses such as:

- 'Accountabilities are unclear; the structure just doesn't work.'
- 'I need to have end-to-end accountability to make it work.'
- 'It [insert team, business unit, division] will work better if it reports to me.'
- 'We need all of those people in one place.'

And on and on and on.

On its own, a restructure — without simultaneously pulling other levers of change — seldom achieves much, other than to give the executives with new reporting lines either bigger egos or bigger headaches, and it's generally demotivating for those who lose responsibilities. An unjustified and poorly implemented organisation structure change is a perfect way to set a harmonious team of executives against one another and almost guarantee that no work gets done.

Every time I've talked with the people actually doing the work in large organisations, a change in organisation structure has actually had very little impact on them. They come in, they do the same work, and that's it. Depending on the impact of the restructure, they may have to identify someone else they need to communicate with or send/get work from. They'll find this unsettling because up until the time of the restructure they knew how to do their jobs and get things done, but all of that's now up in the air, so they're working harder and they're busier just to produce the same work. Oh, but what the hell, the new executive has called a meeting to meet their new team, tell them why the restructure was necessary, and so now they have even less time in their day to get that product or service out to the customer, who is themselves wondering why everything is late.

And another thing to ponder as a senior executive: the further down your organisation you push, the less likely that the people actually doing all the work are to know your name. So go easy on the restructures. The front-line person in any large company is likely to know, obviously, their direct boss, definitely their boss's boss, and then it all becomes a bit hazy ... and then they generally know the chief executive officer's name. As a divisional head or group executive, they probably don't remember your name unless someone reminds them.

Obviously, organisation structures are important. They're an important lever to ensure that people are aligned, that there's transparency of roles and accountabilities, and that there are clear measurement regimes in place to ensure that everything works according to plan. But organisation restructures should be used sparingly. They should be used when you fully understand the strategy of what you're trying to achieve and the business processes that transcend organisation structure boundaries, and when you have a clear goal about what you're trying to deliver with organisation culture, facilities, and so on. In summary, if you change the organisation structure *too much*, it may feel like you're making progress, but it will inevitably actually prevent or delay real transformation.

8. People and culture

The people and culture lever is one of the most powerful levers of change. It's mostly concerned with the quantum and character of the people employed within the organisation, the common skills they possess, and their potential to take on the new skills required to deliver a successful transformation. Because 'culture eats strategy for breakfast' (Peter Drucker), the set of cultures that exist within the organisation must also be supportive of the strategy.

While a powerful lever, it can also be extremely hard to pull as you face directly into all of the human resources processes, mental models, personal biases, inertia and opposition that exist in all organisations. This is because many large organisations will naturally have an HR function that's focused on all things 'people', such as recruitment, training and development, alignment and retention to support the status quo. Like other corporate functions, the HR department will have an established way of performing all the elements it's responsible for, and these will typically be designed, staffed and evaluated based on the support they provide to the existing business as usual operations.

Sometimes the existing HR department is less focused and capable of supporting the needs of a company-wide transformation. After all, it's not the HR department's responsibility to sensitively identify the disruptive forces likely to affect the operations and future viability of the company. A transformation will typically require the identification and recruitment of new skills and people, and these requirements may not be well defined by the traditional BAU managers who have flourished and occupy senior roles within the HR hierarchy and the senior executives they support.

It's therefore the role of the transformation leader to face into this and shake it up a bit, as was done by General George Marshall upon assuming overall command of the US army in September 1939, although 'shaking up' is probably an understatement.

An anecdote early in Marshall's career provides a sense of his talents and potential. One of his earliest commanders was Lt Col. Johnson Hagood. Hagood was asked if he would like Marshall to serve under him, to which he replied, 'Yes, but I would prefer to serve under his command.'

Marshall famously developed a clear view of the characteristics of the leaders he thought would be required to lead the US army to victory in World War II. Within a month of being sworn in as the new leader, and already knowing many of the senior leadership ranks of the organisation, he came to the realisation that most of the leaders had out-of-date ideas and would not be likely to change to meet the new conditions they faced.

As a transformational leader, Marshall didn't simply look at what was required through the lens of the existing BAU operations of the army or the senior people who were in situ. Instead, he looked through the lens of what would be required of his leaders and people in the context of the transformation that he knew was required. He focused on what he needed rather than what he had inherited.

As a result, writes Thomas Ricks in *The Generals: American military command from World War II to today*, 'at Marshall's behest, in the summer and fall of 1941, 31 colonels, 117 lieutenant colonels, 31 majors and 16 captains were forced into retirement or discharged from the active-duty force'. When it came to the most senior general officers, the cuts and reliefs were even more pronounced, continues Ricks: 'Only eleven of the forty-two generals who commanded a division, a corps, or an army [during the Louisiana Manoeuvres in August-September 1941] would go on to command in combat.' The rest were reassigned to different roles more suitable to their skills or removed altogether if their temperament and skills were likely to slow or reduce the scope of the transformation the US army required.

The upside of all this was the identification and rapid advancement of those leaders — such as Dwight D Eisenhower, George S Patton, Omar Bradley and Matthew Ridgway — with the potential to adapt, grow and deliver the requirements of Marshall's new army, and who would go on to win the battles and ultimately the war.

Luckily, the needs of a transformation effort are not as dangerous, demanding, arduous and all-encompassing as mobilising an army for warfare on an industrial scale. However, a transformation will generate the need for a new set of skills and people different from the BAU operations, and this requirement must be first acknowledged, and then carefully and seriously addressed, to ensure a successful foundation is created.

There are several questions a leader must reflect on:

- What skills will be required of the new organisation, and do you have them? If not, where can you get them?
- What are the most important roles that delivering the strategy is dependent on?
- Do you have the right people in these roles, as measured by their temperament and skillset?
- What culture is required of the new organisation, and how will you evolve towards it?

New skills

Given the disruption happening in your industry, what's the likely impact on the skills required to be successful? Disruption will require more of some skills and less of others.

Whatever your industry, disruption is guaranteed to change the skills required to be successful. The existing BAU skills will eventually be supplanted by a new set of BAU skills. The role of the transformation leader must therefore be to pre-empt and forecast these skills, and then to work with their colleagues and the human resources department to actively develop or acquire them as soon as possible.

Transformation skills

When did your organisation last embark on a significant transformation?

By definition, many companies do not undergo transformation regularly, and therefore do not have people with deep transformation skills sitting on shelves waiting to be deployed. Over time, the BAU skills required to run the company take precedence over the skills required to change the company. This is logical and normal.

Some companies, though, — think General Electric under Jack Welch with its famous Crotonville leadership institute — develop transformation skills as an executive competence that's expected in all existing and future leaders. This is both unusual and expensive.

Therefore, when contemplating your own organisation transformation, you must consider the degree of skills you already have in-house, the speed at which you can develop them in your existing cadre of leaders, and the external sources of these skills that you can recruit.

Fulcrum roles

Once you've predicted the new skills that will be required in your newly disrupted organisation, together with the skills that will be required to lead and effect the change, you must then identify the roles and individuals who are most critical to achieving both.

I call these fulcrum roles because they're the roles upon which the transformation effort will succeed or fail. The individuals in these roles can identify and recognise the disruption that could negatively affect the company's future, and debate and agree the strategy that will address the disruption. Once the transformation begins in earnest, they're also the individuals who have decision rights over the design and timing of the transformation.

An easy example will illustrate the point. While leading the design and implementation of one of Australia's first large-scale finance shared services organisations, encompassing four business divisions of one of Australia's largest industrial companies, it became apparent that the four divisional CFOs were the specific fulcrums against which all the levers of change would hinge. Their support would be critical for success because they had to give up some of their existing empires and deliver outcomes using a new shared services organisation.

Unfortunately, one of the divisional CFOs had a toxic reaction to shared services models. He'd grown up in a finance function equating the size of his team with his own importance, and simply couldn't get his head around the change in role associated with shared services, whereby he would be responsible for decision support to his CEO rather than running his own large finance team.

He shit-canned the project from morning to night, and had one of his senior managers double check every calculation and business assumption in an effort to discredit the consulting team. Fortunately, his guy had high integrity, ran the numbers and endorsed the project. Because he was in a fulcrum role as one of the divisional CFOs, if he couldn't support the transformation then he'd have to go. And go he thankfully did.

If you have the right people in these fulcrum roles, with the right transformation skills and temperament, then you're off to a good start. Your role as the transformation leader is to think through which roles are most critical to success and ensure that you have the right people in them. If you don't, then call it early and take action. Remember, no-one ever said 'I wish I'd taken longer to get rid of the white ant'.

Culture

All of us have our own definition of culture and instinctively understand what it is. Culture can be defined as the set of behaviours, symbols, rewards and sanctions that are unique to running your existing organisation.

As we have seen, culture is a powerful force for enshrining the status quo and actively resisting any kind of change or transformation. Remember that Machiavelli referenced the 'lukewarm allies' and 'enemies' that all have a stake in the status quo. The temperament and energies of those who actively resist change, combined with the power of the existing culture, form a powerful force that must be either overcome or at least harnessed to deliver true transformation.

If you're leading change within an organisation, there's a good chance that you understand the existing culture. The questions to ask are:

- Can you define the new culture you'll require?
- Can the culture change at a fast enough pace?
- How will you reinforce the new culture via who you keep, promote and reward?

At the heart of this statement are two important concepts:

- what you invest in (capital budgeting)
- how you keep score (performance appraisal and scorecards).

As the leader, it's also important to acknowledge that sometimes, to change the culture, you may have to change the people. Although this may seem harsh, a transformation is an opportunity to clear the decks, send new messages as to what's valued and important, and ensure the organisation is filled with people who believe in the need to change and are individually supportive of it.

Managing redundancies

In an episode of *The Simpsons*, the new German owners of the Springfield nuclear plant completed a thorough review of the facility. Naturally, all employees were waiting for the announcement of layoffs with anxiety. The new owners then proceeded to read out the names of those made redundant in alphabetical order:

'Simpson, Homer. That is all.'

Because we've not yet reached peak change and disruption, leaders of all organisations will need to transform their business models and operations, and this will inevitably have an impact on the composition, skill and size of their workforce. In other words, some of them will be made redundant.

Transformation leaders must therefore know how to manage redundancies, and must also understand the unique organisational context that employees play in their company.

The employees working in any company or organisation can be considered in either of two ways:

- an expense that's part of the profit and loss statement, or
- an asset that's part of the balance sheet.

In simple terms, if a company's leaders characterise the workforce as an expense, then they're more likely to make short-term decisions that affect these employees and their subsequent engagement and connection to the company and its goals, in a casual manner. For some companies (for example, fast food and grocery retailing) comprising low-skilled roles or a traditionally transient workforce, this may be entirely appropriate, and the company and the workforce know this and conduct themselves accordingly.

By contrast, companies that categorise their highly skilled workforce as an asset (for example, a prestigious law firm) are far more likely to take a longer term perspective, and to invest in the development and engagement of their workforce. This builds strategic capability, culture and a solid foundation for the company's continuing operations. Again, the firm and the workforce understand this approach, and each makes decisions and accepts trade-offs reflective of this reality.

Regardless of whether employees are characterised as either an expense or an asset, emerging disruptions are going to pressure the business models of all organisations. To continue extending the industry examples mentioned above, technological advances such as radio frequency identification tags and robotics have been disrupting grocery retailers for some time, and the looming revolution in artificial intelligence is going to inject significant pressure into law firms.

There have always been two sides to the leadership coin. One side is energising and positive, such as giving promotions, pay rises and bonuses. The other is challenging because it entails telling people that they've lost their jobs. Transformation leaders need to be adept at both.

While obviously developed for humour in a cartoon sitcom, the example from *The Simpsons* mentioned above is a textbook case in how not to communicate redundancies. I've seen leaders who do not want to talk about or face the reality of redundancy management. They find it uncomfortable and difficult to have the right conversations at the right time. Or they're impersonal or deliver the message in a clumsy or inauthentic manner.

There are also leaders who try to ignore the reality of redundancies for as long as possible, to blame the need on someone else's decision or to communicate the need for it in corporate-speak that's belittling to those directly affected and bewildering to those who remain in the organisation after the redundancies are complete.

None of this is necessary or desirable.

Here are some broad principles for managing redundancies associated with transformation programs, recognising that no-one enjoys telling someone that they're losing their job:

- acknowledge that redundancies hurt people
- redundancies need to be carefully managed
- own the messages and lay out the case
- appeal to pragmatism and adulthood
- find a little more in the budget
- be determined and don't get distracted
- get them all done as soon as possible.

Acknowledge that redundancies hurt people

People being made redundant are not numbers or statistics. They're real people who are going to be negatively affected by loss of income, emotional distress, a damaged ego, and a sense of humiliation. They typically didn't vote for the change or disruption that's affecting them, nor is it a result of decisions that they have made. Even when being paid significant redundancy payments, their futures are rarely certain, and they're inevitably in for a period of deep reflection, significant change, potential reinvention and the discomfort of having to re-skill or reinvent themselves. All in all, for most people, being made redundant is very tough.

The remaining employees who know those made redundant are also negatively affected by their colleagues being made redundant, especially if the process appears unfair or poorly managed.

Redundancies need to be carefully managed

Redundancies must be managed carefully, fairly and as kindly as possible. Transformation leaders need to absolutely know that when they're managing a redundancy program they're managing two distinct, but equally interested, sets of stakeholders: those being made redundant, and those who while not directly impacted will remain employed by the company.

Those being made redundant are interested in what will happen to them, and the degree of generosity and care that's shown to them. Those who remain are watching with interest in the full knowledge that this could be them one day soon. For those staying, any negative aspect of the redundancy program will affect their residual engagement, trust in leadership and commitment to the company and its transformation objectives.

If you or your company does the wrong thing by those being made redundant, it will be remembered and leave a negative residue on staff engagement for a long time afterwards. The 'wrong thing' could be careless or misleading communications, trying to artificially minimise redundancy payments or treating those made redundant poorly.

Own the messages and lay out the case

The transformation leader must own the redundancy program and its messages. This is a time to be respected rather than liked, and it's important that you're out in front. You need to own the messages and carefully lay out the case for change. Your communications should be along the lines of:

> There's significant disruption occurring in our industry, caused by factors x, y and z. As a result, our company has been affected by a *[drop in sales]* or *[increase in costs]* or [loss of customer relevance]. This means that *I've* made the decision to transform our operations, processes, technologies and culture to better position our company for the future. Regrettably, this means that I'll be leading a program to significantly cut costs, and unfortunately that's going to result in job losses. I remain committed to open, honest and transparent communications, and when I know something more, or have made a decision, I'll communicate it to you.

You should craft your own message, look people in the eye and deliver the message. Don't be one of those delusional leaders who wants to be liked by the very people they are making redundant. Or worse, start a redundancy conversation with 'This is hard for me to say, Bill, but... blah, blah...'. Rest assured, it's always much harder to hear 'your job is being made redundant' than it is to say it.

Appeal to pragmatism and adulthood

It's easy to limit communicating with people because you think they can't handle it. I've seen leaders act in a parent/child dynamic and withhold information from their workforce because they don't believe they can handle knowing the truth, or they don't want certain people to leave, or they think it inappropriate to share news until they know every single aspect of it.

I call bullshit. Instead, level with people. Tell it as it is, and don't sugar coat the message or deliver it in corporate speak. If you put yourself in the shoes of an affected employee, wouldn't you like to know what's happening as soon as possible? If you think that there's a possibility of being made redundant wouldn't you like to know? With the right knowledge, you can start to manage your downside risks: perhaps you won't buy that car or go on that expensive overseas holiday.

It's pretty simple: treat your employees how you'd like to be treated. If you want people to do the right thing by the company, then you start by doing the right thing by them.

'Oh, but we'd better not talk about redundancies with those people who have marketable skills and might leave now before we're ready for them to leave,' I've heard some say. The answer is not withholding information. If there are people you need to retain, then have an adult conversation with them and put a conditional retention payment in place to keep them.

Find a little more in the budget

You're obviously within your rights to pay the bare minimum redundancy. However, if you choose to also manage the program to win the hearts and minds of those who remain, it's a very good approach to pay those affected more than the statutory minimum. And to communicate that you've paid for some outplacements, training and re-skilling to help them adjust to the shock of redundancy.

After all, you get what you pay for. If you pay the minimum to those leaving, you may well have those who stay give you the bare minimum back. Paying a little more is obviously good for those who leave, but excellent for those you choose to keep. It's money well spent.

Be determined and don't get distracted

Let's face it, if you like making people redundant then you're a psychopath. It's hard. But when you need to do it, then do it. Be clear on what you need to achieve, the level of job losses required and the overall business case that has to be met.

Those affected should fall into one of two buckets: they're either staying because the role they fill is important to the success of the company, or they're not. Don't make up jobs, especially bullshit jobs as described in chapter 2, for people who are popular, or between roles, or on a never-ending project, or because you like having them around.

Asking for voluntary redundancies is tricky. The leaders of the company should know who is good and who is not. Don't outsource the difficult task of identifying people for redundancy to the employees themselves. This is a recipe for all of your best and most talented people to put their hands up because they back themselves to get another job quickly and bank their redundancy cheque. Those less talented or who don't back themselves tend to stay. This is a pathway to losing your best and retaining your least talented.

Instead, make a list of individuals, together with their remuneration, and then ensure that they leave the company with a redundancy, and you bank the savings you identified. Don't be a psychopath, but equally don't be weak. You need to be determined, fair and resolute.

Get them all done as soon as possible

There are few things more erosive to employee engagement and enthusiasm than having a never-ending redundancy program. You need to get it done. Rip off the band aid and aim for as many redundancies as possible in a short period of time. Once they're complete, everyone can get on with business without the fear of redundancy hanging over them.

When you're leading a transformation program, acknowledge that it's going to hurt people. Get out front to deliver the messages, be as generous as you can and recognise that everything you do and don't do will be evaluated by those who stay. Above all, treat people like adults and don't bullshit them.

9. Facilities

It's 1913 and the Registrar General's Building, now also known as the Land Titles Office, has just opened on the corner of Queens Square and Macquarie Street, Sydney. Construction commenced in 1909 in the Federation Gothic architecture style, with a distinctive sandstone facade containing elaborate gables and turrets. The building was purpose designed as the repository for all births, deaths and marriage records, as well as a huge collection of property title deeds reaching back to the formation of the original colony of Sydney.

The land titles office commenced operations in the building in 1915, and generations of highly skilled surveyors, specialist examiners and legal experts worked in its hallowed, fireproof halls and generous colonial-era executive offices across floors connected by graceful sweeping marble staircases, all busy registering the release and transacting of land titles across the state of New South Wales.

On the building went through time, unchanged, slightly tired, a sense of formal permanence and meticulous aloofness. Like the last days of the British Raj, perhaps an emerging sense of physical decay seeping in, providing a clear conservative link back through time to when the Registrar General, as the controller of all things land, had once been one of the most senior officials in the colony.

The specialist employees and managers within felt a strong kindred connection to this permanence, formality and unchanging ways, and jockeyed for the largest light-filled offices and the relative hierarchy associated with every square metre of the place.

And then, at the stroke of a pen in 2017, the NSW Land Titles Office was privatised. Everybody out. The privatised operator certainly doesn't get the chance to keep this precious building, so sayeth the state government.

The culture of the organisation had built such a strong relationship to the facility that some people now mirrored the building's own staid, change-resistant features. When my duty as the first post-privatisation CEO arrived to inform the staff of the need to vacate, one of the outraged employees actually stood up and said, 'That will be impossible.'

Now 'impossible' is a strong word, so my natural response was to reply with, 'Well, they've put a man on the moon, so I don't think it's beyond *our* capacities to move offices.' And thus Project Apollo, our plan to successfully move the organisation out of its 100-year tenancy, began.

The size, type and location of facilities obviously plays a huge part in the performance, efficiency, teamwork, cost base and culture of an organisation. There's a reason why high-end retailers project their brand promise through their retail shops, why supermarkets design their stores around the back dock to improve their supply chain outcomes, why fast-food companies saturate the suburbs with their outlets to maximise reach, why startups use group working areas to drive collaboration and teamwork, and why manufacturers of all types carefully lay out their factories to maximise the efficient flow of materials and assemblies through the production line. Facilities matter.

Unfortunately, because of the sunk cost nature of property ownership, combined with the relative disruption and cost of either moving or decommissioning real estate, property and facilities can also drive your strategy instead of being driven by the strategy.

The branch networks of major banks are a potent reminder of the power of a sunk cost physical branch network continuing to attract strategic mindshare and scarce investment dollars long after the economics and customer propensity of digital and direct banking channels has surpassed the physical. The physical dealerships that support the leading internal combustion engine car companies may prove to be equally challenging as electric vehicle makers such as Tesla bypass dealer channels altogether via online purchasing of their cars.

The COVID-19 pandemic has shone yet another light on the already important nature of facilities and how they influence culture, staff engagement and productivity. Mandatory lockdowns across the world forced white-collar workers to abandon the office and work from home. In some circumstances, the employees have benefited from the lack of commute and increased flexibility. This has led to productivity increases and a reduction in absenteeism. In other circumstances, employees have lost connection to each other and to the organisation's culture, have found learning and development more challenging, and the move has reduced the levels of collaboration.

The COVID-19-powered acceleration of working from home has created an additional dynamic that's seldom discussed, and that's the wedge between employees in the same organisation who can work remotely and those who can't. Health, retail and hospitality, construction, logistics, mining and others are all industries where clerical and support employees get to work from home while their frontline colleagues have to continue attending the workplace. This demarcation is real, and many individuals resent those who don't have to keep coming into the workplace.

It's too early to tell the long-term impact that the pandemic will have on the use of business facilities around the world and the responses that companies will take. Some companies have taken very public stances already: the software company Atlassian has committed to a 'work from anywhere' policy, while electric vehicle manufacturer Tesla has called *all* of its workers back into the office.

Whatever the answer turns out to be for the strategic options and competitor dynamics within your industry, and for the post COVID-19 decisions that have to be made, the importance of facilities is not likely to diminish. Your overall organisation strategy must drive your facilities strategy, and it's a powerful lever to pull to effect significant cultural change and shareholder value.

10. Outsourced providers

It's 1928 and Henry Ford has just opened his Rouge River plant in Dearborn, Michigan to manufacture his new cars. Raw sand, iron ore and rubber make their way to the factory by barge and rail. These raw materials go in one end of the facility and come out the other as fully assembled Model-T cars with glass windscreens, metal body panels and engine, and vulcanised rubber tyres. The workers onsite bring the first modern production line to life, making every part of the car on site in a vertically integrated supply chain entirely controlled within the boundaries of the Ford Motor Company.

Contrast this to a modern consumer product such as an Apple iPhone. Famously 'designed in California' and 'assembled in China', an iPhone comprises a collection of high-tech parts made by specialist manufacturers including Corning (glassware), Broadcom (computer chips) and LG (cameras), all assembled by Foxconn in China.

Business has now evolved since the manufacture of the Model-T to reflect the simple fact that no one company can be the best at everything required to bring their goods and services to market.

As a result, outsource providers are a key lever of change in any transformation effort.

An outsource provider can be defined as any contractual relationship formed between two parties for the provision of specialist goods and services essential to the creation of the purchasing company's goods and services, or the maintenance of their BAU operations.

Every industry and company is obviously different, and, therefore, will make decisions on those special activities or functions that they choose to perform in-house, and those they're prepared to buy from an open market. Very few companies are prepared to make their own desktop operating platform, and so are happy to buy this from Microsoft. Likewise, many manufacturing companies are unwilling to purchase and maintain a fleet of delivery trucks, so they outsource this to companies such as Linfox. All pretty clear so far.

When making a decision on whether to outsource something, people may look through the lens of whether an activity or service is core or non-core. Core is typically defined as essential to the creation of the company's products, and non-core defines everything else. Core functions should be performed in-house, and non-core functions can be outsourced, so the theory goes.

This is a somewhat clumsy approach. If this were true, then it would be unlikely that The Coca-Cola Company would ever have outsourced bottling operations to a global network of specialist bottlers. Or that Apple would outsource manufacturing and assembly of their products to a Chinese multinational.

Instead, the lens to look through when considering outsource decisions is whether something is strategic or non-strategic. Strategic can be defined as those few things that are absolutely critical to the success of the organisation, and in which it has a competitive advantage above all others. When viewed through this lens, the decisions of Coke and Apple make sense: Coca-Cola's competitive advantage lies in its recipe formula and its global branding and market positioning. As it turns out, as long as the consistency of flavour, branding and packaging are maintained, they're happy for others to bottle and distribute their product.

Likewise, Apple. Their competitive advantage lies in the design of the customer interface, the amazing features of their phone and the global branding that makes every release a must-have product. They too are willing to outsource assembly to a third party as long as they can ensure quality, delivery and price parameters.

When considering your own transformation, it's useful to reflect on what's most strategic to your organisation (the *kokoro*) and put all your energies into protecting this from disruption. Or at least embracing the opportunities associated with a looming disruption and providing this product or service better than everyone else. Everything else required to run and operate your organisation can be evaluated by asking whether there's an organisation for which this activity or function is at the heart of their own business model, and could therefore be better sourced and provided by them.

Rappaport's shareholder drivers

The highest use of capital is not to make more money, but to make money do more for the betterment of life.

Henry Ford, American industrialist (1863–1947)

Since coming across Alfred Rappaport's book *Creating shareholder value* more than 30 years ago, I haven't seen a framework for assessing and improving businesses that's as pragmatic, intuitive and valuable. His model is very simple, and contains seven drivers that can individually or in concert with others drive value for the shareholder:

1. *revenue growth*: the rate of growth over time

2. *operating margin*: the difference between unit sale price and unit direct costs

3. *cash tax rate*: the rate of tax paid

4. *working capital*: the change in receivables, payables and inventories

5. *capital expenditure*: the amount required to maintain and/or grow the business

6. *weighted average cost of capital*: the balance of debt and equity and their respective costs on the balance sheet

7. *competitive advantage period*: the period over which the company can expect to enjoy a competitive advantage, or as Warren Buffet would say, its 'moat'.

Quite simply, a transformation leader should pull the levers of change to deliver outcomes that are then measurable in terms of one or more of these drivers. These shareholder drivers are how you also address the critically important financial objectives of the transformation. The company must retain (or achieve) a strong balance sheet, and a healthy profit and loss/cash flow statement to claim a successful transformation. None of this is rocket science, but let's consider each of these seven drivers in a bit more detail so that we don't leave anything on the table or unaddressed.

Revenue growth

This driver is about the degree to which sales are growing sustainably over time. An example calculation is that revenue next month (or year) consistently exceeds revenue this month (year).

Why it's important:

- Good businesses consistently grow (think Amazon).

- Businesses that are not growing are in trouble (think Kodak).

- Revenue is a surrogate for market relevance (i.e. the customers value the services and they're prepared to pay for them).

- With revenue growth comes strategic options for the business and the people who work in it.

Pulling the strategic levers including customers and markets; products and services; alliances; and platforms can help you drive revenue growth.

Driving increased revenue is a sure-fire way to contribute towards greater shareholder value. The revenue growth needs to be profitable though (see below). In the early stages of a new business, revenue growth is likely to be the only game in town as the founders drive to reach scale and keep cash flowing. Revenue growth may be pursued in defiance of every other consideration. This obviously makes sense in the short term, because each new sale absorbs a share of your early existing fixed and establishment costs, and the sooner you break even the better.

Revenue growth is important, but an infinite focus on revenue growth can't go on for ever. At some point you have to make a profit.

Operating margin

As you know, your operating margin is the difference between what you sell a product or service for, and what it costs to produce it. You can measure it at the transaction level or the company level. Believe me, you'll know if the difference is in the wrong direction. Obviously, the bigger the difference, the greater the profit.

Why it's important:

- Every business needs to generate a profit, otherwise it will go broke.

- The operating margin reflects the degree to which business operations are effective and efficient:

  - effective means delivering a customer outcome that's valued

  - efficient means the outcome is produced with the minimum of cost.

There are two ways to increase your operating margin:

- increase the sale price per item you charge each customer (by pulling levers such as customers and markets; products and services; and platforms)

- reduce the cost of production, or the cost of something else within the company (by pulling operational levers such as business process, technology, organisation structure and facilities).

There's not a lot more to say about it really. Increase your prices or cut your costs.

Cash tax rate

All companies pay tax on their profits. Unlike individuals, who pay tax on income as they go, businesses pay tax after everything else has been tallied up. The easiest calculation to determine tax is:

- sales less costs equals profit
- profit less interest and other deductions equals taxable income
- income multiplied by the corporate tax rate is the cash tax rate.

Reducing the amount of cash you pay in tax obviously means that you're able to keep more of the cash profits generated by the business. These surpluses can then be paid as either dividends or reinvested in the business to grow revenues and/or improve operating margin.

This book is not about tax — heaven forbid — but there are multiple ways to reduce the cash tax rate paid, such as accelerated depreciation of assets, getting professional tax advice and moving to lower cost tax jurisdictions. You know what a reduction in your individual tax rate means for you, and companies are no different. Enough said.

Working capital

Working capital is the money used to finance day-to-day trading. An example calculation involves current assets (think receivables, cash in the bank and inventories), less current liabilities (including bank overdraft and payables). You obviously want this simple math to be positive — that is, your current assets exceeds your current liabilities.

Why it's important:

- Money has a cost (measured by interest rates).
- Interest is paid on every dollar borrowed.
- Interest is received on every dollar deposited.
- Good companies try to optimise their working capital.

In the most basic manner, an improvement in working capital is valuable. It becomes more valuable as interest rates increase. In a nutshell, you want to manage the level of accounts payable, accounts receivable, cash and inventories.

This is an underutilised lever. Many years ago, I consulted to a leading blue chip industrial company. We were re-engineering the finance function around a shared services model. We analysed their receivables and their payables. Incredibly, they were doing a daily and weekly cheque run for the urgent bills (whatever 'urgent' meant?) and a monthly cheque run for the balance of their invoices. On the other side of the ledger, they were granting their biggest customers payment terms based on 30 days after invoice, which meant that in some cases (for example, in the earliest days of the month, they were selling and shipping product, and then invoicing at the end of the month). The astute customer was therefore ordering at the start of the month — let's say the 1st — they were being invoiced on the 30th, and then they were paying on the 30th of the next month.

These two scenarios taken together meant that this company was essentially paying cash out on a daily, weekly and monthly basis, while they were collecting money sometimes 60 days after the customer had actually bought and taken ownership of the product. The money was going out much faster than it was coming in. Insanity. Don't do this.

Capital expenditure

Capital expenditure is the money required to purchase durable assets such as property, plant, technology and equipment required to run the business. Pretty straightforward.

Why it's important:

- It costs money to set up and establish a business.
- You typically have to spend this money before you see a dollar of income.
- If you can minimise the amount you have to spend on fixed assets, it can help you make a profit.
- If you can match the cash you have to pay to the cash you earn, that can help make a healthy business.

Weighted average cost of capital

The cost of money used to finance a business is typically either borrowings (on which you *have* to pay interest) or equity (on which you *may* pay a dividend).

Why it's important:

- Interest on money borrowed must be paid.
- In your life there's a big difference between interest on a credit card and interest on a mortgage, and so it is for a business if the mix of debt is not optimised.
- The higher the rate of interest on capital you pay, the less cash you keep.

Optimising your weighted average cost of capital is important. Ideally you want to use long-term finance for long-term assets (i.e. you get a mortgage to buy a house, you don't use a credit card) and you use short-term finance for short-term assets or expenses (i.e. you take out a personal loan to buy a car). Enough. I'll stop there. You get it.

Competitive advantage period

All companies try to build a sustainable competitive advantage for themselves. The source of this competitive advantage could be:

- *a proprietary patent*: think of the recipe for Coca-Cola, or Amazon's logistics algorithms

- *a proprietary technology*: think Tesla's full self-driving development
- *a brand*: think Apple, Hermes or Red Bull
- *scale*: think BHP or Saudi Aramco
- *relationships:* think Goldman Sachs or KPMG
- *a platform*: think the Apple App Store, Uber or Airbnb
- *a network effect*: think Facebook.

And many others.

Will competitor companies try to erode this advantage and build their own competing advantage? The question is therefore, how long would it take a competitor to build an advantage or erode your existing advantage.

Why it's important:

- The better the competitive advantage, the more profitable the company, and the harder it is to beat.
- However, we now live in a world where competitive advantage is more fleeting than ever:
  - physical bookstore chains with many bookstores vs Amazon online and Kindle
  - Nokia mobile phone vs Apple iPhone with apps and music combined
  - Blockbuster's many video stores vs Netflix online streaming
  - Kodak cameras and film vs Apple iPhone with inbuilt digital camera (you know you're in trouble when someone else is giving your core product away as a feature of their product).
- The current cost of an electric car is the most it will ever be — they'll only get cheaper.

- The current number of petrol cars is the highest it will ever be — electric cars will grow as a percentage of total market share.

Bringing the two frameworks together

The two frameworks of levers of change (by the Price Waterhouse change integration team) and value drivers (by Alfred Rappaport) individually are interesting. Combining them becomes fascinating. The easiest way to bring the two models together is to create a simple matrix and to then develop hypotheses (based on whatever company or industry you're involved in) at each intersection. Some of the intersections will be extremely powerful and opportunistic, while others will be less so, or irrelevant. Nonetheless, spending several hours on filling out this table for your own company will be time well spent, and is likely to yield some interesting results and opportunities.

5. Keep score: use KPIs to align and provide regular feedback

One thing that I have learned is that you must study results, not methods.

Henry Ford, industrialist (1863–1947)

The final piece of this chapter is to use metrics and Key Performance Indicators (KPIs) to align and keep score as you proceed to change your organisation.

Develop a couple of clear KPIs for the three key elements required for any successful transformation: disruption, strategy and execution. They will provide a simple dashboard to highlight the progress that's being made against these three elements. They can also be cascaded across the company to ensure people understand the expectations that have been placed on them, and critically, that they're all moving in the same direction. It's also imperative that these KPIs and scorecards are used to assess the actual performance of the individual executives and the overall change effort itself, to ensure that transformation is in fact being delivered. Without clear metrics it's easy for everyone to bullshit themselves that they're making progress.

There's a difference between measuring the performance of a transformation program (i.e. changing the business) and managing the existing BAU (i.e. running the business). This is especially relevant because many people who may be expected to govern a transformation project, may never have managed one, and may therefore approach this accountability with an unrealistic view of what the project should look like, the scope of its objectives, the degree of precision possible and the inevitable ambiguity that's inherent in all transformation efforts.

This appears so self-evident that you may wonder why they're even included in a blueprint on how to get big strategy done. After all, the importance of measurement is key to organisational and corporate life. However, when it comes to transformation, it's often tempting to use existing measures, to assume that everyone — including those doing and those overseeing the work — will know instinctively what's expected of them, to include assessment of overall performance within the normal management fabric and to be either too hard or too soft when assessing actual performance.

It's therefore prudent to unpack some of this detail and ensure that you set up the governance framework for success. This means:

- acknowledging the difference between transformation and BAU
- reconfirming your transformation goals
- identifying the right KPIs
- cascading the right KPIs to the right people
- ensuring everyone has skin in the game
- building alignment across the team
- removing all doubt: setting clear expectations
- assessing performance and alignment
- understanding the ambition paradox.

Let's consider each of these.

Acknowledge the difference between transformation and BAU

As we know, the status quo never has to argue its own case. It plods along until someone or something actively changes it. The status quo also already measures and assesses itself, and there's a whole infrastructure, culture and cadence that's in place. As Stephen Bungay writes in *The art of action*, 'The two most important organisational processes are budgeting and performance appraisal. They form part of the corporate body language, more powerful than anything anyone says, which shapes organisational culture.' The status quo will be safely protected by these annual budgets, which have already been set at the start of the year, inclusive of the existing strategy, and the corporate assumptions and cultural beliefs that underpin them. These budgets will have been converted into scorecards for all of the senior executives, and they'll be earnestly and conscientiously trying to deliver them each day. The status quo therefore has everyone striving hard to retain it.

Feedback in such a BAU environment typically starts by asking questions such as:

- What were the objectives and goals for this month/year?
- What was performance like against budget?
- What was performance like last month/year?
- What resources were consumed to produce it?
- What has changed this month/year?
- How did we go?

It's pretty straightforward to review and compare performance in this kind of environment, and a high degree of precision, predictability and causality is possible. After all, there are historical results, established scorecards and a clear monthly or quarterly rhythm with supporting KPIs and metrics already produced by specialist teams for review. For example, if sales go up, it can be directly tracked to greater customer demand, new marketing efforts or higher prices. If costs go up, it can be directly tracked to input prices, inflation, wages growth or efficiency levels. The relationships and causality are typically linear and historically well understood.

Everyone is no doubt familiar with this.

By contrast, a transformation program is ambiguous. There's less certainty and less precision. There are mysteries and risks. There are creative blind alleys, unexpected complexity, and when actively transforming a business you will run into unexpected problems that are difficult to plan for, such as:

- Your working assumptions were just plain wrong.

- Decisions will take longer than planned because of the resistance of corporate characters.

- Deliverables take longer to approve as the scope, reality and gravity of the change become more apparent.

- The complexity of technology systems is greater than expected (recognising that in transformation, when digging in the legacy technology environment you never turn over rocks and find buried treasure). Unpicking and replacing systems is *always* more time consuming and expensive than first thought.

- As the transformation proceeds, there's always another part that could be added. After all, if the bonnet of the car is up and we're replacing the engine, why not also paint the car and change the tyres at the same time?

And all the while the project clock is ticking with a degree of transparency of direct costs, time and expectation for new outputs that the BAU may not be typically subject to.

This doesn't mean you don't need to assess performance and provide feedback in a transformation environment. Far from it. Performance assessment and feedback becomes even more important. It just means that the governance and feedback has to take these more challenging circumstances into account.

Prussian Field Marshal Helmuth Von Moltke (1800–1891) is famously quoted as saying that 'A good plan lasts until first contact with the enemy.' What he's describing is the ambiguity associated with planning a military campaign in advance, with all its unknowns, frictions and factors that simply can't be forecast. And while we can agree that leading a corporate transformation is not as challenging, dangerous or of such gravity as managing a war, we can also concur that a corporate transformation will be ambiguous, imprecise and difficult, and therefore it too cannot be planned, estimated and budgeted with perfect precision. You simply cannot anticipate every issue, problem, human response or obstacle in advance, and have a plan up your sleeve for what you will do. You will inevitably have to assess, contemplate and respond as required, and do so transparently so that key stakeholders are aware of what is happening and learn to appreciate and be comfortable with your approach.

What you can always be clear on is what you want to achieve, and how you want to achieve it. You can then have appropriate feedback loops to ensure you learn from the inevitable mistakes and blind alleys you'll encounter, and to set up pragmatic and practical mechanisms for ensuring that you achieve your transformation goal.

Reconfirm your transformation goals

As the leader of a transformation, your strategic goals and objectives will be unique to you. However, it's useful to outline some general principles for reconfirming your goals while looking through the lens of disruption, strategy and execution, and to pose a couple of questions that will help you develop a useful set of metrics.

When it comes to disruption within your industry, what's the emerging point of differentiation? For example, in the car industry it might be the migration from internal combustion engines to electric vehicles. In power generation it might be renewables versus fossil fuels. In retail it might be digitally enabled sales versus physical store sales. Whatever your industry, you can start tracking some of the main metrics that illustrate the degree of change in the industry and the speed of this change.

Having identified these disruptions you'll also have developed your own strategy and objectives. It's obviously impossible to predict what they might be in a book like this, but they'll no doubt be reflective of the new company or organisation that you wish to create and/or transform to.

You should restate your strategic objectives through the lens of the levers of change. For each lever that you think relevant — which may not be all of them but should be over five or six — you should attempt to write a simple statement that illustrates the 'from/to' story that you'll be looking to achieve.

An example transformation blueprint can illustrate the point (see table 4.6). The summary is intended to get to the very heart (the *kokoro*) of what you're trying to achieve and describes the essence of the change. It should be clear that the company or organisation is going to move away from one state of being to another, transformed state of being.

Table 4.6   example transformation blueprint

Change lever	From	To
• Products and services (I)	• Manual/paper based	• Digital/auto registered
• Products and services (II)	• Existing regulated	• New/unregulated
• Markets	• NSW only	• NSW only (no change)
• Customers	• Existing	• Existing and new
• Business processes	• Inefficient/manual	• Efficient/automated
• Technology	• Legacy/data centre	• Cloud/SaaS
• Organisation structure	• Tall/hierarchical	• Flat/flexible
• People (I)	• Excess to requirements	• Balanced to needs
• People (II)	• Disengaged/resentful	• Engaged/motivated
• Culture	• Seniority based	• Meritocracy based
• Facilities	• Old tired building	• Contemporary office

A simple table such as this can summarise much of what you're trying to achieve. It describes what you want rather than how you're going to deliver it, and it serves as an objective checklist for measuring the success of the transformation effort.

As we've seen, the longer a transformation project takes to deliver its goals, the more expensive it gets, the more fatigue people feel and the more likely that accountable executives will prematurely call success. Having a statement of intent in a simple table such as this one will keep everyone honest, facilitate effective planning and scheduling, enable the communication of clear intent, and serve as the final yardstick for calling completion. Done is done.

Once you've summarised your simple transformation goals, you can then proceed to develop a set of metrics to measure the degree to which you've achieved them.

Identify the right KPIs

Austrian-American consultant and author Peter Drucker's observation that 'What gets measured gets done' appears to have become a truism of corporate theory. Having recommitted to the overarching strategic goals of the transformation, you should now start identifying the metrics that are going to provide real objective evidence that you're achieving these goals.

Right up front you should develop a *'Change* the Company' dashboard that's distinct and separate from your existing *'Run* the Company' dashboard. This recognises that there's already a detailed set of metrics, scorecards and apparatus in place to run the company and highlights the need to use a different set of metrics to measure the degree of change that's being delivered.

Again, this book cannot possibly predict the metrics that will be most suitable for your industry, organisation context or point in time. However, universal principles and questions can still be useful to facilitate the development of your own set.

The most important thing to remember when setting KPIs is to choose metrics that are:

- objective (i.e. hard to bullshit)
- linked to an outcome (the ends) rather than the means
- simple to calculate

- movable with the resources you have available
- assignable to people and/or teams
- relatively few in number
- *observed to move one of Rappaport's shareholder drivers.*

This list of metrics can now form the basis of a dashboard that will keep track of the transformation and its delivery of the original strategic objectives. It does not, however, necessarily track or translate the financial benefits of the transformation into an easily digestible and clear format. This is where Rappaport's shareholder value drivers can complement the original Price Waterhouse levers of change to bring an essential financial lens to the dashboard.

Table 4.7 shows complementary financial metrics from Rappaport.

Table 4.7 complementary financial metrics

Shareholder driver	Simple metric
• Sales growth	• $/% growth ONLY from new products
• Operating margin (I)	• $/% gross margin ONLY from new products
• Operating margin (II)	• $/% cost reduction ONLY delivered by program
• Working capital	• $/% improvements ONLY delivered by program
• Fixed capital	• $/% improvements ONLY delivered by program
• Weighted cost of capital	• % improvement ONLY delivered by program
• Cash tax rate	• % improvement ONLY delivered by program
• Competitive advantage period	• Relative position based on disruption metrics

Inclusion of Rappaport's value drivers grounds the transformation in financial results and the delivery of shareholder value. It's a great way to keep score to ensure that you don't gold plate the transformation program or pursue pet projects that will never deliver shareholder value.

A quick point to complete the discussion on KPIs and metrics: the *'Change* the Company' dashboard approach outlined is designed to facilitate reflection on what you're trying to achieve strategically and how you'll measure success in an absolute sense (for example, have you really digitised and automated your business processes?). It doesn't provide guidance on the metrics you need to govern the different parts of the transformation journey, such as scope, schedule, budget, and so on.

The transformation will require an iterative approach whereby you break the journey down into its constituent phases and reset the metrics iteratively for each phase. The program metrics appropriate to governing the transformation approach are pretty well known, and typically comprise the 'seven project keys' across:

1. *Scope*: the outcome of what you're trying to achieve. Obviously, the scope of transformation must be the North Star of the program, and all decisions reviewed and made while looking through that lens. Elements of the scope will need to be ranked, because if they're sufficiently ambitious, they cannot all be completed simultaneously. I use the term 'ranked' instead of 'prioritised' on purpose. They're not the same. It's very easy for business leaders to communicate their many 'priorities' without being specific. Ranking demands a disciplined approach to setting a definite *order* of priority.

2. *Schedule*: the forecast timings anticipated to complete the work. Set an ambitious but reasonable schedule. Build in time for the inevitable delays associated with unexpected issues, unanticipated complexity, and the constructively fierce debate of ideas and decision making. If you think the schedule is too long, then demand quicker decisions before you ask for quicker deliverables.

3. *Budget*: the forecast cost anticipated to complete the work. Revisit the budget within the overall business case to ensure that it remains worth it. Review the project budget through the lens of the scope and satisfy yourself that the program is not wasting money. Keep it ruthlessly lean and transparent

so that there's no gold plating and it's effective and efficient at delivering the transformation. As unanticipated issues arise ensure that they're dealt with transparently.

4. *Stakeholders*: the people, internal and external, who will be affected. Ensure all stakeholders are identified, together with their 'stake'. Be clear on the winners and losers and manage all of them accordingly.

5. *Risks*: the events that could affect the success of the program. Be realistic about the project's risks, including the strategy (does delivery of the project matter?), execution (are there capability and resources to deliver it?), scope (will it deliver what it says?) and benefits (will it be measurably complete?).

6. *Issues*: the events that have arisen and which could affect the success of the program. Ensure that there's a clear mechanism to identify and escalate issues, and then hold the executives accountable for deciding in a timely manner how to resolve them.

7. *Benefits*: the financial and other benefits that you have committed to achieving. Every executive should be on the hook for delivery of the transformation. They must be inspired, aligned and rewarded for achieving the change required to address the disruption and deliver the organisation's strategy.

By tracking these metrics, you can manage and measure the programs of work required to conceive the corporate strategy, understand the current state, design the detailed future state, and then implement the changes required to deliver the transformation.

It's also important to be honest about which metrics are going to be negatively affected by the transformation and to be transparent and objective about this. Unless you acknowledge these, and adjust executive scorecards accordingly, you can inadvertently create misalignment among the executive team and have senior people unfairly and counter-productively working at cross purposes.

An example illustrates how easily this can happen. In a consumer bank transforming to be more digital, it's a reasonable expectation that the weight of capital investment will be directed at the digitisation of key products and business processes. In such an environment, threadbare carpet in the branch network should be taken as a sign your strategy is working, not a cause to reinvest in the channel that customers are evolving away from, or to sanction the executive responsible for managing the physical branches.

Cascade the right KPIs to the right people

As the transformation leader, you simply cannot do it all. You would be deluding yourself if you think you can have a positive influence by continually intervening. You therefore have to select the right people and delegate work to effect large-scale change.

Equally, you need to ensure that the people you task with different parts of the organisation are not working at cross purposes. In a corporate environment there will always be 'rationalists' who come in each day and deliver against their scorecards. They may not care about context, purpose or what everyone else is doing. They just want to do their job and deliver their scorecard goals. It's therefore critical that you capture all of these personality types with scorecard goals that are clearly aligned to the transformation. For these rationalists, if the goals change, then so does their behaviour and direction of energy. You need to harness this.

Companies and organisations are theoretically based on everyone pulling in the same direction; however, as the many corporate characters described in section 3 of this chapter ('Build the team: get the right people') attest, there will always be those who put their self-interest first, regardless of what their company is trying to achieve. Altruism and ambition among executives and employees are great for building support. However, to be truly successful, and engage everyone in the effort, you also have to appeal to self-interest.

That's because, as Jack Lang, former premier of New South Wales, famously said, 'In the race of life, always back self-interest — at least you know it's trying.' It's through the right metrics and their inclusion in an individual's scorecard that you build alignment between all executives and the transformation program. If you don't reset their scorecards, then you'll always have the rationalists determinedly delivering their scorecard outcomes even if they're at odds with the transformation. They'll be working against you.

This is where the right KPIs for the right people comes in. You need to identify those people in the organisation who occupy the fulcrum roles (discussed earlier) and insist that they have the right KPIs assigned to align their energies and efforts. You need to get them lined up behind the effort so that they know what the objectives are, they agree and buy in to the transformation plan, and they care deeply and accept the new definition of what the organisation will look like.

You should also review the scorecards of all other executives and ensure that none of them are likely to delay, obstruct or duplicate the transformation. Both of these steps are critical. The first is relatively common, the second not so much.

Once you've converted the transformation goals to scorecard elements and then cascaded them to the necessary team members, you should require them to report back to you. There's an art to explaining the transformation goals, converting them to succinct and digestible tasks and activities, linking this to scorecards and communicating it to others. You need to deliberately practise and have clarity of thought to ensure that everyone understands what you're trying to collectively achieve.

A formal and personalised letter to each executive in your team to open the coming performance year is an excellent way to set up the KPI cascade. In such a letter you should:

- outline the context of the transformation for the company
- explain what you're trying to achieve
- cascade the actual KPIs and scorecard expectations
- reinforce the degree of latitude that each executive has to work out how they'll deliver their accountabilities for the transformation
- close with a personalised message reinforcing the trust you have in each executive.

When you then sit down to discuss the points in the letter, you can have a constructive discussion about the year ahead and how success will be measured. You should also ask your team member to repeat what you've told them back to you to ensure that everyone is on the same page, and there is no doubt as to what is expected. There's nothing worse than getting to the end of the performance period and having someone say, 'I didn't know what you expected of me!'

So you've now explained and agreed with the overall strategic context in which the transformation is taking place, been clear with your requirements and expectations and decided how you intend to measure progress. Great! With each executive having equally communicated their understanding back to you, you have collectively created the perfect environment for the objective assessment of actual performance into the future.

Ensure everyone has skin in the game

Okay, so far so good. You're leading the transformation, and you've been assessing your own progress using the transformation mechanics.

- You're personally committed. Check.
- You've developed and communicated a clear strategy. Check.
- You've selected your team, and they have the right temperament and skills. Check.
- You've cascaded the KPIs to them. Check.

Having got to this point, how much of each executive's scorecard should be related to transformation? There's no simple or easy answer to this question, but perhaps another question will shine some light on this critical topic.

The key consideration is, simply: how important is it for the company that this transformation is successful? Is the disruption on the horizon likely to permanently and terminally affect the company unless the change is acknowledged, a clear strategy set, and most critically, the correct actions implemented?

It's the answers to these questions that should drive the allocation of weight to each executive's scorecard. Many companies say stuff like 'this transformation will be the most important thing we need to do' but then when you look at the executive scorecards, its delivery is assigned 10 per cent for a couple of the executives. The rest of their scorecard is based on them successfully managing the business as usual. Said another way, the executives have 10 per cent at risk linked with leadership through uncertainty and change, and 90 per cent at risk linked to management of the BAU that continues to plod along. This is not a good approach for alignment around making a transformation a success.

Transformation-focused leaders are comfortable linking their scorecards to the actual change that's required. Less ambitious managers may find linking their scorecards to transformation very uncomfortable.

If the company is serious about transformation, then the leader's scorecard should have well over 50 per cent allocated to it. That means, for the leader to be successful, the company must transform. Managing the existing BAU component successfully is not enough and shouldn't result in a big bonus payment. Leading a transformation is difficult, it's risky and it's likely to make the hair on the back of your neck stick up from time to time. For the executive looking to quietly hit their BAU scorecard and pay for their holiday house and private school fees, this is not always good.

Transformation-focused leaders delegate the BAU so they can personally spend more time leading and shaping the more difficult change effort and putting their efforts into making sure the program is ambitious and meaningful, that the entire executive team is aligned, and that it's fully resourced to be successful.

No senior person in the company should be able to be 100 per cent successful while delivering only the BAU. Additionally, a transformation program should be an 'all boats make it to shore' effort whereby everyone makes it or none do.

You must also understand how your people may react to being given scorecard targets relating to a challenging transformation effort.

People can respond to transformation scorecard objectives and the ambiguity associated with them in either of two ways:

- they're up for it; or
- they're not.

It's a simple fact of organisational life that not everyone can deal with the ambiguity of challenging goals without a clear roadmap. As we saw earlier in the 'Build the Team' section, the 'Care Free' and the 'Authoritarian' are two personality types that are simply not cut out for transforming an organisation. Both of these traits are going to make a transformation more difficult than it needs to be. For those not up for it, or who are not suited to the ambiguity associated with transformation, you — as the leader — will need to decide whose needs are most important: those of the company, shareholders, customers and employees who benefit from the transformation, versus those of the individual executive who is not up for it, because it's unlikely that the needs of both group can be simultaneously satisfied.

Build alignment across the team

Because you've selected high performers with high energy and ambition, and you've cascaded their scorecards, it's a safe bet that they'll all now be aligned and on you all go to transformation success. Sounds easy, doesn't it? Well, it is — and it isn't.

By taking personal accountability, the leader must start to build team cohesion around the effort. Team cohesion is built off a common understanding, agreement and commitment to all elements of the transformation, including:

- *the disruption:* everyone agrees that the forces identified will negatively or terminally affect their company, and their roles, and therefore change is required

and ...

- *the strategy:* everyone understands the options that could be pursued and agrees and aligns to the option that's proposed as the way forward and ...

- *the execution*: everyone agrees with the way the transformation will unfold and the implications it has for their role and their part of the business.

It's very difficult to achieve a successful transformation unless the team agrees on all three of these elements. Otherwise, the project will be pulled in different directions or stalled altogether. Should an executive team be unable to discuss, debate and agree on all three elements, then either:

- the transformation goals, methods and approach must be adjusted until they can, or

- failing this, if after there has been a thorough, open and honest analysis of all aspects of the transformation, the dissenting executives should be replaced by people who are totally committed to the transformation (i.e. they recognise the disruption, agree with the strategy and support the execution approach).

As a leader of transformation, which is already difficult, the last thing you need when the going gets tough or you hit an unexpected obstacle, is a whole heap of 'I told you so!' personalities that will offer lukewarm public support, and simultaneous private steadfast resistance.

When the disruption is real, and transformation of the company urgent, the program and its outcomes are more important than any particular individual. And let's not forget that graveyards are full of indispensable people. No current individual is worth the entire company's future.

Once you've got the right people on the transformation program, you need to get the right metrics in their scorecards, *and* you need them all to understand one another's scorecards and metrics. You also have to adjust the scorecards of those not involved to ensure that they also support the effort. This is especially magnified if not everyone on the executive team is directly involved in the implementation of the strategy. It's critical that everyone understands the objectives and is required to put the full executive weight of their roles and their personal energy into the transformation to trigger a scorecard and bonus outcome.

Remove all doubt: set clear expectations

Given his amazing business success, Sam Walton, founder of major retailer Walmart, built some credibility around the importance of being direct with people, expectations and his belief that 'high expectations are the key to everything'. But clearly no-one believes that 'low expectations are something'. What's most important is *clear* expectations.

It's obvious, but often forgotten, that before you have a performance conversation, you must have had an expectations conversation. Clear expectations are critical to setting direction, evaluating performance and adjusting the approach. You know this. The only reason it's worth reminding ourselves is because we all get busy, and clarity of expectations can often be the first casualty.

Expectations can be considered in three ways:

- the leader's general expectations of everyone in the team (regardless of role)
- the team's expectations of the leader (as their people leader)
- the leader's expectations of each team member (reliant on role).

General expectations

It's 2006 and I'm on a plane flying across the Tasman Sea. I've just joined the Bank of New Zealand as the GM Technology and Operations. I've left my home in Sydney, and I'm preparing myself for my first day in the role. Overnight, the size of my team has increased from 10 to about 850 people. From accountability for developing strategies, ideas, white papers and governing projects in head office, I'm now responsible for the operations of the BNZ encompassing technology, mortgage processing, payments, fraud and security, property and customer account services and administration. It's daunting.

I knew upon landing and launching into my new role that my leadership team would want to know what was important to me. On the plane, I took out a piece of paper and wrote down a list of expectations that best described the standards I expected of myself, and of the people on my team.

In the years since, I've reviewed it regularly on entry to new roles, but it essentially remains as written, because I've never really thought it necessary to change it:

- *Confront reality.*
  - Let's look at the empirical data — what are the facts?
  - What are the metrics trying to tell us?
  - Hope is not a strategy.

- *Remember that trust once broken, is almost impossible to repair.*
  - So don't break it.
  - As the leader, assume trust.
  - People not trusting someone is usually a function of one or more of the following three elements: lack of character, lack of competence, lack of communication (most common).

- *Have no surprises: communicate.*
  - I'll keep the CEO/chairman/board in the loop.
  - I expect you to keep me in the loop.
  - Keep each other in the loop.

- *Act like a team.*
  - Be courteous — to each other, to employees, to our regulator, etc.
  - Don't blindside each other in meetings or in front of me.
  - Put things down by the side of the road.

- Empty the files you've gathered on each other.
- Pick up the phone, or even better, visit. Carelessly written emails/SMSs can be like corporate hand grenades because they lack context and emotion.

- *Take a whole-of-company view.*
  - All boats should make it to shore.
  - We are collectively smarter than individually — no-one has a monopoly on good ideas.
  - Know what success for the whole company looks like.
  - Whether the division or the company... there's only one share price.

- *Make yourself independently accountable.*
  - Get out of the river and stand on the bank regularly.
  - Be a leader (adapt to change) as well as a manager (adapt to complexity).
  - Take some personal and professional risk (though not with the integrity of our performance).
  - Leading should sometimes feel dangerous... what is it you'll want to remember from all of this time you've spent in the office over the years? I bet it won't be when you were comfortable or cruising along day to day.

- *Keep learning: empty your cup.*
  - Be open.
  - Be curious.
  - Reserve the right to get smarter.

- *Make your people successful.*
  - Use the data.
  - Extend a ladder, don't close a hatch.
  - Reward the 'doers' who get shit done.
  - Have the hard conversations.

- *Create an environment where people can get things done.*
  - There's no such thing as 'no decision'.
  - Don't step over things — fix them at point easy.
  - In my experience, the things you kick down the road get harder, not easier, to fix.

- *Have fun.*
  - Take the job seriously, but not yourself.
  - We'll all be a long time looking at the lid.
  - Be careful of context when you crack a joke and pick your time: I learned first-hand that apparently the chairman doesn't like jokes in his board meetings.

These are my 10 expectations and while you'll have your own, what I've found particularly useful is:

- they tell my team who I am and what I stand for
- it leaves them in no doubt about what I value, what I will tolerate and what I will reward
- they provide a yardstick for me to live up to — I absolutely abhor hypocrisy, so I'm equally bound to live by them.

The simple fact that they're written down and I've shared them with my team means that I can't escape them, and they become a foundation for assessing how we're all turning up each day. Sharing these with my team was not easy at first. However, I soon realised that the easiest way to get into them was to design a very short session for the team to cover:

- my expectations of the team
- the team's expectations of me
- the team's expectations of each other.

After I've spoken about my expectations, and answered any questions, I then facilitate a session on the team's expectations of me.

Team expectations

None of this is rocket science. The easiest way to facilitate this conversation with the team is to request them to take some sticky notes, write down some expectations they have of me and be ready to discuss them (too easy).

You might think my list of 10 expectations is long, but what inevitably happens is that the team's list of expectations on me is *always* longer. The team write up their sticky notes, we stick them in groups on the wall, we summarise and before long we've got a workable list. What's also interesting is that in every team I've led, one of the first expectations that the team members require of me is that I give them honest feedback on their performance. Absolute gold, because this is the gem that you want. In the near future, when you sit down to have their next performance conversation, you can preface your comments with:

> As you requested, I'm going to give you some honest and direct feedback. You need to think about blah blah blah. And here are the things I'd like you to stop, start and continue.

The importance of setting clear expectations cannot be overstated, and it provides a clear yardstick for living up to and for holding everyone accountable. And while we're on the subject of expectations, another very useful exercise to do with your team is to ask them to take some sticky notes and list everything that you can think of when you've felt most supported by, or you've admired or really liked your boss.

Again, group them on the wall, and pretty soon you'll have a workable list. This is where the session gets interesting. Now ask them to make another list of everything that you've absolutely hated in a boss or how they've behaved or operated.

Human nature being what it is, I guarantee that despite writing furiously, people will ask for more time, they'll get out of their chairs and search for more sticky notes, they'll look across at what their colleagues are writing and the energy and laughter will crank up a notch. Again, sticking them on the wall will ultimately translate to a summarised list.

Once done, it's then easy, as individuals and as part of a team, to commit yourself to aspiring to do more of list 1 (the positives) and less of list 2 (the negatives). And if you want to then use this to build momentum on the employee engagement front, and hold yourselves accountable for living up to them, simply share both lists with everyone in the company and say this is what we aspire to.

Specific expectations

You should be up front about what you want each executive to actually do. The individual scorecard is typically used for this. It's also good practice to write everything in a personal letter so that there can be no doubt about what's expected. In this way, you can have a very tailored conversation with each executive that covers the coming year or quarter. You can then use this letter as the basis for subsequent discussions throughout the coming period as you assess their performance against it. Sounds simple, but in my experience, it's rarely done in a thorough or consistent manner.

These expectations and scorecards then get cascaded down the organisation so that everyone knows what's going on and what's required of them. Writing it down is more important than only saying it. It provides a record, and there's no room for 'But I didn't realise' or 'I didn't understand' or 'I forgot about that'.

Building employee engagement around a transformation is partly grounded on everyone knowing where they stand and what's expected of them. If you take the view that 99 per cent of people want to do a good job and contribute to organisation success, then having them understand how their work and what they do fits into a greater whole is critical. Everyone has the right to understand what they're expected to do, and how their contribution will be measured and assessed. It's impossible for people to be engaged unless they understand the expectations that have been placed upon them.

Assess performance and alignment

Jack Welch, the long-serving CEO of General Electric, was right when he said that managers who don't provide feedback to their people are cruel. People need feedback. Direct and honest feedback is critical for people and businesses to thrive. Together with the setting of clear expectations, it's the basis of high-performing organisations. If you don't get feedback, then how do you improve either as an individual, as an organisation, or to take the necessary corrective action on a transformation project?

It's the role of the transformational leader to continually set the tone and reinforce clear accountability to the standards and expectations that have been set and agreed to. In most cases this is done by role modelling the behaviours and rewarding and celebrating those who most deliver. Pay rises, bonuses and promotions are all mechanisms to reinforce and set the tone for what's expected.

In corporate life, it's very energising and enjoyable to deliver the great news to someone that they're being promoted or paid extra. But sometimes people step outside the boundaries, sometimes a little and sometime egregiously. This is when leadership can become lonely. As Jocko Willink and Leif Babin write in their book *Extreme ownership*,

> *If an individual on the team is not performing at the level required for the team to succeed, the leader must train and mentor that underperformer. But if the underperformer continually fails to meet standards, then a leader who exercises extreme ownership must be loyal to the team and the mission above any individual. If underperformers cannot improve, the leader must make the tough call to terminate them and hire others who can get the job done. It is all on the leader.*

A couple of months after joining NSW Land Registry Services I sat down with one of my direct reports to close out the financial year. He'd worked for the old NSW Government Land Titles Office since leaving school, and he'd been appointed to the leadership team during the privatisation to help the organisation transform and navigate through what was obviously a sensitive and dynamic environment.

Having joined the company and worked with him for only three months before the financial year end, and not having been involved in setting his scorecard or the transformation objectives, there was not much context for me to work with, but I pressed on. I asked him some questions about how he thought he and the company was going, what he was pleased with, what he would do differently, and so on. Based on the things I'd observed I also provided some feedback about things he might want to stop, start and continue to keep developing his career.

We finished the meeting, and as he got up to leave, he said to me 'You know, Adam, I was a bit nervous about this meeting when I saw that the subject was performance review.'

'Why?' I asked innocently, because I certainly didn't read too much into the subject.

'Well, I've been working here for more than 33 years, and I've never received any formal feedback on how I'm going and how I could improve,' he said.

He left the room and I sat there thinking about what he'd just said. It got me wondering about how many people throughout their careers might not receive feedback at all or might receive ambiguous or superficial comments that don't help them improve.

The need for honest and regular feedback is even more important during times of transformation. Having set expectations in section 3 of this chapter ('Build the team: get the right people'), it's critical to hold others to account, while being sensitive to the reality that a transformation is more ambiguous and difficult to predict than that of a BAU environment, and therefore requires a slightly different approach.

Having set up the environment for effective review, and given that the very future of the organisation is at stake, assessment of performance must be:

- honest and objective
- clear and transparent
- regular and timely
- based on outcomes *achieved* not efforts made
- direct but sensitive.

The easiest way to measure progress against the transformation is to be ruthlessly honest and use either:

- green: achieved
- red: not achieved.

Do not use amber.

This simple binary approach removes all subjective interpretation and ambiguity. You're either achieving your goals or not. In the adult world, transformation measurement is about achieving results and outcomes. It's not about giving someone a ribbon for working hard and putting in a big effort. It's the results that matter, not how hard you worked.

Therefore, be clear, direct and objective about whether a deliverable or change objective has been achieved in absolute terms, and consider whether it's been delivered on time, on budget and on schedule. And this means it's either green or it's red.

Only after you assess actual performance should you then dive in and interrogate the results or reasons for not achieving them. Without taking this approach, everything will tend to become amber over time. A good definition of an 'amber' issue or deliverable is one that doesn't yet know it's 'red'. And let's not forget that there will always be some executives who have a preference for being rated amber over red, particularly if their performance is being transparently reported to a board. Beware the so-called watermelon project that's green on the outside, and red in the middle.

However, this is also where — and when — judgement and leadership are required to accurately and objectively call out deliverables and issues that are 'red', but to simultaneously create an environment within which executives (unless they're continual repeat offenders) are not crucified and can safely reach out for more support or resources to get them back on track.

When governing a transformation, never forget that it's inherently difficult because the status quo is determined to preserve its place via the corporate structures and customs already in place, and because there's often a cadre of corporate characters — including the losers, defenders and wimps — who are actively or passively resisting the change.

Tracking progress in a transformation environment is going to be different from the day-to-day BAU because the objectives are far more fluid, ambiguous and often times more ambitious. There's also no blueprint from the previous year to gauge progress against, nor are all of the resources for measuring performance as well matched and allocated to objectives as they are for the BAU. Remember that the status quo already has, by definition, all of the resources that it needs to proceed because that's exactly what it has successfully done in past years.

Transformation is therefore, by definition, paraphrasing Machiavelli, 'difficult and dangerous' to lead, and 'dubious of success'. Mistakes will be made, blind alleys pursued, and it's inevitable that even the most capable and motivated leader will stumble.

Transformation therefore requires the creation of an environment and culture of curiosity, the assumption of trust and continuing support to make the difficult decisions. When people stumble, they need support, not sanction, and this need to acknowledge and encourage leaders battling under difficult circumstances has a long tradition.

Von Moltke sought to create a culture that was designed to build individual initiative and organisational resilience, transparency and accountability in the 19th century. As Stephen Bungay writes in *The art of action,*

> *Superior officers were instructed to refrain from harsh or wounding criticism of mistakes lest it undermine the self-confidence of subordinates, to praise the fact that they did show initiative, and to correct them in such a way that they learn. 'Otherwise', as one general wrote, 'you will extinguish a hundred positive initiatives in order to prevent one error, and thereby lose a tremendous amount of energy.*

The difficulty in a transformation environment — where there are no existing guideposts and no established way of doing things — arises because there is an almost infinite variety of ways to get these things done, some of which may be very different from how you may have done them. Okay, let them be different. Create an environment of rigorous review of the outcomes achieved rather than only the methods or inputs used, and you may be surprised at how fast the transformation proceeds.

Ongoing transformation governance is critical. It should be based on common sense and reflective of the realities and difficulties inherent in the overall effort, be designed to build confidence in the respective leaders and create momentum for material change. This governance should also recognise that the feedback cycle is continuous. In *The strategist: Be the leader your business needs*, professor of strategy and corporate governance Cynthia Montgomery writes,

> *Good strategies are never frozen — signed, sealed, and delivered. No matter how carefully conceived, or how well implemented, any strategy put into place in a company today will eventually fail if leaders see it as a finished product. There will always be aspects of the plan that need to be clarified. There will always be countless contingencies, good and bad, that could not have been fully anticipated. There will always be opportunities to capitalise on the learnings that a business has accumulated along the way.*

For those directors and executives tasked with governing large transformation projects, it's important to acknowledge the realities associated with them. This is especially important if those on the governance forums haven't been involved in leading or delivering transformation. Ironically, these executives and directors may well be those people whose own personal home kitchen renovation project triples in price and takes twice as long because they simply don't understand how to manage projects.

Directors and executives tasked with the oversight of transformation projects should approach their responsibility with both humility and reasonableness. They'd do well to remember the words of US

President Theodore Roosevelt that, 'It's not the critic who counts' or the people sitting in the somewhat sterile governance forum with the benefit of hindsight or additional information that wasn't available when certain decisions were made.

Instead, according to Roosevelt,

> *The credit belongs to the man who is actually in the arena, whose face is marred by dust and sweat and blood; who strives valiantly; who errs, who comes short again and again, because there is no effort without error and shortcoming; [and] who spends himself in a worthy cause.*

The metrics, culture and cadence established around transformation, and all involved, should seek to be ambitious, honest and transparent, while simultaneously being supportive and sensitive to the challenges that will be encountered along the way.

Understand the ambition paradox

The Italian Renaissance painter and sculptor Michelangelo di Lodovico Buonarroti Simoni said, 'The greatest danger for most of us is not that our aim is too high and we might miss it, but that it is too low and we reach it.'

It's a fact of corporate life that not everyone will be ambitious. Some like to play it safe and achieve conservative goals with little stretch. Others like to set ambitious stretch goals and give everything a red-hot go. Who is right and who is wrong? This dynamic creates the perennial question of how ambitious we should be in the context of the ambition paradox.

The ambition paradox is the emergent requirement that we all be ambitious when we set our goals, but there's then zero tolerance for missing them. Or in other words, it's better to set a small goal and achieve it, rather than set a big goal and miss it. Zero tolerance for missing goals rewards conservatism and punishes ambition.

In corporate life we often hear statements like:

- 'You must deliver on your commitments' and
- 'We need consistent financial performance.'

These are both reasonable requirements. They form the basis of all budgeting and scorecard evaluation processes whereby you'd set a (quantitative) target, you'd measure the performance, you'd tally up at the end of the period and you'd determine the reward. The scorecard would probably have some different percentages for 'meets', 'exceeds' or 'outstanding'. All of it designed to be clear, transparent, somewhat binary, and to remove objective judgement. Seems fair at first glance.

Equally, we don't often hear statements like:

- 'We must shoot the lights out' or
- 'Let's double our existing performance.'

Imagine if your boss gave you these goals in the context of a 'normal' performance evaluation system. They might then seem like unreasonable requirements. If you used exactly the same approach as described above, word for word, would you still feel comfortable? Would the level of ambition seem equal, because the degree of difficulty is so much harder?

Are we setting goals designed to make evaluation easier rather than our ambitions higher?

Here's a theoretical example.

	Existing sales	Target sales	Final result
Executive A	$100 m	$102 m	$103 m
Executive B	$100 m	$110 m	$107 m

Who is the better executive and who should be most rewarded?

Under the ambition paradox, if your culture and corporate objectives most reward hitting targets, then executive A is the hero. Executive B clearly missed their target. No soup for you!

On the other hand, if your culture and corporate objectives most reward ambition, then executive B is the hero. While they missed their number, they actually delivered 4 per cent more than executive A, despite executive A actually exceeding their target. Executive B delivered more value in absolute terms.

Such a scorecard evaluation process is tricky because it requires debate and alignment when setting the targets, and then judgement and deep consideration when assessing final performance. But this system is now being more ambitious. It's acknowledging and rewarding ambition, rather than the steady state. It's a much more exciting system for the company, for their project and for themselves. For the transformation leader, it will be very energising. For the steady state manager, it will be very intimidating. This is the ambition paradox.

All things being equal, the right amount of ambition, combined with systems that acknowledge and promote it, is better for generating and rewarding true transformation.

Key points from chapter 4

- Identify potential disruptions and opportunities and discuss and debate logical and pragmatic strategies to address them. Having the right mindset, while providing an excellent foundation for transformation, will not of itself move the needle.

- Until you make a choice and actually commit, and then take appropriate *action*, the status quo will continue unchanged. Even the best strategy ever conceived will make no difference to the real world unless it is *implemented*.

- There are five key 'mechanics' that will help you successfully take action to drive your transformation forward:

  1. *do the work*: personal commitment of the leader

  2. *make decisions*: choose, own and communicate a clear strategy

  3. *build the team*: get the right people

  4. *be thorough*: follow a proven methodology and approach

  5. *keep score*: use KPIs to align and provide regular feedback.

- There is no substitute for the personal involvement of the leader.

- The transformation leader must choose, own and communicate the strategy. This cannot be delegated to another internal department or outsourced solely to consultants.

- The transformation leader must own and be prepared to communicate and argue for the strategy. That means the strategy must be clear and focused on the 'ends' and not just the 'means'.

- If success cannot really be tracked or is expressed in something that can't really be measured, it will be hard to make the strategy resonate with people.

- One of the most important accountabilities every transformation leader has is to build the team and select the right people.

- When evaluating people, try to deal in facts, and have your own objective set of criteria that you can use to determine the value people can contribute. Build diversity in all its forms into your teams. And remember: no individual is more important than the collective success of the company.

- The transformation leader must be thorough and follow a proven methodology and approach such as the 'levers of change' I've adapted from Price Waterhouse.

- Critically, you must ensure that pulling these 'levers of change' delivers a measurable result and increases shareholder value. You must be able to show how your changes increase shareholder value.

- You must keep score and use KPIs to align people and provide feedback. Your KPIs should be transformation focused and measure progress against the strategic destination that you want to implement. No-one should be in any doubt as to what's important and what they must personally contribute to the transformation.

- You must regularly confront reality and measure how you and your team are going. Give honest and candid feedback on what each person should stop, start and continue. Your job is to be clear, fair and hold people accountable to their commitments.

- While there are no silver bullets and no guarantees, by following the five 'mechanics' in this chapter you'll give yourself the best possible chance of a great transformation.

CHAPTER 5

Creating your 90-day blueprint

Even if you're supremely sensitive to the world around you, and subsequently capable of developing an awesome strategic response, many of the people you lead will judge you on what you do in your first 90 days. This is the period during which your closest team will judge your character, competence and overall cultural style. They will scrutinise the decisions you make (or not), the confidence and professionalism of your approach, and ultimately, whether they're prepared to follow you. It's therefore critical that you have a thorough plan for how you'll approach your first 90 days so that you finish it with a clear understanding of the major issues at hand, you make a meaningful connection with the people in your new team and you build a sense of momentum that the future will be positive.

| Making an impact

It's early 1951, and General Douglas MacArthur, commanding Korean war operations from his headquarters in Tokyo, Japan, has taken a gamble. He has ordered his seven US infantry divisions (when the United States has only 12 divisions in total across the globe) north towards the Communist Chinese border, where an army of 253 divisions — totalling five million men — awaits his arrival. What could possibly go wrong?

By mid December 1951, 30 000 US troops have been encircled and attacked by 120 000 Communist Chinese troops. The battle of Chosin Reservoir has just played out, being fought over some of the roughest terrain of Korea, during some of the harshest weather of the entire war. A cold front has even blown in from Siberia, plunging temperatures to as low as −38° Celsius. Medical supplies have frozen solid, wind chill is causing frostbite and weapons are continually malfunctioning.

The battle has left the United States with nearly 10 500 battle casualties, and the US Marines report another 7300 non-battle casualties due to the cold weather. The allies are in full retreat, trekking through treacherous and freezing mountain passes, crossing rivers frozen solid, up and down hills as they make their way to the port town of Hungnam 80 kilometres south. They abandon 50 000 square kilometres of previously hard-won territory in the process.

Winter has well and truly set in and morale is rock bottom. What's more, MacArthur's senior local representative, General Walton Walker, has just been killed in a car accident, his speeding jeep slipping on the icy roads and colliding with a truck.

To use the technical term, the US and the combined United Nations armies are in the shit.

Back in Washington, US General Mathew Ridgway receives his orders to move out and take command of US and UN forces in Korea. As he's preparing to travel, the last US forces depart Hungnam, blowing up the port facilities as they leave to prevent them falling into the hands of the enemy. It's not clear whether the situation can be saved, and the entire US and UN front could collapse at any moment.

Cometh the hour, cometh the man.

General Matthew Ridgway has enjoyed a meteoric rise through World War II, beginning the conflict as an aide to General George C Marshall, the most senior general in the US army. He rises to command the elite 82nd Airborne Division, campaigning through Sicily and the Normandy invasion, and then commands the entire airborne corps during the Battle of the Bulge.

Ridgway has already won fame as a highly successful, but humble and authentic, leader. Thomas Ricks writes in *The Generals*:

> Once explaining why he did not like to speak to his soldiers from steps and platforms, he said, 'I always disliked standing above people. I'm no better than they are. In rank, yes; in experience, yes; but not as a man.' Instead, he preferred to stand on the ground and look into their eyes: 'Looking into their eyes tells you something — and it tells them something too.'

After leaving the United States, he stops off in Tokyo on his way to Korea to confer with his old — and now current — boss, General Douglas MacArthur, one of the most controversial generals of the 20th century. Ridgway has worked for MacArthur before and knows full well the size of his ego, and how jealously he guards his reputation. The war is going badly, and he's under no illusion that he's on dangerous ground with the pompous MacArthur, and that if he puts a step out of line, he'll be fired.

Ricks continues, 'Ridgway's actions in the weeks after his arrival were a model of how to revitalise the spirit and reverse the fortunes of a sagging military force.'

Ridgway's first 90 days as commander

Let's examine a quick timeline from Ridgway's appointment as commander of UN forces just before Christmas, 1950, and get a feel for how he navigates his first 90 days.

Ridgway leaves Tokyo and flies straight to Korea. Within a day of arriving, he jumps into a B17 bomber aircraft and orders the pilot to fly across central Korea at 3900 metres so he can study the terrain over which he'll have to fight. He meets with South Korean President Syngman Rhee and assures him that the United States will not abandon him.

Ridgway then spends three days out in the field visiting local battlefield commanders, evaluating them and assessing how much they know about the enemy, the terrain they'll have to fight on, their level of aggression and enthusiasm, and the state of their own forces. He quickly realises that there's a significant lack of confidence throughout the ranks and that there's a unanimous desire among the forces to get out of there. He also discovers that his own headquarters is in a warm, comfortable, well-lit building hundreds of kilometres behind the front lines.

Only after having scoured the terrain, consulted with his senior people and made his own first-hand observations, does Ridgway start executing his plan.

He immediately moves his headquarters far closer to the front line and establishes his office in a tent. He orders his men to start patrolling aggressively, but he knows that they're not yet ready for a full offensive. Despite the state of the forces now under his command, he messages his boss back in Washington (as recounted by Thomas Ricks in *The Generals*): 'We shall be in for some difficult days, but I am completely confident of the ability of [my forces] to accomplish every mission assigned.'

Within two weeks of his arrival, he makes an early example by sacking a commander who was focused on withdrawal rather than holding or attacking. Despite the protests of the army and its civilian leadership back in Washington, he sacks not only his first divisional commander (who had only been there 39 days) but also another four generals over the coming months. Ridgway writes to Washington asking for three 'young, vigorous, mentally flexible Brigadiers already marked for high command by reason of demonstrated leadership', in the words of Ricks.

Ricks continues:

> *In a few short months of dynamic action, Ridgway turned the Korean War around. At the end of January 1951, the Americans for the first time not only stopped a full divisional assault by the Chinese but virtually annihilated the attackers.*

With pretty much the same set of resources that MacArthur had had at his disposal, Ridgway was able to first stabilise the front, and then push the more numerous Chinese forces right back over the 38th parallel.

In less than two months General Ridgway had quickly understood the strategic situation on the ground, aligned his army from top to bottom around new objectives, and then led and motivated the execution of a series of military manoeuvres that inflicted grievous casualties on his opponent.

And in an interesting side bar, Ridgway's success destroyed MacArthur's standing, making MacArthur seem far less indispensable. MacArthur would himself be fired several months later in April 1951.

General Ridgway didn't just turn up and wait to see what happened. However, nor was he fixed about what he'd find and what he'd do.

He had a flexible plan that he refined and executed brilliantly to reverse the losses incurred by the US and UN forces, and to lay the groundwork for a negotiated peace that has secured the division of North and South Korea at the 38th Parallel ever since.

His plan encompassed many of the mindset and mechanics outlined in chapter 4 — for example:

- *Selected 'mindset' elements*:
  - *Ambition*: Ridgway was ruthlessly ambitious for his army to prevail against the enemy, and this ambition was tempered by not wanting to put his forces at unnecessary risk. Unlike MacArthur, he didn't put his personal ambitions ahead of the organisation's.

  - *Curiosity*: he maintained an 'empty cup' and was sufficiently curious that he got out to the front lines to assess the terrain and condition of his forces before developing his plans.

  - *Kokoro*: he certainly got to the heart of the matter by identifying leadership as his army's greatest challenge, and then he worked forcefully to solve that problem. He put the organisation's mission and objectives before the personal comfort of its officers/executives. It was the soldiers and army that were most important, *not* the ego and comforts of the senior officers.

  - *Urgency*: he hit the ground running and displayed urgency to put things right. He realised that time was of the essence, and that failure to act quickly could get people killed. He didn't delay in personally assessing and then firing other generals who he didn't believe had the temperament and skills to help win the war.

- *Selected 'mechanics' elements*:

  ○ *Personal commitment of the leader*: Ridgway personally did the work. He managed his boss's expectations by visiting MacArthur in Tokyo. He also managed his 'client' — in this case, the President of South Korea — by visiting him upon arrival into Korea. He didn't float across the top of everything statesman-like or hire management consultants. Instead, he hopped onto an aircraft and went to the front line to see the terrain with his own eyes. He consulted with people — from privates to generals — to get a direct and very personal sense of what was happening, how people were feeling and what they needed.

  ○ *Choose and communicate a clear strategy*: Ridgway made his standards and objectives clear and he used the initial firing of a division commander to reinforce these standards.

  ○ *Get the right people and get them aligned*: Ridgway fired those generals in his team who didn't have the characteristics required to be successful. He recruited junior officers into the organisation to inject new energy, new ideas and a different style of leadership. He also led by example and moved his headquarters further towards the front and out of a comfortable, warm and well-lit building into a basic army tent. He sent a message to his men that he would experience the same living conditions and food rations as they did. This built alignment and connection to his troops.

  ○ *Follow a proven methodology and approach*: Ridgway was able to leverage the lessons, methods and experience that he'd gained across his entire career, from when he was a junior instructor at the US Army's infantry school through the furnace of World War II to then apply them in the Korean campaign.

In summary, Ridgway landed in Korea with a sense of courage and grand ambition to turn around the fortunes of his army. He knew he had to act with urgency, so he melded this ambition with a pragmatic plan to create a virtuous cycle of observation, thought and action. He very quickly identified that the heart of the matter (the *kokoro*) was leadership within his army, rather than a lack of resources. The US and UN forces, although significantly outnumbered, enjoyed superiority in equipment, training and logistical support. Ridgway was then able to get the right people into the critical leadership roles and focus (*kime*) all of these forces in a way that his predecessors could not. Then, with the same army and equipment, he completely reversed the tide of the war.

Ridgway was resilient. Despite being landed into a very physically difficult, threatening war zone, with a disheartened army and with success or failure hanging in the balance, Ridgway didn't panic or let the circumstances grind him down. Instead, he wrote to his boss with confidence saying that he could achieve his mission, and when he arrived at the front lines to visit his troops he was considered a refreshing change.

Your first 90 days

If you fail to plan, you are planning to fail.
Benjamin Franklin (1706–1790), US Founding Father

Before starting any new role, you should develop and document a plan addressing such things as priorities and hypotheses, and identifying stakeholders. You should then develop, inform, update and challenge the 90-day plan during the course of your first couple of months in the role by considering these three aspects:

1. mindset

2. mechanics

3. mistakes.

Next, we will walk through each of these aspects.

| Mindset

We've already discussed the mindset required to effectively tackle transformation, which can help you accelerate into your first 90 days. Intellectual humility and curiosity, a sense of urgency and being aware of your own biases are all traits that will help you enter a new role with a sense of purpose and balance. In the context of the first 90 days, you should also:

- be alert but not alarmed
- promote yourself into the job
- look in the mirror
- give up the 'expert' title
- want to win
- know what success looks like
- confront reality.

Let's consider each of these in some detail.

Being alert but not alarmed

As you come into your new role, it's useful to remind yourself that transformation is difficult, and by acknowledging this up front, together with the reasons why, you'll be far better mentally prepared to navigate these challenges.

Flex your mental muscles as you consider whether the power of the status quo, corporate factors or any of the personalities you'll meet or already know will work to prevent transformation.

You can get into the right mindset by asking yourself early questions such as:

- How strong is the status quo?
- How long is it since there was a successful transformation?

- Is the company seeking to transform from a position of strength or is there a burning platform?
- How strong is the existing culture?

Think about the corporate factors that might hinder the transformation. Challenge yourself with some critical questions such as:

- Is everyone aware of the signals suggesting that transformation is required?
- What's currently being invested in and does this need to change? Are there competing priorities?
- Are there existing projects that need to be stopped?
- What are your competitors already doing?
- What unwritten assumptions in this company may need to be challenged?
- What are the prevailing cultural norms that must be either harnessed or challenged?
- What people are available or looking for new opportunities in the company?

Lastly, think about the personality types that you might encounter. As you plan the interviews that will help you to understand what's going on and who's who in the zoo, think about the questions and interview techniques that you'll use to deeply understand the level of support for the impending transformation. Be prepared to encounter the corporate personalities — such as the potential losers, the defenders, the wimps and rationalists — who could either actively or passively resist the change. Assume trust and constructive engagement, but equally, make sure that your bullshit antenna is up and sensitive.

Promoting yourself into the job

Be inspired by Michael Watkins' excellent book *The first 90 days: Critical strategies for new leaders at all levels*, and get into the mindset of the new role as quickly as possible. This means you need to promote yourself mentally (it doesn't mean you hire a publicist). It also means that once you accept the role, you accept the obligations and accountabilities of the role, and that you'd better start earning your keep as soon as possible.

A great anecdote on the importance of taking ownership is the fable of the three envelopes. According to this story, the newly appointed CEO meets the outgoing CEO, who shakes her hand and says, 'Here are three envelopes, marked one through three. When something bad happens, or you miss your annual plan, open an envelope'.

The new CEO settles in, and everything is going well, but a downturn in the past month means the company misses its annual plan. The new CEO opens the first envelope, and it says: 'Blame your predecessor'. After several months, the company is once again missing its numbers, so the CEO opens the second envelope: 'Blame the market'. On the company goes, until it runs into a big issue with one of its products. The CEO opens the last envelope, which says 'Prepare three envelopes'.

Looking in the mirror

As you embark on this transformation journey, what's on your own mind, and what are the mental challenges you may need to be aware of? Ask yourself some hard questions:

- What do you want to achieve from all of this, and why?
- Are you being sufficiently curious, and are you listening more than you're talking?
- What biases might you be bringing to this role and/or transformation effort?
- What 360-degree feedback have you been given before? Did you agree with it, or have you sought to address it?
- Do you have the personal energy to drive urgency for transformation, and how will you maintain your own resilience levels?
- What are you prepared to focus on? How are you going to actively assign your time between the business as usual and the transformation? What might you have to delegate?

- Are you already getting all serious and losing your sense of humour?
- Above all, will you be open to people giving you surprising feedback on either yourself or the way you're leading the transformation?

Giving up the 'expert' title

With executive seniority comes the expectation that you'll give up the mantle of being the technical expert, and instead become a more generalist leader whose job it is to get the best out of all of the newly emerging leaders and technical specialists. Again, this doesn't mean you don't draw on what you've learned. It just means that you grow to be more generalist.

This can be challenging for someone who has spent their career self-referencing as the expert in their field, and then wants to retain this reputation in a new more senior role. Instead, aspire to acquire the next set of skills to complement your existing technical skills. A small example illustrates this important principle.

In most armies around the world, young officers join a branch of the army — such as infantry, artillery, engineering, armour — and all their badges of rank and sense of belonging are related to this branch. However, once they're promoted to the rank of general, their badges of rank drop anything that's specific to a particular branch because the requirement is that they become a more 'generalist' leader who is now able to and expected to co-ordinate all branches without prejudice to achieve the mission and its objectives. People in business would be well served to adopt a similar perspective and view the role of 'General' Manager as less about seniority and epaulettes on the shoulder, and more about 'Generalist' Manager responsible for combining all parts of their company to achieve its objectives.

Wanting to win

Personally, I'm very ambitious and competitive for my company, and therefore I find it hateful to think that a competitor company could be regularly beating mine. Successful companies should be seeking to promote people who like to win, and who are competitive (but to also have this competitive streak directed to those outside the company). Then, in their first 90 days, they should be imbuing their new teams with a desire to win.

I see winning as less of an event (i.e. 'remember when we were #1') and more of a habit (i.e. 'What are we doing today to be excellent, and to beat the competition, and to keep beating them tomorrow?'). When selecting people for teams, and then managing and leading them, I have a firm view that people who like to win don't need to be motivated. Instead, people (and teams) who like to win need to be aligned and unleashed, and then acknowledged for what they've achieved.

Knowing what success looks like

When entering a new company or role, you should form a clear and early view of what success and winning looks like for your company and how it will be measured. As leaders, our job is to translate this view of winning into something tangible for our teams. Explore what metrics and objectives demonstrate winning, regardless of what part of the company you're working in.

Confronting reality

You have to identify what's preventing the current or future success of your organisation and, once it's up and running, the transformation program itself. It could be process, technology, structure or it could be culture. Or, it could be your products. Whatever it is, having identified it, you need a plan to fix it. You need to be clear on what you want to achieve, what you have now and where you're starting from.

| Mechanics

Reflect on a role you've entered, and what the first 90 days were like. Everyone wants some time with you. You're drinking from the fire hose to get across everything that's important, and there doesn't seem to be enough hours in the day. Each Monday morning, you step into the metaphorical river, and it carries you along for the week, spitting you out onto the bank late Friday night, where you lie panting and recharging your batteries until Monday morning sees you repeat the process. Eventually, you get the hang of things, everything starts to settle down and you're in more control.

If you're motivated and ambitious for the success of your company and its transformation, then there's no way to completely avoid the sensory and intellectual overload that comes from plunging into a new role. You can, however, apply some planning principles and mechanics to get things in control and try to accelerate yourself to the breakeven point where you're adding more value than you're consuming.

Some mechanics and techniques to use in your first 90 days include:

- be clear on context
- write down your plan
- consider all the levers of change
- build allies
- consult across the company
- leverage the value of symbolism.

Let's dive a bit deeper into each of these.

Being clear on context

All jobs have a context, and it's important to understand it. It might be building on the success of a predecessor or turning a role around after someone else failed to deliver. Your predecessor might have done a great job initiating improvements to the business. It has momentum and provides a great foundation for you to build on and improve it even more. By contrast, it might be a basket case, with low morale, confusion over its mission, inefficient, ineffective, fat and expensive: a turnaround case that's a completely different situation.

In all cases it's necessary to understand the context because this will impact the mechanics of your 90-day plan. What you need to do in an emergency environment (think General Matthew Ridgway) is very different from taking over responsibility for a company that's running with the efficiency of a Swiss watch.

Recap your definition of transformation: what disruption or opportunities do you see affecting the company, and how do you intend to respond? Are others seeing what you're seeing? Are the disruption signals obvious, or is it a slow burn?

Writing down your plan

Developing your first 90-day plan should commence upon accepting the new role and proceed by drawing on a combination of 'mindset' and 'mechanics'. It's an opportunity to get your head in the right place, identify any potential skill deficiencies or blind spots, understand the unique context of the company and role that you're entering and actually document your 90-day plan.

It's worth spending some time on this because the actions you take during your first three months in a new job will largely determine whether you succeed or fail. When starting a new role, or starting a transformation project, it's critical to have a plan. Over the years, my approach to a new role has been informed by:

- historical stories, such as the one about General Matthew Ridgway

- books, such as the excellent *The First 90 Days: critical strategies for new leaders at all levels* by Michael Watkins. I re-read this book every time I get a new job

- my consulting career at PwC, where I'd prepare a formal pre-engagement briefing deck to ensure that my team knew about the client, their industry and the latest news, followed by a detailed walk-through of the project plan so that everyone knew what we were trying to achieve, and their role within that

- my executive career at NAB, where I typically changed roles every three years or so, and which included joining the Bank of New Zealand, where I had a fixed two-year assignment to work on improving the bank's technology and operations division, presenting a time-boxed opportunity to get things done

- five years at NSW LRS leading a newly privatised government department staffed by many people very resentful of the change, and stakeholders fearful for what would happen to its services.

All new leaders take time to get up to speed in a new context, and they therefore consume more value than they contribute to their new organisation. We've all experienced that first day in a new organisation or job where you don't know how anything works, or who to ask for help. It takes time to be briefed, to understand who's who in the zoo and to learn the 'way' that the new organisation works.

The objective of a clear 90-day plan is therefore to get you to what Michael Watkins describes as the 'breakeven point' as quickly as possible. This is the point where you are starting to generate more value to the company than you consume. It's a sobering reminder that every single executive must continue to represent a mini business case and generate greater value than they consume. Unfortunately, some senior executives never reach this breakeven point, often due to a lack of ambition, urgency and a clear plan of action. Ironically, having achieved their dream job, some executives seem to have no idea of what to do when they get it, or why they wanted it in the first place.

I suspect that most people think about what they're going to do as they enter their new role, but based on my experience, not everyone actually develops a 90-day plan. Having a loose list of activities and tasks in your mind, while better than nothing, is not a substitute for a written document. Deeply reflecting and thinking about the new role in a comprehensive way, and then writing down your thoughts and plans in a logical and thorough manner, will force you to a better outcome. The blank, empty page that confronts you at the start of the process will provide a useful challenge to the loose collection of tasks, activities and intentions potentially swirling through your mind, and force structure, logic and consideration of time commitments and possibilities. Writing things down will help you focus, rank activities, and identify dependencies and priorities.

Additionally, as you enter your new role, people in the company will inevitably ask you, 'What are you going to focus on?' It's therefore important to have a cogent answer. An easy way to talk about and describe a 90-day plan is to break it down into three distinct months:

- *month 1:* understand the current state
- *month 2:* develop some hypotheses
- *month 3:* confirm the team.

To build additional momentum, these three steps can be preceded by a Pre-entry Information Request, which could include obtaining, requesting and/or generating the following.

Pre-entry Information Request

Objective

To develop a list of materials that you'd like to read before entry to ensure you hit the ground running with some momentum on day one.

Example notes and tasks

- Get all the minutiae and logistics squared away, such as desk location and laptop. Be clear on logistics. (Boring I know, but you'd be surprised at how the lack of basic things will slow you down.)

- Advise the organisation of the information you'd like to obtain before you start. You typically have time before your new job starts, so use it to get up to speed with the new organisation that you'll be leading. It also sends the team a strong message that you're organised, and it gives them time to reflect and think deeply about how they'll answer some of your questions. As a minimum, you should be able to get hold of the following information:

- a management reporting dashboard outlining monthly operational and financial performance
- the latest board report, including CEO and CFO reports
- the strategy presentation discussed at the board
- customer satisfaction scores
- a scorecard and end-of-year letter for each executive/ direct report
- employee engagement scores
- capital budgeting/monthly investment slate reporting.

- Set some 'homework'. Formally request that each of your new direct reports prepare a briefing for you on their area of accountability. This enables you to start assessing the quality of the team you're inheriting: who has read and prepared answers to your questions, versus who claims that unfortunately, the dog ate their homework.

- Obtain the details of any external stakeholders you'd like to meet. This may include customers, regulators, suppliers and industry stakeholders. You will want to proactively email or telephone the individuals on your stakeholder list on your very first day and have a quick 'greeting' style conversation, so get their names, titles and organisations in advance.

- Make a list of the meeting agendas and questions that you'll run through with these stakeholders.

- Pre-prepare a personal message that you'll send to everyone in the organisation to introduce yourself. This provides everyone with a sense of who you are as a person and what you think is important, and starts to introduce your professional standards. By communicating this up front, you're accountable for living up to these standards and it avoids you being a 'do as I say, rather than as I do' style leader.

- Develop some loose hypotheses to be tested and added to (or quickly abandoned if unsuitable or wrong). Again, the point here is not to have strongly held pre-conceived notions of exactly what you'll find and what you'll do. Instead, it's designed to be like mental gymnastics to get your brain warmed up and working through the opportunities that might present themselves.

While it's important to be seen to do the work, no-one expects you to do everything, so think about whether there are some management consultants who can help you make an early impact and augment the work you do personally. However, be careful not to outsource or delegate your first 90-day plan activities to them.

Key points	Ask yourself
• You need to hit the ground running and build urgency. • You need to embrace the role of 'transformer in chief'. • Prepare your plan but remain flexible and ready to adapt to what you learn. • Get mentally and emotionally ready to delegate the BAU as much as possible and immerse yourself in addressing the changes and threats impacting your company.	• Do you truly understand the industry forces at play, and what disruptions and opportunities could present in your company? • What new skills may you need to acquire to be successful in this new role? How will you acquire them? • What new mindsets may you need to adopt to be successful in this new role? • What 'sacred beliefs' do you have that may limit your transformation goals? • What level of ambition do you have for the company and your role? • Are you ready to get to work?

With the above items and information in hand, the first month of your 90-day plan might look something like the following.

Month 1: Understand the current state

Objective

To quickly understand the current state of the company and its challenges, opportunities, strengths and weaknesses, across a broad range of factors. Note: this is not about trying to become some kind of expert in every facet of the company. Don't deceive yourself that this is possible within a month. Your goal is to become familiar with the organisation so that you build momentum towards your personal 'breakeven point' as quickly as possible.

Example tasks (day 1)

- Send out your introductory message to all staff within your organisational unit.

- Contact external stakeholders. Don't go into any details. You only want to lay some pipe for the next meeting that you know will come. Do this on your first day for two reasons:

  o First, it sends a message — on a very personal and individual level — that you're acknowledging them as people and the importance of their role to your future success, and you're legitimising their 'stake' in the company or organisation that you're now leading.

  o Second, it allows you to control your first 90 days, because you can then manage the timing of your next interaction to understand their perspectives and the relationship you'll have.

Example ongoing tasks

- Visit your major customers for both the symbolism and because you will gain some critical insights on how your company is perceived.

- Set up meetings with internal stakeholders. This is obviously not rocket science, and the easiest way to start is to work your way down the organisation (you can try to set up the meetings before you arrive). As a minimum, set up interviews with:

- each director (one on one)
- each executive (one on one)
- each of the direct reports of the existing executive team
- frontline employees and middle managers, in groups of five to seven people over morning/afternoon tea.

- Ask everyone the same questions:
  - What do you hope I change?
  - What do you hope I keep?
  - What do you think of the team?
  - What's the biggest opportunity for driving the organisation forward?
  - What's the biggest obstacle to driving the organisation forward?

    (Take written notes and ensure that the people you are meeting with see you taking notes.)

- Get control of the capital budgeting process to understand governance, scope, financial burn rate (and so on) and ensure that these are not about to make some decisions that can't be unwound.

- Schedule a discussion on talent management to learn who is in the talent group and why.

- Review the BAU management reporting to understand current performance.

- Schedule individual meetings with your new direct reports for them to talk you through their 'homework' and explain the details of their business.

- Use the levers of change as a mechanism to quickly familiarise yourself with all facets of the company. Try to consider them all within your first 90 days, and drill down on those you think are most relevant to your role, the company's context or your developing plans. (See the section titled 'Month 2: Develop some hypotheses' for an example set of questions to ask regarding each lever.)

- Try to resist making any big decisions during this first month that you may have to unravel. This doesn't mean you're indecisive — it means that you're thoughtful and smart.

Key points	Ask yourself

• Do not shit-can the past as you enter the company, because it annoys everyone and makes them switch off, or worse.
 	
• Take a balanced view: seek to identify both strengths and weaknesses in both the company and the team.
 	
• Evaluate all of the people you meet — find the hidden gems and the psychopaths.
 	
• Remember the 'silver bullets' of communication:
  o appeal to people's self-interest
  o make people want to be part of something bigger
  o make it feel 'right'.
	• How do you want your new team to experience you?
	
	• What early symbolic messages have you sent?
	
	• Are you promoting an environment where people will speak up? Are you encouraging constructive dissent and disagreement?
	
	• Are you doing all the talking?
	
	• Are you controlling your pace of learning and the documents that you read?
	
	• Are you considering all levers of change, or only those you're most familiar with?
	
	• What have you learned that most surprises you? What is something that happened as expected?

In the second month, your 90-day plan should move to developing some hypotheses.

Month 2: Develop some hypotheses

Objective

To validate and/or abandon some of the early hypotheses you developed pre-entry; and to build a new, more comprehensive set based on what you've learned so far. This new emergent set of hypotheses can then be further iterated, analysed and tested as you proceed through your first 90-day period.

Example tasks

- Carry forward and continue the consultation process with internal and external stakeholders that you started in month one, and ask people what they think should change.

- Use the levers of change as a mechanism to develop your hypotheses, and express them as a broad statement of intent to be further tested and refined. For example:

  - *Products and services*: 'Double down on profitable product X' or 'It looks like Product Y is not delivering; something will have to change.'

  - *Customers and markets*: 'Customers are saying we are too expensive/unresponsive/disconnected, so we need to address this.'

  - *Business processes*: 'Division X appears inefficient and may need some improvement' or 'The following policies (X, Y and Z) could be simplified to send a symbolic message.'

  - *Technology*: 'The technology model looks complicated' or 'Too much/too little of the technology function has been outsourced' or 'I am concerned about cyber threats.'

  - *Organisational structure*: 'There are too many layers between the CEO and the frontline' or 'There appear to be too many middle managers and a resultant lack of accountability and drive.'

  - *People and culture*: 'The culture appears to favour the status quo' or 'The culture is biased towards X, Y and Z.'

  - *Facilities*: 'These facilities appear old/expensive/fit for purpose.'

...and so on

- Develop some hypotheses regarding the organisation's ability to change, based on a review of recent change programs and the measurable results they delivered.

- Develop some hypotheses regarding the executive and workforce's ability to change, based on who has been leading and experiencing change, and the results achieved.

- Continue to critically evaluate your executive team against criteria such as transformation temperament and skills, ability to get things done, how they work with colleagues, and so on. Watch how they treat more junior people who visit or present to the executive team.

- Continue to watch the team dynamics and how the organisation structure works. What are the tension and friction points? Why?

- Begin to confirm broad-brush executive roles, but still reach out to a trusted recruiter to accelerate gauging the market for talent (this doesn't mean you have to change the team).

Key points	Ask yourself
• You want to achieve a solid understanding of the issues combined with a broad hypothesis for what could be transformed.	• Are you keeping your mind open and curious?
	• Are you being realistic but also ambitious?
• You are not looking to immediately address every issue you find, nor pursue every hypothesis you develop.	• Are you self-referencing as the expert who cannot be challenged?
• The objective is to work your mental muscles and identify a range of potential options that can be assessed in more detail later.	• Could you be displaying traits such as 'Thank God I'm here', or 'You're all shit'.
	• Are any serious or critical themes starting to emerge?
• You want to demonstrate that you are out and about meeting people and building credibility that you are identifying the real issues.	• What are the most tightly held mindsets among the people you're meeting?
	• What factors are present in the company that may prevent transformation?
• Be seen to be doing the work.	• How enthusiastic are you about leading the change?
• What corporate characters — both positive and negative — are you seeing emerge?	• Are you controlling your time and what you focus on, or getting drawn into everyone else's priorities?

In the final 30 days of your 90-day plan you need to confirm your team.

Month 3: Confirm the team

Objective

Recognising that the people you field will probably be the biggest determinant of your success, you need to quickly take a position on your team: who should be kept, who may need to change roles, who may need to be exited. Your objective is to deal with your team fairly, objectively and decisively, so that everyone can then settle down and get behind your agenda as quickly as possible.

Example tasks

Note: You may well inherit a perfect, well-functioning and collegiate team filled with absolute corporate superstars. If this is the case, then great. Lucky you. If this is not the case, then continue to identify the superstars or the psychopaths, and consult (with discretion) with others to gauge their views.

- Continue to evaluate your people and take written notes. Observe them across a range of circumstances and how they treat people at all levels in the organisation. Review the actual results of what they've achieved, and their scorecard/ appraisal history.

- Revisit your hypotheses on the organisation's structure — does anything have to change quickly, or can you wait and evolve it?

- Meet with the direct reports of all of your executive team to gauge their views and ideas, and to get sense of the depth of talent.

- Review the talent program and assess both its integrity and efficacy (do you believe in the process?) together with the talent that's been identified (do you rate these people too?).

- Based on your loosely held hypotheses, do you have all the diversity and skills you need in-house? Do you have to inject new external talent for both the symbolism and new energy that results?

- Commence mapping your executive team to confirm roles and to identify movements and/or exits. Engage with HR to map the process for communicating with impacted people, and to prepare the required termination calculations and exit letters.

- Identify interim or internal succession to keep the existing operations and organisation structure going.

- Schedule and conduct all meetings required to both confirm the team and exit (with dignity) those who need to leave the team.

- Prepare your first major communication back to the entire employee base (in your team) and aim to do it in the last week of your third month. The symbolism of hitting your own milestones will not be unnoticed and it demonstrates your urgency and ability to meet your commitments. This communication should outline your:

  o views on the current state

  o developing hypotheses

  o intentions regarding the executive team.

- Schedule and conduct your first offsite to share your expectations and commence team building. Be prepared to continually revisit these expectations as new people join the team.

- Start documenting your goals, objectives and approach to your next 90 days, covering the initiatives you'll launch, who will lead them and their intended scope. (Don't hold this meeting too early, with people that you may then have to exit. It's far better to wait until you've got the team you want in place.)

Key points	Ask yourself
• Your people decisions will be among the most important decisions you make.	• Who are the people most likely to embrace transformation and change?
• Most people within your organisation unit will be heavily focused on your entry to the role, and the people decisions that you might make. The rumour mill will therefore be working overtime, so get at it.	• Who are the people most likely to resist and sabotage the transformation?
	• When evaluating your team, what could you be missing?
	• Are you being independent and objective?
• Build allies and find the hidden gems — both always exist in any extended team.	• Are you putting off the hard conversations?
• When evaluating your team, trust the data and your instincts: any doubt on someone is no doubt.	• Are you creating a truly diverse team, or assigning/ recruiting in your own image?
	• Have you retained/assigned/ recruited people to cover off the skills gaps that *you* have?
• Most leaders regret not moving on the 'white ant' type personalities sooner.	• If one of your existing team members resigned, would you talk them into staying? (If no, then that's a sign they should be exited.)
• Be aware of the flow-on effects of all promotions, exits and movements — none of this happens in a vacuum.	

Remember that you're not seeking to develop the perfect plan. There is no such thing. The real world will interfere with even the best plan in ways that cannot be predicted. As heavyweight boxing champion Mike Tyson said when interviewed ahead of a bout, 'Everyone has a plan until they get punched in the face.'

As you go through the process of documenting your own 90-day plan, be prepared to maintain flexibility, roll with the punches and adapt to what you subsequently learn and the natural rhythms that emerge in your new role. Documenting a plan is not intended to make you mentally rigid or have you slavishly follow your original plan at all costs. The documented plan is only the 'means'. The 'ends' is for you to enter your new role with momentum, take a thorough approach to understanding what's going on, and make a positive impact that starts to win the hearts and minds of your new stakeholders.

Considering all the levers of change

Use the 'levers of change' (see chapter 4) as a checklist. Try to consider all of them in your first 90 days, and formally address each one you think is relevant.

In addition to the meetings and interviews, you'll inevitably sit with your directors, direct reports and key people throughout the organisation. You should also initiate some high-level reviews to build momentum during your first 90 days. You can then do detailed deep dives during your second 90 days on things that grab your interest and curiosity. Example reviews (in rough order of importance) include:

- *Customers*: identify your most important customers and reach out to them early to reinforce their importance.

- *Products*: find a way to personally experience your company's service proposition as though you're a real customer. This builds immediate credibility and rapport with the workforce and puts your team on notice that you'll be prepared to 'lead from the frontlines' rather than 'manage from the chateau miles behind the front'. Get to know your three most important products and the people managing them, and walk through the high-level business processes that deliver them.

- *Strategy*: review the latest strategy and business plan to gauge the degree of sensitivity to external factors, how the world is perceived, and what's being done to address the emergent opportunities and threats.

- *Financial analysis*: initiate a ratios-based review of the company's balance sheet and profit and loss to identify potential hotspots and opportunities about working capital, cash flow and overall financial health. Be sensitive to what the numbers are trying to tell you. The numbers have more credibility than the anecdotes.

- *People*: review the scorecards of your direct reports to understand the degree of alignment and what's valued and ask to see the scorecards of their direct reports. Review and understand the payout ratio on scorecards from last year. Review the details and papers of the last talent management meeting to gauge how talent is defined, identified and managed, and importantly, get to know who they are.

- *Regulator*: reach out to the regulators to introduce yourself and take control of the agenda.

- *Business processes*: mentally walk through the core business processes of the company to understand what they do and how they all fit together.

- *Technology architecture*: meet with the enterprise architects to get a sense of the state of the technology stack, where it's going, and what strengths and weaknesses exist.

- *Technology security*: meet with the cybersecurity team to gauge the relative and absolute vulnerabilities that might exist.

- *Suppliers*: reach out to the strategic suppliers to introduce yourself and take control of the agenda.

- *Capital budgeting*: take a detailed look at the capital budget and investment slate to familiarise yourself with what's important and where capital is being allocated. Find out what major projects are underway, what they're trying to deliver and how they're going.

- *Facilities*: what's the status of your property portfolio? Are there buildings coming off lease, and what flexibility is there for property decisions?

Building allies

No transformation can be delivered by a single person no matter how talented they are. Day-to-day leadership can be lonely, and transformation leadership even more so. It's therefore important to build coalitions with people who can help you do a good job and want to see you do a good job. You'll find these people internally and externally. Engage with them, consult them and ask for their advice and perspectives. When you meet talented people who might be suitable, consider hiring them to the impending effort.

Seek out the views and support of strategic suppliers and your best customers. Engage with your regulators, bankers, auditors and legal advisors, and seek their professional opinion on the state of the external market in which you operate, and your company's position and challenges within it.

Coalitions of likeminded people will help you get things done and help maintain your own personal energy and resilience levels.

Consulting across the company

It's important to get out and consult many stakeholders — up, down and sideways within the company — and key people from outside. Keep the interviews simple and ask the same questions: what's going well, what would they like to see change. Hold morning/afternoon tea with groups of people to get a Q&A going to learn about themes relevant to your new role. This kind of personal consultation is essential for understanding what's actually happening in the company. When you see people from across different levels of the company it sends a couple of important messages to everyone, including:

- You're interested in seeing things with your own eyes.
- You're not hierarchical, and you believe that everyone has a legitimate voice.
- You'll understand reality and not get a distorted or filtered message.

Carefully plan who you need to meet, and keep a record of who you met and what they said. Share this with your team at the end of your first 90 days so that they know whatever changes are happening are grounded in facts, data and the views of a broad group of people.

Leveraging the value of symbolism

Senior leaders cast long shadows: everything that you do will be observed and interpreted by the people in your team. As a result, there are typically positive symbols that can be sent early on to assert the change in leadership and to change the culture. For example, you can acknowledge and reward the behaviours that you want to see more of, and you can call out those that you think will slow your progress.

These messages can be powerful, such as General Ridgway removing a senior officer who was not sufficiently prepared or aggressive towards the enemy. Equally, they can be simpler: when I first joined NSW LRS, I went to see the head of our legal operations department around lunchtime. When I walked into that part of the office, there was a beautiful old sign saying that it was closed for lunch. I enquired why we closed at lunchtime, when that was clearly the only time that many people would be able to see us.

Apparently, we'd always closed at lunchtime because that was 'what law firms did', and because it made scheduling easier when everyone in the department could take their lunchtime together. I told the head of legal that as of tomorrow, we would be open for lunch because that was when customers could see us more conveniently. As intended, the early decision spread through our building with a clear message that customer service was now important. This was the exact symbol of a refreshed customer service ethos that I wanted to send.

| Mistakes

During your first 90 days, it's very easy to make mistakes, such as annoying everyone through ill-thought-through or clumsy communications, pursuing the wrong priorities or forgetting to undertake certain activities that are critical for success. Or just not having a plan or demonstrating sufficient urgency.

Here are some of the mistakes to avoid.

Reading everything you're given

As you enter a new role, you'll have well-meaning people (together with others with an ulterior motive) hand you reports, personal essays and documents that they've prepared, together with previous strategies. This is the quickest way to drown in detail and get bogged down. It's important to only read the things that you need to, when you need to read them (i.e. according to your own 90-day plan); otherwise you'll lose momentum and initiative and find yourself operating to someone else's timetable and priorities. This obviously requires balance and judgement because hidden within this paper pile might be nuggets that you didn't necessarily know to ask for.

Pretending you have all the answers

Entering a new role with intellectual humility and curiosity is critical and will deliver significant benefits, such as:

- People will feel empowered to share their own perspectives, many of which will be extremely invaluable because they've been developed by people who deeply understand the current challenges and opportunities that exist in the company.

- This openness and curiosity will start to permeate the corporate culture (it's a very powerful cultural symbol).

- You'll learn more.

There's nothing as liberating as admitting that you don't have all the answers. Whenever I've done this, people tend to think more highly of me rather than less. It shows honesty and a certain level of personal confidence to admit that you don't know everything. It also gets you off the hook from making decisions about things with which you're not yet familiar, it removes the temptation to pretend or bullshit, and it also provides early space for your people to step into and exert their own leadership.

Failing to leave your old job behind

Whether you're joining a new company, or you've been promoted within your existing company, you need to shed your old job like you would an old coat. Take it off, put it on the floor and back away.

If you've been promoted within a company, taking off your old job will leave a clear runway for the new person in it. If you've previously done a good job, then you should have set it up so that the function will be in good hands. You should be intellectually gracious and ambitious for your company, and by being so, you should hope that the best days of your old function are ahead of it.

If you're new to the company, then everyone, and I mean everyone, will quickly tire of hearing about how things worked at your old employer. No-one cares. What they care about is what you are doing to address the circumstances of your new job at *this* company. Don't be that annoying executive who is continually banging on about how things were back in the day at their previous company.

Making early decisions that you have to unwind

Write on top of the first page of your 90-day plan: 'Do not be tempted to make a long-term decision too early'. I learned this the hard way when I went to Bank of New Zealand. Soon after joining, I was confronted by the need to make a structural decision in my first 30 days. The person pushing for the decision was very persuasive and mounted a very solid case. I made the decision, and within days I regretted it. As I found out more facts, I learned that the person had really used my ignorance as an opportunity to quickly push through something that they wanted. Once I'd learned more, I had two choices:

- let the decision stand and carry on, and thereby look easily led or ego-driven, or
- reverse the decision, eat humble pie, but at least get to the right place.

Neither of these decisions was a good outcome. In the end, I chose to reverse the decision, and get things back to a better place.

Not moving fast enough on your team, and then their teams

The entry of a new leader into a senior role is the catalyst to review the team and ensure that everyone in it has the right skills and temperament for the task at hand. I've described at length the process for evaluating people and listed the kind of corporate characters — both good and bad — that you're likely to encounter, so there's no need to repeat them here.

Starting into your first 90 days is a good time to review the organisation structure and to ensure that the senior leader population is the right one. I've learned over time that any doubt on someone is no doubt. You have to trust your instincts, temper this with first-hand observation and review the hard evidence of what each person has done and how they behave.

Once you've made up your mind, it's then important to move quickly. Get the right team in place, ensure they get their teams in place and get on with it.

Annoying everyone with blunt messages

As you come into your new role, it's inevitable that you'll find things that need improving, just as whoever comes into your old role will find things that need improving too. This is to be expected and welcomed. The key to effectively calling out things that need improving is to be diplomatic. As I described in chapter 3, this is an opportunity to be seen as a straight shooter by providing direct feedback without sugar-coating, and it's also an opportunity to present things positively. Do not shit-can the past.

Key points from chapter 5

- Your new job should not start on the morning of your first day in the role. Instead, you should commence planning your first 90 days and initial impact as soon as you get the job.

- Your first 90 days provide the opportunity to grab hold of the agenda, understand the potential disruptions and opportunities, and start developing a pragmatic strategy that will deliver transformational results.

- Everyone will be watching you closely. The actions you take will send their own messages. Are you organised, are you competent, do you have a documented plan or are you trying to 'wing it'?

- It's critical that you have a documented plan, and that you accelerate your breakeven point.

- Write down your plan. It should be clear on context: is this BAU or a turnaround scenario? Your plan should also be thorough, consider all of the levers of change, and set aside time to consult with people up, down and across the company.

- Avoid the most common errors that many leaders are prone to, such as reading everything you're given. Instead, take a step back, develop a simple and yet comprehensive plan, and enter your new role with confidence and momentum.

Conclusion:
I wish you luck
with your choice

Don't explain your philosophy — embody it.

Epictetus (50–135 CE), Greek Stoic Philosopher

Well, here we are at the end of the book, and the big question looms: what's next?

What's next indeed.

There are an almost infinite set of forces and factors that will inevitably affect your industry and your organisation. We've not yet reached peak change, with a range of geopolitical forces, technology and innovation, industry agitations, societal forces and the characteristics of your own company all jockeying with one another to see which will create the biggest disruptive threat. The climate crisis, population growth and technology are just some of the forces that will fundamentally change your organisation's future.

There's always a choice between embracing that which might be uncertain, risky and dangerous, but that we acknowledge deep down is the right thing to do, compared to that which is easy, certain and comfortable, but which we know will not lead to progress or a better outcome. It's always been easy to kick the hard choices down the road.

The choice for our current generation of leaders is important for our existing and future standard of living. The disruptive forces emerging and already challenging our industries and companies will require the very best of our energies to confront them. To assume that our companies will continue to flourish in the face of this disruption without major transformation is either naïve or negligent. The importance of a profitable corporate sector that generates valuable products and services, provides meaningful employment for our citizens, generates wealth for our shareholders and superannuation funds, can afford to address and reduce climate impacts, and can pay the taxes that underpin our society and all of its wonderful offerings, cannot be overstated.

Hence the choice that now confronts all of us: what type of leader do we each want to be?

Are you prepared to step into the ambiguity and uncertainty of transformation? Can you identify these disruptive forces even when they're potentially knocking softly on the door of your company — even as your colleagues are not listening or prepared to acknowledge them — and do something about them? We know that these forces are persistent and emotionless, and they don't at all care whether anyone gets up out of their chair to answer.

To paraphrase Machiavelli, even though transformation is 'difficult and dangerous to administer', we need to get at it.

Without transformation — and an understanding of all three elements including identification of disruptive forces, the crafting of strategy and the successful implementation of change — our leading organisations are destined to fall behind their more nimble and ambitious competitors or become marginalised by the disruptive forces arrayed against them. This has far-reaching impacts.

Leaders at all levels are therefore going to have to choose a side: are they the conservatives trying to preserve the status quo, or are they the worthy custodians of their company's ability to grow and prosper, with the spirit that their organisation's best days are ahead of them?

People at every level must embrace transformation by understanding its three core elements and being sufficiently ambitious to give it a crack. Everyone has a role to play.

Directors and boards should be even more sensitive to the disruptive forces at play in the world and appoint chief executives who are familiar and comfortable with transformation. They should work with them to demand ambitious goals and objectives, while being sensitive to the challenges that, in the words of Theodore Roosevelt, 'the person in the arena, their face marred by dust and sweat' confronts as they embrace the ambiguity and uncertainty of driving transformation. Let them at it, get them to report back, hold them to account, but don't argue the difficulties. After all, as Winston Churchill said, 'the difficulties will argue for themselves'.

Chief executives have to choose too. Do they want the quiet harvesting of economic rents from their senior role and pay packet, too timid or afraid to set an ambitious transformation agenda, or will they choose to marshal the best and brightest from within their company's ranks and chart a course that results in an objectively and measurably better future?

Leaders and employees at all levels, are you ready to put your hand up to get involved and embrace the excitement, pressure and heavy responsibility of transforming your companies to deliver better products, opportunities, returns and outcomes to all stakeholders, whether financial or societal?

Acknowledging the reasons that make transformation hard, including the power of the status quo, company characteristics, and most critically, the corporate personalities — such as the losers, defenders, wimps and rationalists — means that you'll recognise ahead of time their shallow, self-serving and timid excuses for getting in the way and understand the actions that you'll need to take to drive progress forward around, under or over them.

We should seek to do the hard things.

Have a clear ambition for your company, for your transformation project and for yourself. As leaders, as people who want to be winners, we should be seeking to sign up for the hardest assignments available, not only because they're typically the things that matter most, but also to prove that they can be delivered. And after all, if you expect a small challenge, you should equally expect a small bonus, notwithstanding that without a successful transformation, the ability of your company to continue its payroll may eventually be at risk.

President John F Kennedy said it best:

> *We choose to go to the moon, not because it is easy, but because it is hard... because that goal will serve to organise and measure the best of our energies and skills...*

And last, as you mentally fire up and get into gear to become involved in driving these changes, remember that there's a WAY of transformation encompassing the mindset and mechanics required to make meaningful and sustainable change.

Maintain your curiosity and *shoshin*, your beginner's mind, to generate unconstrained possibilities. Challenge your own sacred beliefs and biases that might limit the ambition that's possible. Focus (*kime*) on the *kokoro*, or the heart of the matter, but equally, don't become fixated, and be ready to let go and try something else when necessary (i.e. renew). Along the way, give someone the gift of trust, and you'll be surprised at what they'll do for you and the company. Above all, keep your sense of humour, and find resilience; you're certainly going to need it. Be ready to put things down by the side of the road. There will be no shortage of negative corporate personalities and psychopaths in your way. Believe me, you can't fit all of them in your backpack.

The mechanics are also clear. Be ready to personally do the work. You simply cannot outsource or delegate the kind of leadership that you need to inject into the transformation. Make decisions: you have to choose, own and communicate a clear strategy. Obviously, you can't do all of this work on your own. Transformation is a team sport that requires the identification, recruitment, alignment and direction of talented and energetic people, so get the right people on board as quickly as possible.

You must also be thorough: use a well-proven methodology and understand the strategic and operational levers of change that you can pull to ensure the transformation is meaningful, successful and sustainable. Measure your success using clear shareholder value drivers so you can show empirical progress and keep score. Use KPIs to align the team and provide a mechanism for regular feedback. Ground your transformation in reality, and never bullshit yourself or others about its real progress.

When you weave all of this into a thoughtful, urgent and active 90-day plan, you'll be off to a great start.

Leading transformation, while difficult, at times stressful and requiring lots of hard work, will not be a punishment. I guarantee it will be exciting, intellectually stimulating, challenging, meaningful and purposeful. Above all, it will be fun. To quote American journalist and author Hunter S Thompson, who founded the gonzo journalism movement (strikethroughs added):

> [Your] ~~Life~~ [career] *should not be a journey to* ~~the grave~~ [retirement] *with the intention of arriving safely in a pretty and well-preserved body, but rather a skid in broadside in a cloud of smoke, thoroughly used up, totally worn out, and loudly proclaiming 'Wow! What a ride.'*

Bibliography

Aaker, J. & Bagdonis, N. (2020). *Humour, seriously: Why humour is a superpower at work and in life*. Penguin Business.

Axelrod, A. (1999). *Patton on leadership: Strategic lessons for corporate warfare*. Prentice Hall Press.

Bernstein, C. & Woodward, B. (1974). *All the president's men*. Simon and Schuster Paperbacks.

Bondanella, P. & Musa, M. (1979). *The portable Machiavelli*. Penguin Books.

Bungay, S. (2011). *The art of action: How leaders close the gaps between plans, actions and results*. Nicholas Brealey Publishing.

Christensen, C. M. (1997). *The innovator's dilemma: When new technologies cause great firms to fail*. Harvard Business Review Press.

Collins, J. (2001). *Good to great: Why some companies make the leap and others don't*. Random House Business Books.

Cray, E. (2000). *General of the army: George C. Marshall, soldier and statesman*. Cooper Square Press.

Dalio, R. (2021). *Principles for dealing with the changing world order*. Avid Reader Press.

Dixon, N. (2016). *On the psychology of military incompetence*. Basic Books.

Duke, A. (2022). *Quit: The power of knowing when to walk away*. Penguin Random House.

Gates, B. (2021). *How to avoid a climate disaster: The solutions we have and the breakthroughs we need*. Penguin Random House UK.

Graeber, D. (2018). *Bullshit jobs: The rise of pointless work and what we can do about it.* Penguin Books.

Gulati, R. (2022). *Deep purpose: The heart and soul of high performance companies.* Penguin Business.

Johnson, S. (2021). *Extra life: A short history of living longer.* Riverhead Books (Penguin).

Kaplan, R. S. & Norton, D. P. (2008). *The execution premium: Linking strategy to operations for competitive advantage.* Harvard Business Press.

Kotter, J. P. (2008). *A sense of urgency.* Harvard Business Review Press.

Le Guin, U. K. (1997). *Lao Tzu Tao Te Ching: A book about the way, and the power of the way.* Shambhala Publications.

Lewis, M. (2003). *Moneyball: The art of winning an unfair game.* W. W. Norton & Company.

Lovret, F. J. (1987). *The way and the power: Secrets of Japanese strategy.* Paladin Press.

McKeown, G. (2014). *Essentialism: The disciplined pursuit of less.* Crown Publishing (Random House).

Montgomery, C. (2012). *The strategist: Be the leader your business needs.* Harper Collins.

Musashi, M. (trans. Brown, B. J., Kashiwagi, Y., Barrett, W. H. & Sasagawa, E.). (1982). *The book of five rings (go rin no sho).* Bantam Books.

Parker, G. G., Van Alstyne, M. W. & Choudary, S. P. (2016). *Platform revolution: How networked markets are transforming the economy and how to make them work for you.* W. W. Norton & Company.

Perry, R. (2004). *Monash: The outsider who won a war.* Random House Australia.

Price Waterhouse Change Integration Team. (1995). *Better change: Best practices for transforming your organisation.* Price Waterhouse.

Rappaport, A. (1986). *Creating shareholder value: A guide for managers and investors.* The Free Press (a Division of Simon & Schuster Inc.).

Reid, H. & Croucher, M. (1986). *The way of the warrior: The paradox of the martial arts.* Century Publishing.

Reps, P. (1998). *Zen flesh, Zen bones: A collection of Zen and pre-Zen writings.* Anchor Books, Doubleday & Company.

Ricks, T. E. (2012). *The generals: American military command from World War II to today.* The Penguin Press.

Rogers, M. B. (1998). *Barbara Jordan: American hero*. Bantam Books.

Rosling, H. (with Rosling, O. & Rosling R. A.). (2018). *Factfulness: Ten reasons we're wrong about the world—and why things are better than you think*. Sceptre.

Sandbrook, D. (2020). *Who dares wins: Britain, 1979–1982*. Penguin Random House Books.

Thompson, Sir R. (consulting editor). (1982). *War in peace: An analysis of warfare since 1945*. Orbis Publishing.

Watkins, M. (2003). *The first 90 days: Critical success strategies for new leaders at all levels*. Harvard Business School Press.

Willink, J. & Babin, L. (2018). *Extreme ownership: How U.S. Navy SEALs lead and win*. MacMillan.

Yang, A. (2018). *The war on normal people: The truth about America's disappearing jobs and why universal basic income is our future*. Hachette Book Group.